SHINE BRIGHT

ONE WORLD · NEW YORK

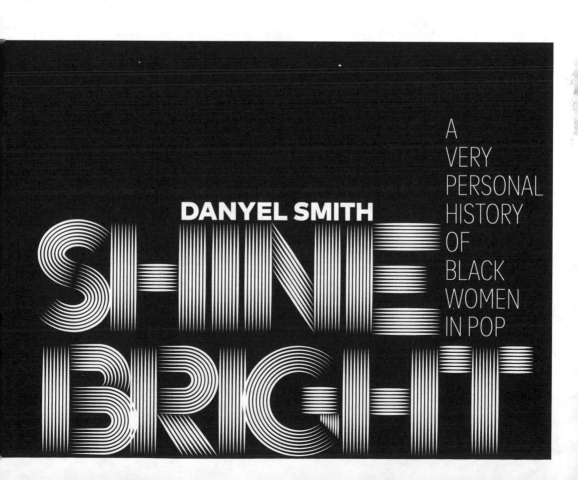

DANYEL SMITH

SHINE
BRIGHT

A
VERY
PERSONAL
HISTORY
OF
BLACK
WOMEN
IN POP

Published in the United States by Roc Lit 101, a joint venture between Roc Nation LLC
and One World, an imprint of Random House, a division of Penguin Random House LLC,
New York.

ONE WORLD is a registered trademark of Penguin Random House LLC.

ROC LIT 101 is a trademark of Roc Nation LLC.

LIBRARY OF CONGRESS CATALOGING-IN-PUBLICATION DATA
Names: Smith, Danyel, author.
Title: Shine bright : a very personal history of black women in pop / Danyel Smith.
Description: New York : Roc Lit 101, 2021. | Includes index.
Identifiers: LCCN 2020057494 (print) | LCCN 2020057495 (ebook) | ISBN 9780593132715
(hardcover) | ISBN 9780593132722 (ebook)
Subjects: LCSH: African American women musicians. | Popular music—United States—
History and criticism. | African American singers. | Women singers—United States.
Classification: LCC ML82 .S615 2021 (print) | LCC ML82 (ebook) |
DDC 782.42164092/2 [B]—dc23
LC record available at https://lccn.loc.gov/2020057494
LC ebook record available at https://lccn.loc.gov/2020057495

Printed in the United States of America on acid-free paper

oneworldlit.com
randomhousebooks.com

9 8 7 6 5 4 3 2 1

First Edition

Book design by Debbie Glasserman

THIS IS FOR ELLIOTT

CONTENTS

DELROY RUSSELL'S *PHYLLIS WHEATLEY* (LINOLEUM PRINT, 2008)

INTRO

My love of music is intense. My commitment to it is steadfast. This project is an attempt to figure out why.

When I talk about Black women in music—at colleges, on my *Black Girl Songbook* show, to my husband, my friends—it's normal for me to weep. My voice breaks, I'm looking up because my eyes are brimming. Someone hands me a tissue. It's dramatic but it's real. There are no reasons.

I'm asked, *Why does Tina Turner matter? Why is Mary J. Blige important?* and my answers are passionate and learned because I want credit to be given where credit is due. I weep because I want Black women who create music to be known and understood, as I want to be known and understood. For so long, little that I have accomplished has felt quite mine. When folks show me love, like at a party celebrating my birthday, those glowing candles, lighting up my face, look like doom. I've spent a career—as a reporter, editor, producer, author, host—speaking to Black women who feel the same. But we all love music. Please read this the way Martha Wash sings it in 1990's "Gonna Make You Sweat (Everybody Dance Now)": *the music is my life.*

It goes back to my ashy-knees era. My climbing-plum-trees era. The

1970s in Oakland, California. Me in two long braids and a key on a ball chain around my neck.

Why speak, now, on those Kodachrome days? Because behind my picture-day smiles is a lust for loudness. I go to therapy because I still clench my fists when receiving "feedback." I still smell the Vitapointe vat, and eggs frying in oleo. Hear a bus braking out front? It's a reminder that I don't need a boyfriend to, as Aretha Franklin sings, go someplace far. Recorded music? That I chose, or turned up, or turned off? Back then, it was a bright and rare thrill, up there with holding a sparkler. I liked to sing school songs with my school friends, but the "real" songs, on the radio or on the record player, were breathtaking. Most of the time they were sung by adult Black women—even when they weren't.

Played by my mother on a boxy portable with the speaker in the top, my earliest favorite records were 45s. We didn't have a stereo "system" with turntable, amplifier, eight-track player, and standing speakers. And as my mother didn't yet drive, my sister and I didn't hear a lot of radio. On the portable we listened to a lot of Jean Knight's "Mr. Big Stuff," and King Floyd's "Groove Me." My sister is a blur of hazel eyes and overalls. My mother is haze itself, and she is the DJ.

A granddaughter of Louisiana, my mother may have been responding to the fact that Knight, Floyd, and producer Wardell Quezergue all hailed from New Orleans. Both "Mr. Big Stuff" and "Groove Me" were huge pop hits, loved by millions of Americans, and listeners around the world. Both songs were recorded on the same day in 1970, in a Mississippi studio, in the very same session. I didn't know what horns were on "Mr. Big Stuff," but I liked them. And the background singers had me from the first "Oh-oh ye-ah."

I'd expect the line to arrive, and it would. *Oh-oh ye-ah*. They sang it the exact same way each time. I wanted the song to go on longer than its two and a half minutes. And when the arm with the needle floated into the shiny blank part of the vinyl, I wanted to hear it again. This itch is in every wise definition of pop: young people want it over and over.

Most of the recorded voices I heard when I was a kidlet were men singing alto and soprano, vocal ranges associated with women. From

Eddie Kendricks to Frankie Valli to Philip Bailey, it was the age of the falsetto. It was also the age of me riding a Big Wheel, and reading our neighbor's *Archie* comics. Unless I saw a man singing I pretty much assumed a woman was singing. At the age of, say, six, I could not believe that the person singing "I'll Try Something New"—*I will build you a castle / With a tower so high / It reaches the moon*—was a man called Smokey Robinson, with his group of "Miracles."

My brain backflipped. First of all, what names! Smokey on a man and not a bear. And why was Smokey the Man singing like a woman? Surely he had his own male voice. I did like the song, though. There was talk of playing every day on the Milky Way. But I needed more rhyming and stories and promises of fun.

I got it in morning care at Bella Vista Elementary, where my mother dropped us before her shift as an admin in the dental area of the county hospital. I was one of the free-ish breakfast kids, a gnawer of cantaloupe, down to the rind. Our morning-care teachers taught us to sing the Stylistics' "Betcha by Golly, Wow," Sammy Davis, Jr.'s "The Candy Man," and B. J. Thomas's "Raindrops Keep Falling on My Head." In memory, these teachers are soft. They smell like themselves. I can't recall their race at all.

We kids held sticky hands and sang. The vibrations in my body flowed through to my friends. We saw approval in the faces of our teachers when we were in unison on a series of notes: *Write your name across the sky / Anything you ask I'll try.* I literally had no idea what I was singing about and did not care. When we sang, the happiness was as intense as any I'd felt.

Our little chorus of eight or ten often walked in a loose line around to what we called "the old folks' home" and sang for people who had been alive since the Great Depression and the turn of the twentieth century. When we sang they leaned in, desperate, or overcome. I had great-grandparents, so I wasn't afraid, even when some of the old folks reached toward us, as if we were not quite real.

My sister and I spent most weekends with our great-grandparents. The three of them were in their early seventies, and they were active. Big Lottie and Dorson—they were the parents of my grandmother Little Lottie and my great-aunt Betty (and of my great-aunt Marjorie, who died before I was born). They took us to Mass, gave us the run of the house and yard, and when it was time for Arthur Duncan to tap dance, sat us in front of *The Lawrence Welk Show*. Dorson had worked on passenger trains, usually in the club car. Big Lottie had been a housekeeper in the historically all-white Piedmont area of Oakland.

Dorothy, on my paternal grandfather's side, fed us pot roast and rice, ran a daycare out of her home, and lived a musical life rich with Adventist hymns and Johnny Cash's Blackish gospel. Mother Dorothy had worked mostly as a maid. Her husband, my great-grandfather Pedro, was a Filipino immigrant who'd worked as a houseman and chauffeur. He died the year I was born.

It took a village, in the innocent time when the tall people were watchful and sinless, to raise my sister and me. Our clothes were handmade—and embroidered and appliquéd. Our afternoons were spent dodging bees near the red rosebushes, and drinking apple juice highballs with Big Lottie. At Mother Dorothy's, there was a stone birdbath to monitor, and hydrangeas to deconstruct.

On a dare from my grandpa Dorson, I listened with him to the entirety of game 7 of the 1972 World Series. He was almost blind from diabetes, so the radio was his domain. I loved him for not being surprised I was fascinated by people named Catfish, Blue Moon, and Rollie Fingers. Loved him for talking me through the narrative of the first six games. And when the A's won, it was the first time I felt like a part of a hometown. I'm from Oakland; we can have wild hair and strange nicknames. We win big. And we do it on the radio.

Which I was starting to get into. When I finally heard "Betcha by Golly, Wow" on a car radio, I was psyched to already know all the words. The lady was singing so sweetly about Candyland appearing each time someone smiled. Another household favorite was the Stylistics' "I'm Stone in Love with You," featuring Russell Thompkins, Jr., on lead vocals. Thompkins is still known for his countertenor and for his falsetto, the male ranges similar to the female contralto of singers like Evelyn "Champagne" King or Phyllis Hyman, or the mezzo-soprano of Ella

Fitzgerald, Aretha Franklin, or Donna Summer. As literal as I was back then about lyrics and musical mood, when Thompkins sang "I'm just a man / An average man / Doing everything the best I can," it didn't override the fact of the voice sounding like a woman's. I felt concretely that *she* was singing to me.

When I was eight, after some chaperoned trial runs, my sister and I walked the six blocks to Bella Vista by ourselves. I knew to wait for the green light before crossing, and to look both ways even so. I could also neatly make peanut butter and jelly sandwiches. I read everything I saw, and was known as Chatty Cathy, especially about music. But I of course didn't yet know that "falsetto" is from the Italian *falso:* "false." Didn't know that in Elizabethan times, women were not allowed to perform onstage with men, so young male performers, dressed in women's costumes, acted and sang women's parts. These male teenagers were paid the least of all the actors. "We need you here but don't want you here" was the message.

From the Shakespearean stage to pop music's global arenas, the story has not changed. Pop music is not now, nor was it historically, written for bass or baritone voices. Michael Jackson, Michael Bolton, George Michael, Prince, Bruno Mars, Bob Marley, Tevin Campbell, Paul McCartney, Sam Smith, Usher Raymond, Johnny Mathis, Justin Bieber—all tenors, most often singing in soprano and in falsetto. The bottom-heavy voices of Elvis Presley, Johnny Cash, Nat "King" Cole, Bill Withers, Eddie Vedder, Nate Dogg, and Frank Sinatra are actually exceptions. Throughout pop history, it is the rich, high, strong, womanly voice that is the prize.

I also assumed the Stylistics' songs were being sung by a Black woman because I was a small Black woman, and because the people around me were mostly Black women. Who else but a Black woman would lead me, or at least take me on trial runs?

My young life didn't include a lot of media. I have vague memories of Denise Nicholas on *Room 222*. Out of Chicago, *Soul Train* was syndicated to seven cities in 1971, but Oakland was not one of them. In second and third grade, I was being haunted by *Highlights* magazine fables and zipping through Roald Dahl novels. I was playing under clotheslines out back of our apartment building. Trying to grow radishes in the hard soil along the driveway. Searching couch cushions for wayward hamsters.

Despite what contemporary documentaries about 1970s culture will have you believing, Black music, even big hits like "Groove Me" and "Mr. Big Stuff," were not just always wafting from grocery-store speakers. Blues, soul, R&B, and Black gospel were most often relegated to the backs of record stores, if they were heard at all. Black music has always had to fight for the credit it deserves for the massive impact it's had on American culture. My family was at the forefront, in Northern California, of selling folks the sounds they craved.

My great-aunt Elizabeth "Betty" Reid and her husband, my great-uncle Melbourne Reid, sold "race records" out of their garage in Richmond, California, in the early 1940s. That enterprise morphed into Berkeley's beloved Reid's Records, launched in 1945. Specializing in blues, R&B, gospel, and choir supplies, the record store was one of the oldest record stores in the United States, and, according to author, critic, and editor Lee Hildebrand, "certainly the oldest in the Bay Area." Reid's was not a glamorous business. Aunt Betty and Uncle Mel often protested unfair retail policies in what was then a young music industry. Reid's finally succumbed in February 2019 to racial retail politics, music streaming, and the gentrification of California's East Bay Area.

In addition to the Berkeley store, Betty and Mel had a Reid's stall in Oakland's Swan's Market back when Swan's stayed crowded with an endless variety of people going about the business of buying my aunt's records, purchasing linguiça and cabbage, or, as in the case of my mother, flipping through paper packets of ladies' dress and children's clothes patterns. Candy proprietors handed my sister balloons. We were allowed juicy pickles in waxed paper. Betty—in her nineties an author, a California Woman of the Year, and our nation's oldest park ranger—is our late grandmother's sister, and as those two wavered between impasse and hostility, we took Gramma's side in a long war about which we grasped little. I barely saw Betty or our cousins our entire lives.

In 1989, Lee Hildebrand assigned me my first paid story—a live re-

view of Natalie Cole, who was playing Oakland's Paramount Theatre. I
don't know if Lee knew I was Betty's niece. That I recall, he never spoke
to me about her. But in a town as small as Oakland when Oakland was
a Black city, it would be odd if he didn't know. It also seems like Lee, a
culture reporter in love with nuance, might know that our family of
groups of sisters was not as close as it could seem. My sister worked the
counter at Reid's in Berkeley when she was in her early twenties. We
were roommates at that time, and I never visited her there.

When I called my mother about the Cole job, she was like, "That's
great! How much are they paying you?" I had to call Lee back to in-
quire. At the time I was ringing up Clinique at Saks Fifth Avenue in San
Francisco. Second job was working at a nonprofit serving youth parol-
ees. I'd dropped out of UC Berkeley. My sister was a part-time counselor
at a Head Start day camp. We were on and off food stamps. We had cute
boyfriends, talked our way into nightclubs, and knew all the dope deal-
ers. We got our nails done at hood-ass MacArthur-Broadway mall. Got
guys to drive us to the City for no gas money. Once, we stole a refrigera-
tor. We figured shit out.

But Raquel and I had few plans beyond next month's rent and groceries. We didn't even talk about having or not having plans or goals—
that's how free we were. That's how indigo deep we were into a long
post-high-school era, aswirl as it was in our blues, sandalwood incense,
and survival. That's how broke we were. That's how little we had to
lose.

I would have drowned without Sade's "When Am I Going to Make
a Living." Without sweet bitters from Vesta (who died alone in a hotel
room of a bona fide enlarged heart), without Anita Baker's tenacious
middle-class optimism about love. Caron Wheeler of Soul II Soul ad-
vised us to keep on moving. *Don't stop,* she sang in 1989, *like the hands of
time.*

The Natalie Cole assignment was a beacon, though. My life was
shining back at me from the future. Not so long after the show, the girl
with the ashy knees and a key on a chain around her neck became music
editor of *SF Weekly.* Then a weekly columnist for the *San Francisco Bay*

Guardian, and a monthly columnist at *Spin.* In a new marriage, I moved to New York to be rhythm and blues editor at *Billboard,* and to escape both the warmth and the cold comforts of the city I was born in.

I loved Oakland. I wrote some for the Black-owned *Oakland Post,* but they had very little money. The *Oakland Tribune* had no interest in me. And neither did the *San Francisco Chronicle.* In my untrained way, I had tried to "be a journalist." But I had no bachelor's degree. No journalism school. No network. No friends in high or even medium places. No internship at a proper daily or local television station. No membership in the National Association of Black Journalists. I truly just did not know how to act.

I was a music-and-culture writer. A hip-hop specialist when the mainstream was skeptical at best and hostile at worst to the art form. If Bill Adler—then Run-DMC's publicist—had not recommended me for the *Billboard* job, my come-up would have been even more nontraditional.

And while there, I also started reviewing shows and albums—from Tina Turner to Ice Cube to Neil Diamond to Kenneth "Babyface" Edmonds—for *The New York Times.* Then started work as the second music editor at *Vibe,* and the first Black one. To say I "became" editor in chief of *Vibe* in 1994—and the first woman and the first Black person to have the job, and the first woman to run a national music magazine—is a criminal abbreviation. And I mostly trained myself. Editing people's term papers for money, learning nonfiction writing from Dr. Charles Muscatine, blasting Janet Jackson's "Miss You Much" at obscene volumes while crossing the old Bay Bridge, stomping on a San Francisco pier to Public Enemy's "Can't Truss It"—it all prepared me well for heading the premiere hip-hop and culture magazine of the 1990s and 2000s. I was a journalist. I had been journaling since childhood. I performed fearlessness from memory. I led genius teams. I wrote my ass off. I was everywhere. I loved it. It wore me out.

The girl who created *The 5th Grade Daily Arrow* (that one handwritten edition), who was page-two editor of her junior high school newspaper, *The Far & Near,* and photography editor of her high school yearbook, went on to become an editor at large at Time Inc., and then editor in chief of *Vibe* again, editor of *Billboard* magazine, and a senior editor of culture at ESPN.

I wrote two novels, both published by Random House. I've written for everyone from *The New York Times Magazine* to *Rolling Stone* to *Essence* to *Elle*. I have been to over a thousand live musical events. I haven't paid for music since I was twenty-five. I didn't just edit a magazine that relentlessly covered Death Row Records. I knew boys who are in San Quentin State Prison as we speak. On death row. Boys who have been there since before Natalie Cole played the Paramount that night. I knew girls who rode and, in the crossfire, died.

I didn't have my BA or MFA in hand until I was in my late thirties. Like so many of us, I bounced between achievement and self-stigmatizing sadness. Imposter syndrome and impulsive bravery. I've lost months at a time, even years or more, to rigorously planned self-sabotage, and the ensuing self-beatdowns.

I've loved and supported men who loved and resented me. I "knew too much." "Talked too much." I had "a golden touch." My life was "easy." Why wasn't I thinner? *You quietly ain't shit. Please come back. You make me feel like less of a man. You're the only one I really respect. You don't need me. You're going to die alone.*

I was fortified by songs like Erykah Badu's "Next Lifetime," Mary J. Blige's "Seven Days," and Janet Jackson's "I Get Lonely." When Badu sings (and co-writes), *See, it ain't nothing wrong with dreaming,* she's talking about a guy she longs for. She's also, in this most luminous of her songs, naming the whole of my creative life. I'm weeping right now, reading this aloud to my husband of sixteen years. It can still seem like I'm doing too much when I talk about myself. When more truly, I am rarely doing enough. *Shine Bright* is the name of this book. It is also a mission statement, and a command.

"Ten cents a word," Lee Hildebrand said when I finally called him back, asking about a fee. It was 1988. His voice left no room for negotiation.

I turned up the volume on Cole's second album, 1976's *Natalie*.

I was on my way.

PROLOGUE
Phillis the Precursor

It's not the way it should be / And heaven knows /
It's not the way it could be

—FROM 1978'S "HEAVEN KNOWS," CO-WRITTEN AND RECORDED BY DONNA SUMMER

A kidnapped child stands on Boston's Beach Street Wharf. The girl is eight, nearly nude, and has just stepped from a small Massachusetts slave ship called *The Phillis*. Some recall the child as seven. In any case, she is half-covered in a piece of dirty carpet. This is July 1761, fifteen years before the American Revolution.

I have imagined this girl so many times. My sixth-grade teacher told me about Phillis Wheatley, this child who was responsible for herself. A victim not allowed to be a victim. I used to dream about Phillis as a girl when I was a girl. When I dream of her now, she's an adult. I know it's Phillis because she arrives in profile, in her bonnet, like in the famous etching. And even though I never see the whole woman, I know I'm a part of her story. The essence of Phillis is strong in American music. I hear echoes of her voice streaming from speakers more than 250 years after she was born.

Phillis is a first. She's the model. The archetype of Black woman genius. A singer, with all that title conjures. And a composer of song. I relate to her lack of protection. And loneliness. Her survival instincts. Her belief, under grim circumstances, in love, and in herself. Phillis's urge to perform truths before the masses—to be seen and heard—is as

familiar as a sister's scent. She literally keeps me up at night. And I know
Phillis sees me.

Originally packed with ninety-five humans—Ghanaian, Gambian, Sen-
egalese, Fula, and Muslim are among the descriptors—*The Phillis* arrived with seventy-five. Timothy Fitch of Massachusetts sold the sickly
child to tailor John Wheatley, as a gift for his wife. Susanna Wheatley
was mourning the death of a daughter about the same age.

The new baby slave is assigned "light" work. She is taught English
and Latin and, as she gets older, is given, among other materials, a Bible
and a book of poems by Alexander Pope. *Blessed is he who expects nothing,* this girl might well have read, with resignation and resistance, *for he
shall never be disappointed.* The girl slave is referred to over the centuries
as "precocious." Well.

She carried for her short life the name of the vessel that transported
her unprotected self across the Atlantic, a ship on which 21 percent of
the cargo died of smallpox, fevers, suffocation, bloody infections of the
intestines, exhaustion, and who knows what-all violent and sadistic else.
"They frequently sing," said a mate who sailed on four voyages to Africa
in the 1760s and '70s. Lamentations. Communications. "The men and
the women answering each other. But what is the subject of their songs
I cannot say."

Phillis Wheatley was basically a second grader on a sea basket of
Middle Passage horrors. So perhaps trauma contributed to her sass. Or
maybe her precociousness was in response to the casual cruelty of being
named after the vessel of her terrors. "As to her writing," John Wheatley
said in a letter, "her own curiosity led her to it." Little wonder.

In 1773, the year Sarah "Sally" Hemings was born into slavery on
Thomas Jefferson's slave-run Virginia tobacco farm, Bostonian Phillis
Wheatley's *Poems on Various Subjects, Religious and Moral* is published in
London. Slaves in Massachusetts were beginning to individually petition the colony's General Court for freedom—or, in the case of a slave
known to history as "Felix," to pose the end of slavery altogether. "We
have no Property," Felix wrote. "No Wives. No Children. We have no

City. No Country. But we have a Father in Heaven, and we are determined."

It's no surprise, then, that even with a hard press from John and Susanna, Boston publishers refused to print the slave Phillis Wheatley's work. And regardless of Felix's efforts, there were still ninety-two years until emancipation. Generations. Harriet Tubman's grandparents were likely not yet born.

Yet the slender book, a kind of "greatest hits" of work Phillis had published in Massachusetts newspapers, is a huge success. The book features a pristine drawing of Phillis in a stylish bonnet and wide-collared day dress, sitting at a round desk. She has a book, a quill, an inkwell, and paper, and she looks thoughtfully into the distance.

The image is that of an artist and intellect. Even with the caption "Phillis Wheatley, Negro Servant to Mr. John Wheatley of Boston," the illustration is radical, and elegant. What was known as "society," in both England and the American colonies, loved Phillis Wheatley's work. A young and graceful Black girl who spoke truths in the language of her oppressors.

Imagination! who can sing thy force? This is what the young slave was writing, and performing in parlors and at fashionable salons. *Or who describe the swiftness of thy course?* Swift indeed. By the age of twenty, Phillis's childhood frailty had become a chronic asthmatic condition. She was sent with the Wheatley's son Nathaniel, Phillis's "young master," to London. Her trip back across the Atlantic was partly for her health—sea air had been prescribed by Susanna. With regard to her work, the trip was to be promotional. With regard to her quarters, and the slave-to-master relationship with Nathaniel, little is known.

On her literary award tour, Phillis arrives in London a year after the *Somerset v. Stewart* decision declared that slave owners could not legally compel their slaves to return to the colonies. And the thirteen in America—working their way toward a Tea Party in Phillis's adopted hometown—were getting restless. All this had to be on her mind as she performed her poetry among London's literate classes. She is fêted. She is lifted—by her work and perseverance and Blackness—to success. One of the very first of what will become the religiously chronicled and revered "firsts" of African American history, Phillis Wheatley is the first published African American poet in America. In London, her legal status is decried by progressive whites and free Blacks alike: "A genius in bondage."

A slave in fact. Phillis was in Europe living the kind of temporary freedom from slave-based American Blackness that would be experienced by so many Black American artists in the coming centuries. Included among her creative progeny would be the singer and songwriter Donna Summer. Summer fled Black Boston's gospel circuit for Germany on the promise of performing in a rock opera. Two hundred years after Phillis, in the 1970s, Summer felt the same need to leave in order to find freedom—the Me Decade was not meant for the Black Me. Even in the wake of the Black Power and Civil Rights movements, Black pop performers were rarely allowed narcissistic introspection and badassery, let alone unabashed individualism, until a decade later, in hip hop.

This motherless child, "Phillis," reportedly had one memory of her mother in Ghana/Gambia/Senegal. It was of water being poured over her, as if in a bath, or a ceremony. Perhaps this image was a dream, a notion. Surely it was a lifeline.

> Should you, my lord, while you peruse my song / Wonder from whence my love of Freedom sprung / Whence flow these wishes for the common good / By feeling hearts alone best understood / I, young in life, by seeming cruel fate / Was snatch'd from Afric's fancy'd happy seat.

For six weeks in London, while it may well have felt like the fish were jumping, being owned by her traveling companion had to curdle her soul.

Even as she tore from one appointment to the next, through filthy London with its theaters and hot air balloons—London with crowds so thick that maybe she could just . . . blend. How might Phillis have dreamt of losing herself among the servants and pickpockets and sales boys, among the pig carcasses, and silk shops. *What if,* she may have wondered, *if I could just stay here, and be me.*

She might have—she would have—left behind the biblical influences and the yoke of Alexander Pope had she her life, however terrifying, as her own. "In every human breast," Phillis wrote in a letter, "God has implanted a Principle, which we call Love of Freedom; it is impatient of Oppression, and pants for Deliverance." These were slave days, though, even in England.

And in Boston, Susanna was ill. Phillis returned to the colonies earlier than scheduled. The colonies were also about to be at war with the Crown. By some reports, Phillis negotiated for her freedom before she returned to the American colonies. Some say it had long been planned for Phillis to be "given" her freedom on the death of her senior owners.

In any case, Phillis "secures" her freedom from the Wheatleys upon Susanna's death, and begins work as a seamstress. In 1778, Phillis marries the handsome and educated John Peters—a man described as a lawyer, a physician, and most often as a free Black grocer. He is also described, as if he were white and free, as being "unable to settle in any vocation."

What vocations were available to John Peters? The job of a Black person in that era was to be a slave. Anything else was criminal. Not much is known about his and Phillis's courtship, but that there was one, and that it led to marriage is a kind of miracle. What is known is that the couple lived in great poverty. It is often reported that Peters deserted Phillis when she was pregnant with their third child. Their other two children had died in infancy.

Other historians make an important distinction: that Peters was just as likely to have been traveling—extremely dangerous for a free or enslaved Black man in those times—searching, without much success, for any kind of paid work. Did he desert her? Was Peters killed? Kidnapped and taken to another colony as a slave? Who can know?

Phillis was trying, unsuccessfully, to find other patrons. The woman who had in 1776 written a poem praising George Washington—one that got her invited to his Cambridge headquarters—was trying to write, and still taking in sewing. She had a few poems published in local publications—about the horrors of slavery, and about "expanding the liberating expectations of the American Revolution to everyone"—but she had no steady income of any kind.

How far away London's busy streets must have seemed. How much further away the mirage of Africa's "happy seat." Alone in a boarding house, and maybe because of her recurring asthma—or maybe due to the mix of physical and spiritual ills that Black women died of during slave times, Reconstruction, Jim Crow, the Civil Rights Era, the bright, turbulent seventies, the crack-y eighties, the rise of hip hop in the nineties, and the Obama dynasty of the twenty-first century—at about the age of thirty-one, Phillis Wheatley is dead.

At the time of her death, against good sense and contra to the mores of the times, Phillis had written a sheaf of new work. Until the end, she was like, *Let's try to get this second volume of poetry published*. No Boston publisher would have it.

Did the Wheatley children reach out to Phillis, to help her toward publication as their parents had? Did they take bread or cabbage to the Black girl who had been purchased as a balm for their mother, Susanna, who had lost a daughter of her own? Did Nathaniel or his sister provide even the mildest comfort as Phillis's first two children died, one after the other? Or were their minds spotless of responsibility? Who can know? What is known is that in those rugged revolutionary years, as chattel slavery was moving into its highest gears and all men were being declared equal, Phillis's third child died soon after she did.

Yes, I do know how I survive / Yes, I do know why I'm alive. This is what Donna Summer hurls out two hundred years later, in a 1982 Quincy Jones–produced song called "State of Independence." She's interpreting the lyrics of two Englishmen, and her mood is grounded in history: Summer's 1970s European sojourn worked. It allowed her to break out of a cramped gospel-and-soul lane in which Black artists had to live and for which Black women artists had to carry water.

Summer was in Germany, married to an Austrian, when she co-wrote "Love to Love You Baby" and reenacted the moaning sounds of Black female orgasm that shocked the world and made her a star in the country of her birth. The freedom to be and to create—to say, *Yes, I am alive*, to say, *I am human and feel pleasure as well as pain,* to claim the name and rank of poet or songwriter or MC or disco diva or pop star— this was another stretch in the wretched climb up from slavery.

Phillis Wheatley is buried in Boston's still active Copp's Hill Burial Ground, home to the remains of ministers from as far back as the Salem Witch Trials. "Countless free African-Americans," says the graveyard's site, "are buried in a potter's field on the Charter Street side."

Since 2003, a life-sized statue of Phillis rises from the concrete of Boston—in 2015 considered one of the top ten most racially segregated cities in America. She is near like figures of first wife and first mother Abigail Adams and abolitionist and suffragist Lucy Stone. Wheatley was chosen, according to *Black Art Depot Today,* "because of her progressive ideas, commitment to social change and the impact of her legacy and writings. Her statue represents youth and imagination."

The monument is a part of the city's Women's Memorial. Phillis looks serene and beautiful, and focused on the near distance, as if nothing could upset her creative process, let alone her life. She is briskly bonneted. Her scars and anguish are invisible under folds of bronze and granite. For survival and for her art and for success, she smoothed and sculpted her pain. From a junction of desperation and hope, of staged equality, she sang her songs.

There would be no justice or tranquility for the human Phillis Wheatley. *There in one view we grasp the mighty whole / Or with new worlds amaze th' unbounded soul.* How must it have been for her, our first star, as she tried and tried again to let shine her unbound light? Phillis died alone. But not in vain. For she is tied to me, and makes herself mine to imagine. *Let it shine / Let it shine / Let it shine.*

PART I

THE DIXIE CUPS

If you as a female—I don't care how many hit records you've had—if you're out there, still working, if you accept anything that [a] promoter throws at you, and you never say anything to lift yourself up, first as a female, second as an artist— then what's going to happen? His next clients that are females, he expects them to take it because you took it.

—ROSA LEE HAWKINS OF THE DIXIE CUPS, 2015

Until we moved to Mid-City, Los Angeles, with my mother's lawyer boyfriend, who was not practicing law, I was not sure that girls—outside of my sister and me—were teaming up in the world and making mischief.

Quel and I got up to ours with our new friends at Carthay Center, then an experimental magnet school. I was in a "gifted" program run by my teacher, Roberta Blatt. My mother and her well-connected semi-lawyer boyfriend moved us to the Miracle Mile–adjacent neighborhood specifically so we could attend Carthay.

I loved that school. It was about kids having freedom. My mother's freedom came in the form of a used cream-yellow Monte Carlo. She looked cool in it, played her music in it, and on hazy Los Angeles mornings, seemed on her way to some kind of peace.

My sister's Carthay class had rabbits. In my classroom, beneath tendrils of Mrs. Blatt's ivy, there was a carpet square designated for silent reading. I gulped essays printed on card stock, and answered the attached questions. With every correct answer, one moved up a color to the next comprehension level. Simple. I wanted to live on that carpet square. Because the duplex on Hi Point Street, with the bold tile in the long kitchen, was not a home.

At Carthay, where there was softball, and chorus, my sister's teachers noticed that she wasn't speaking. Not even to say "Here" at roll call. They called my mother in. Who knows what was said. But my sister, who talked to me about the rabbits during recess and lunch, was soon sent to counseling. I was amazed by this turn of events and had a feeling that my li'l tide was about to turn.

I don't know when I first heard the Dixie Cups, but it was likely on the radio in my mother's car. By the late 1970s, 1964's "Chapel of Love" was a new oldie, and popular on "gold" and "easy listening" stations like Los Angeles's K-Earth 101. My mother, who hadn't learned to drive until her midtwenties, drove to work and ferried groceries while leaning in to the jams of her youth. When she was driving we were allowed to adjust the volume, but we rarely changed the station.

By the time I got to high school, my mother was into the jazz-esque pinings of Angela Bofill, Marlena Shaw, and Michael Franks. But when I was a tween in the Monte Carlo, there was a lot of Motown and Elvis, and groups like the Shirelles, who, with 1960's "Will You Love Me Tomorrow," became the first girl group—of any race—to hit number one on the pop charts. I liked the song, but it was an inch too whiny.

The Marvelettes hit number one with "Please Mr. Postman" in December of 1961. A deeply danceable blues co-written by original member Georgia Dobbins, "Postman" is Motown's first number-one hit. At the 1:42 mark, when Gladys Horton doubles down on *You better wait a minute / wait a minute / Oh, you better wait a minute,* it's a demand of her man, not a request of the postman. I used to scream those lines with her, and I see Dobbins in the shine of Chrissie Hynde's vocals on The Pretenders' 1979 "Brass in Pocket."

I tolerated the Chiffons' 1963 number-one hit, "He's So Fine," as I did the Supremes' first number-one, "Where Did Our Love Go" from 1964. But the Dixies' "Going to the Chapel," recorded in February 1964 and released that April, was America's number-one pop song for three pealing weeks. It ruled in the Monte Carlo as an oldie, and gleams still with a kind of confidence in romantic commitment that—were it not for songs like this—I could doubt exists at all.

Rosa Lee Hawkins and Barbara Ann Hawkins are sisters, born and raised in New Orleans. They are two-thirds of the Dixie Cups. Barbara Ann is the older by three years. They share a modest home. In 2013, they're in their seventies and have survived Hurricane Katrina together. With their cousin Joan Marie Johnson, the trio recorded "Chapel of Love."

"Chapel of Love" sold over a million copies, dominated radio, unseated the Beatles' "Love Me Do" from number one on *Billboard*'s pop chart, and propelled the young women to a brief and hot stardom that could not compete with the more lasting impact of the Supremes. From the short a cappella rise to the finger snaps to the alternation between the soft *g* of *Gee I really love you* and the hard *g*'s of *gonna get married*—the cadence of "Chapel of Love" is consistent, and mesmerizing.

Spring is here, the
Sky is blue
Birds all sing as
If they knew

If "Chapel of Love" is confection, it is each listener's own individual favorite, and most of the later covers of the record—the Beach Boys' in 1976, Elton John's in 1994—basically align themselves with the Dixies' vocal arrangement. But Bette Midler went in a different direction.

Midler's cover of "Chapel of Love" appears on her 1972 debut, *The Divine Miss M,* an album on which she, with expressive freedom, braids Barbra Streisand, Broadway, and the earnestness of girl group songs like the Shangri-Las' 1964 "Leader of the Pack" and "Chapel." *Divine* begins with Easter-worthy bells, skips the slow intro, and rips into a Blackish, raucous delivery. Even with tongue in cheek, Midler's homage is weighted with the irony of a white woman covering a song by a group of Black women who in their original are deploying strategic enunciation.

"Proper" English diction is associated with white people in general and rings off in the pop of white stars from the Andrews Sisters to Doris

Day. "Properly" is what Blacks have been accused of being unable to speak since their chained arrival in the colonies. Midler, with a wink, goes with an ad-libbed churchiness. How free she sounds singing in ways Blacks were pressed to dial back—if they wanted to succeed.

"We grew up in the Calliope Projects," Barbara Ann Hawkins tells me. "Which, back then, was nothing like projects are today."

Completed in 1941 over what had been a city dump, Calliope is the original name of what became in 1981 the B. W. Cooper Apartments in Central City, New Orleans. It was for many decades known as one of the most violent housing projects in the nation. Rapper/entrepreneur Master P and his brother, the rapper Silkk the Shocker, grew up there in the 1980s.

In the Dixie Cups' era, the projects and 'hood known as Calliope had its own Boy Scout troop. Kites flew in open areas. Folks ate at Joe's Po Boys, and knocked back a few at the Rose Tavern. Black kids swam at nearby Rosenwald Center, then the "only such facility available to African American children" in New Orleans. The Neville Brothers also grew up in Calliope, near the Dixies—Art Neville won a talent show at Rosenwald.

The Hawkins sisters' parents were separated. "We were fortunate . . . to have a strong mother," says Rosa Lee. "She was not going to allow us to go down that road of *'I can't get into school because I'm Black,'* or *'I can't do this because I'm Black'*—that was forbidden in my house. My mom was . . . a Girl Scout leader."

Her mom, Mrs. Hawkins, was from Crowley, Louisiana—population less than ten thousand. All-Black schools situated among meticulously maintained antebellum mansions featured outdated books from all-white schools. Mrs. Hawkins got herself away from the old rice plantations to New Orleans and sang in cornetist Papa Celestin's Original Tuxedo Jazz Orchestra. She also sang with her daughters.

"We knew we could sing when we were kids," says Barbara, "because we used to do trios in [our Baptist] church with mom. And Rosa and I were always in whatever choir they had for our age bracket. . . . We knew we could sing, but we thought everybody in the world could sing. I thought it was something that came natural to everybody."

But Mrs. Hawkins's ambition couldn't protect her daughters from the truths of their environment.

"Yes. Yes," says Barbara Ann, exasperated by my obtuse segregation questions. "On the bus, the public transportation, there was a sign that said For Colored Only. It didn't say for what color, but it said For Colored Only. And all the seats on the bus had two little holes in it where you put the screen."

"The screen?" I ask.

"If a Black person was sitting too close to the front, and white people got on and wanted to sit down, they could ask you to move."

"And would they? How did that work?"

"You had to move back," she explains, "and they would put the screen back."

"It didn't even have to be a police officer, or the bus driver? Any white person could say, 'Move'?"

"Exactly."

"Sometimes [they were polite], and sometimes they weren't," says Rosa Lee. "Depends on what side of the bed they got up on. Some of them took advantage of the fact that the law . . . was on their side. So they wanted to act real nasty." But, she says, "I give my mom kudos. She taught us not to hate people."

The Hawkins family nimbly navigated New Orleans's apartheid policies. Rosa Lee recalls going to the Cabildo, a state museum in the French Quarter. "We probably were able to go on a special day [when African Americans were allowed]," she says. "She made sure we . . . saw all of the exhibits that any white child . . . made it to." Mrs. Hawkins also took them to the Ringling Bros. circus every year. "It didn't matter if you had enough money to buy a ticket to sit down front," says Barbara Ann. "You couldn't sit down front. You had to sit in the nosebleed section."

Some are good at writing obituaries. I'm among them. I've written obituaries for Michael Jackson, Bobbi Kristina Brown, the Notorious B.I.G.,

Gerald Levert, and more. When my maternal grandmother, Lottie Charbonnet Fields, died in July 2010 in Pasadena, California, I wrote hers.

Not long after Little Lottie, aka Gramma, was born, my great-grandparents—Dorson and Big Lottie, aka Gram—got their family from Louisiana's Orleans Parish to East Oakland, California. Much of my great-grandparents' family is still in Louisiana, proprietors of a Treme-based triplet of funeral homes that has been serving families since 1883. For homegoing services there are ivory carriages drawn by white horses.

My grandmother was light and often mistaken for white. Her gray-eyed father, Dorson, was as well. My mother is sometimes mistaken for white. During my childhood, she often told a story starring my sister, who as a toddler loved helium-filled balloons. Quel and I were on an Oakland AC Transit bus one day with my mother. This was when windows on city buses slid open. This was when psychic muscle memory had Blacks sitting at the back of the bus.

Raquel let the balloons bounce along on the current, and then opened her fist to let her "foons," as she called them, float up to the sky. Depending on my mother's mood, either Quel then cries out because she no longer has the balloons, or she just watches her foons for as long as she can see them—and then immediately asks my mother for more. But the story's kicker never changes. A white lady calls back to my mother in commiseration: "Times must be really hard if you have to babysit two colored girls." I was barely five and have little memory of the moment. This was three years after California's Summer of Love.

Two colored girls of my mother's generation dined quite formally in Calliope's projects. "It may sound simple," says Rosa Lee of 1950s Black New Orleans, "but just setting a table for dinner, you know? For a four-course meal, and all the way up to eight courses. We'd ask her, 'Mother, why do I have five forks?' She'd say, 'Just because you're living in the projects today does not mean that when you grow up, this is the only place you're going to live.' She told us that we never know who we're going to sit at the dinner table with. She wanted us to be able to handle ourselves, as young ladies."

This keep-yo-consonants, napkin-in-lap charm school for which Motown is famed has, since forever, been going on in Black homes of all classes. Manners are being taught, but so is strategy, and self-worth. There's a direct line from the Hawkins family in Calliope to my grandmother's no-hair-kerchiefs-outside to the infamous 2002 "Look the part, be the part, motherfucker" moment from *The Wire*.

These lessons become lifestyle, and culture. The overpreparation. The clenched hours of expecting the worst. The labors involved in actually working twice as hard to only get half as far. Straight A's from kaput textbooks. Comfort at the back. Ownership of spaces from which the rest of the world is unnecessarily far away. Nose bleeding fast and hot, and you don't even know why.

One Tuesday during the mid-1980s, I was going dancing. I lived in Oakland, and my grandmother happened to be in town from Los Angeles. She noticed how carefully I was applying mascara.

"Where you going?"

I named the spot. And I told her that the place was always the most fun on Tuesdays because it seemed like all the Black people in Oakland were there. They played all-Black music, even rap music, there are drink specials—

"Does someone organize it? It's someone's party?"

Me, exasperated: "No, Gramma! It's not like that, it's just a bunch of cool, fun people getting together. It's, like, organic! That's why I love it so much. It's like we all just know, and we go."

"We used to go over there every Tuesday. When I was nineteen or twenty. Dancing."

"It wasn't even there, Gramma!"

"It was right there. It was called something else. That space been called all kinds of things. Owned by different people. When I went on Tuesdays, it was the only night Blacks were allowed to go. Never on a Friday, or a Saturday, the typical party nights. Those nights were whites-only. We had Tuesdays. When we all had to be at work the next day."

This is one of the reasons my grandmother and her girlfriends started a club called "The Women." They rented halls and paid caterers, and sometimes gave parties at each other's homes. In photos, The Women are sparkling and hair-sprayed. The men are suited and shoes are shined. It's Saturday night. No place to go but late to Mass the next morning.

It can seem very Southern—this tendency of Black grandmothers like mine, or like Jamie Foxx's, who famously taught him to "act like you've been somewhere." But African Americans in all fifty states have a mystic recall of the Confederacy and Jim Crow. We know that the place we're to act like we've been is out from under the yoke of those evils, and free.

It's that "somewhere" we respond to in the precision of "Chapel of Love." It's what we feel in the urgent patty-cake of "Iko Iko." It was an international hit, and one for which the Dixie Cups fought James "Sugar Boy" Crawford for songwriting credit. The Dixies partially won.

My grandma told your grandma is how "Iko" goes, itself based in folkloric Native and African New Orleans Mardi Gras traditions. *I'm gonna set your flag on fire.*

On a block that could have been cast for *Sesame Street,* I have a dozen friends. We put on backyard talent shows. *Can you tell me how to get / How to get to Hi Point Street?* We actually sing this in a show. In a breezy moment of sobriety, Alvin—the lawyer boyfriend who is not being a lawyer—suggests the name "Crispy Critters" for our crew and we accept it, half in fear and half as proof of the humanity my mother insists lives within.

"Outside" on Hi Point Street is Critter Country. We first-kiss in garages. We lock legs in skateboard catamarans, and for our boards we dream of clear Cadillac wheels. The Gardens, the Cannadys, the Lewises, the Sussmans, the Donahues, the Bartons, the Porters. We are Black and Jewish and Catholic, and more than a few of us are adopted. Michael G. wears mascara and blows his hair out to Leif Garrettville. Michael L.'s father hates being Black LAPD and keeps his hedges in upside-down triangles.

This is 1975, 1976, 1977—and the Critters are tight. This is back when everyone called me "Dany." We go to Disneyland with Temple

Beth Am. We bike nine miles to the Venice Beach boardwalk. We pack liverwurst sandwiches, stay out past dark. For us there is KC and the Sunshine Band and the Whispers. We crib nickels for Cactus Coolers, for tickets to see *Jaws,* and for *Right On!* magazine. Michael L. kisses me hard in that garage.

Nearby Carthay Center is a reflection of our block. Key words being: creativity and integration and self-pacing. We definitely learn to tie-dye. I do math in my head with a Krypto deck in hand. Teachers jog into one another's classrooms shouting ideas, and they chat us up—about Irving Berlin, about Phillis Wheatley, about Judy Blume—like we're adults. There are semester-long choral projects, and intensely rehearsed productions of *Fiddler on the Roof* (fifth grade) and *The Music Man* (sixth). I melt into the love affair of the rebels Hodel and Perchik. Every rehearsal, when they defy tradition for travel and love, I know which *Fiddler* daughter I am.

I still know all of the lyrics to all of the songs in both plays, as well as the lyrics to Berlin's "Cheek to Cheek" and "Play a Simple Melody." The reason I can still recite the sonnet engraved at the base of the Statue of Liberty is because I learned it to the music Berlin wrote for the Broadway production of *Miss Liberty*. This was Carthay Center Elementary. This was me, happy.

Yet all of this learning and performance happened on the thinnest of ice, because my sister and I were arbitrarily forbidden from after-school practice and as arbitrarily allowed to return. Even during the heady camaraderie of dress-rehearsal week, Alvin was: *All that theater shit is bullshit and that fiddler is the main one all those teachers your teachers are Jews you're out of that bullshit never should have started you off in it. You're not wearing that shit stop reciting that shit.*

Days of screaming and snot and begging and Mrs. Blatt calling the Hi Point duplex and my mother negotiating behind closed doors with Mr. Not-a-lawyer, who beat her, beat us, and hated joy. Hi Point's sunken living room smelling of burped artichoke hearts and hidden bottles. My mother rushing us up to the school in the Monte Carlo before Alvin's mind could change or he erupted from coma. Us limp and tearstained in the school auditorium singing "Seventy-Six Trombones."

In 2020, I run into people I know from Hi Point Street. I occasionally hear from Crispy Critters: *You don't keep up with the kids we went to Carthay with? You should call such-and-such, she has pancreatic cancer. Remember the one with the long eyelashes? He has grandchildren with the same ones! You didn't see on Facebook?*

I don't *be* on Facebook unless I have to be, for work. For my whole life, I have been cutting off the kids I was in school with. Not just Carthay; every school. And for so long, I cut off people after every job. I don't want to see *nobody* after I have moved on. At first I had real shit to be ashamed of. And then shame became lifestyle.

Walter Louis Cohen (1860–1930), was born free before the Civil War. His mother, Amelia, was a free woman of color, and his father, Bernard, was Jewish. Walter rolled cigars and worked in bars before becoming a page at the New Orleans State Assembly, and eventually registrar of the U.S. Land Office and comptroller of the Bureau of Customs. Cohen might have been tickled to know that in the 1950s and '60s, at the high school named for him, there was a yearly talent extravaganza called the WaLoCo Show.

One year, Barbara Ann Hawkins, with her friends Barbara Phillips and Eula Barnes, won a trophy for singing. "And after that," Barbara Ann says, happy with the memory, "there was a citywide talent show, and we represented our school, and we won [another] trophy." Segregation was still the rule in New Orleans schools. Cohen High was all-Black, and the teachers and administrators were Black as well. "Public school was so different than it is now," Rosa Lee said when we spoke. "When there was a PTA meeting, all parents went to the PTA meeting. It was a big deal."

Barbara Ann, at the suggestion of neighbor girl Joan Johnson, formed a singing group with Howard Johnson and two other boys lost to memory. When one of the boys dropped out, Rosa Lee, an alto who could sing bass, joined up.

Barbara Ann made the outfits: iridescent green satin dresses that fell just above the knee. A-line, with a camisole bodice. There were matching pumps, and Barbara even found green netting and made overskirts. "Everyone called us 'the group with the green dresses,'" she told me. Barbara Ann even made a tie and cummerbund for Howard. "And we had our gloves. We were just cool, okay?"

The girls came by sewing via family. "My grandmother," says Rosa Lee, "I don't think she finished school . . . but she had a way with her. We'd go to the bigger stores and look in the showcase. She'd say, 'You like that dress?' And I'd say, 'Yeah . . . but we can't buy that.' She'd say, 'Do you *like* the dress?' And I say, 'Yes.' Then we'd go down the street . . . and she'd buy fabric . . . close to what she saw, and she'd go home and take the newspaper and cut out the pattern and cut the dress, and [then] there I was, wearing the dress."

At St. Augustine High School—founded in 1951 by the Josephite Fathers and Brothers "for the education of young men from African American Catholic families of New Orleans"—the group with the green dresses performed in the yearly talent show. In the audience was a talent scout named Joe Jones.

Jones had served in the navy, spent time at Juilliard, and been valet, pianist, and arranger for B. B. King. In 1960, Jones had a number-three pop hit for Roulette Records called "You Talk Too Much." The girls went to his house.

"And when we walked in," says Barbara Ann, "he kept looking at me. He said, 'Weren't you in that group that had the green dresses?'" Joe found the program from the talent show. "He showed me," says Barbara Ann, "that he had circled our names. At that time we were the Meltones."

Barbara Ann told Joe she held rehearsals at her place every day with neighbor girl Joan and the rest of the crew. The place was always jumping. Even Barbara Ann and Rosa Lee's grandmother was often there.

Barbara called her mother and asked if she could bring Joe Jones by. "We didn't know at the time," says Barbara Ann, "that he was the biggest crook God ever created. But he came to our house and talked to us. He talked to our mom . . . we sang for him, and he asked my mom to use the phone. He called Sylvia, of Mickey & Sylvia."

Mickey & Sylvia had a number-one pop hit with 1956's "Love Is

Strange," which Patrick Swayze and Jennifer Grey famously lip-synch in 1987's *Dirty Dancing,* and which in 2004 was inducted into the Grammy Hall of Fame. Mickey Baker and Sylvia Vanderpool were also off-and-on nightclub owners, music publishers, and indie label owners. Vanderpool eventually became Sylvia Robinson, and in 1979, she and her husband, Joe Robinson, founded Sugar Hill Records.

A founder of hip hop as much as the more famous Russell Simmons, the relentless Sylvia Robinson (who died in 2011 of heart failure) invented the Sugar Hill Gang. And—though the song's origin is stacked with accusations of thievery—Robinson is credited with co-writing the culture-shattering 1979 "Rapper's Delight." The international hit brought rap to the mainstream seven years before Run-DMC (managed by Simmons) exploded with Aerosmith and "Walk This Way."

Barbara Ann Hawkins recalls what Joe Jones told Sylvia. "We have," he said, "a gold mine."

Jones received money from Sylvia so the group could go to New York City. "He took us, [still called] the Meltones . . . there was an . . . artist named Vivian Bates." Jones also packed in his own band. They were in two or three cars and a station wagon. As for Howard and his green satin cummerbund? "Yeah," says Barbara. "Joe got rid of him."

Barbara Ann, Joan, and Rosa Lee were still teenagers. Mrs. Hawkins, who'd had that tiny taste of the chitlin music business, knew—as Barbara Ann puts it—"what it entailed." There was hesitation, but Mrs. Hawkins "had talked to Joe, and she said it was okay for us to go," says Barbara. "She wasn't going to stop us, because it was something we wanted. . . . We didn't know anything about making a number-one record or traveling all over the world . . . What was important was for us to sing—and to hear our song on the radio."

In New York City, they went to record companies and sang. "Everywhere we went, everybody wanted to record us," says Barbara Ann. "But we didn't know at the time that Joe was trying to find the best deal for himself."

Our softball team makes it to the schoolyard championship. Many of the Crispy Critters are on my team, or the opposing, or will be in the crowd. We've tie-dyed our jerseys. I'm a captain. We're good. A thing Alvin taught me was not to be afraid of the ball. *It's not going to hit you in your face and if you just watch it you can move out the fucking way. Watch it your eye will tell your brain when to swing. Watch the ball! Don't do this pussy shit don't close your eyes swinging at air like a fucking faggot. Keep your eye on the fucking ball.*

Alvin tells me that morning I cannot play, or go, or be a part of it at all. *You don't need to go up there you need to do what the fuck you supposed to do around here.* No memory of if I actually played. Or went.

Back then, I took my sister to counseling every Wednesday. I had my high hopes. We took the RTD Wilshire bus to UCLA to see Dr. Drapkin. She was a PhD candidate with long red hair. It was from a poster in the waiting room of her office that I first learned about a sliding scale. I wanted to be on that scale. Instead I waited with my feet dangling in the inverted fountain on Franz Plaza. Then Quel would tell me about Dr. Drapkin making her act out our Hi Point duplex times with the dolls.

In the Monte Carlo, reasons for Alvin's evil were delivered by my mother, with the implication that he should be considered with empathy and maybe even understood. This and that about his job. This and that about his father being mean to him. This that this that this that. *You don't leave someone at the first sign of trouble.*

From whom did she learn that last bit? What is the origin of the echo I hear in her voice?

Little Eva's "Loco-Motion" on low in the Monte Carlo. Beach Boys' "Help Me, Rhonda" on low. I'd once heard Alvin's mother tell mine, "If he's not doing it for you and the girls, he's not going to do it." Alvin's mother was talking about her son quitting alcohol, and about him getting married.

> *And then I saw her face.*
> *Jimmy Mack / When are you coming back?*
> *Going / To the chapel / Of love*

In the Monte Carlo, to the new oldies, I thought about ways to murder. Of possible poisons in scouring powder, and in the mold on bread. At the age of eleven and twelve and thirteen, in the Monte Carlo, I was expected to cosign on the idea that a man should be given all benefits of all doubts. Even though it was in our moments of focused effort, of achievement, of joy, that we were most mocked and most attacked.

"Iko Iko." That was August 1965. We were in the studio doing an album, and . . . the band and everybody was gone. We didn't know that Jerry Leiber and Mike Stoller were still in the control room. So, we had been singing this song forever [laughter]. My grandmother used to sing it to us. There was an aluminum chair, a drumstick, a cola bottle, an ashtray— and we played these instruments and sang "Iko." If you listen to it, you'll hear all of that. So, Jerry and Mike say, "Hey, ladies, can y'all do that again?" So, we did it again. They recorded it. They said, "Well, did y'all write that?" And we said, "Yes, we did." So they—we signed a contract, he sent it to Washington, and when Joe came back, he had a hissy fit. Oh, he hit the ceiling. Oh, child, it was nothing nice, you hear me? So then he went into this, how white people are going to steal from you, and blah blah blah blah blah, and we already knew he was the one that was stealing from us! But he didn't know we knew it. We were nineteen, twenty.
— BARBARA ANN HAWKINS AND ROSA LEE HAWKINS

By 1964, future Hall of Fame songwriters Jerry Leiber and Mike Stoller had already written Big Mama Thornton's—and then Elvis Presley's—"Hound Dog." They'd written the Coasters' "Yakety Yak" and "Charlie Brown." The duo worked also with LaVern Baker ("Tweedle Dee") and the incendiary Ruth Brown. Leiber and Stoller are credited with being "first to surround Black R&B music with elaborate production values, enhancing its emotional power."

"Leiber and Stoller," says Barbara Ann, "told us that 'the Meltones' was not a catchy name, and we had to change it." Leiber and Stoller came up with Little Miss and the Muffets. "We didn't want that. So . . . since we're from the land of Dixie, because we have the Dixieland jazz . . . and at that time, the groups were named items. You had the Rolling Stones, and the Animals. We decided on the Dixie Cups."

It was decided the newly christened Dixies would record "Chapel of Love," which had been written by Jeff Barry and Ellie Greenwich for production by Phil Spector.

Spector had already recorded "Chapel" with Darlene Love's Blossoms and never released it. He recorded the song with the Ronettes, but the Ronettes' "Chapel" had not been released either. The definitive version of "Chapel of Love" was recorded and released by the Dixie Cups in June 1964. "I wouldn't know [Spector]," Barbara Ann says later, in 2016, "if he walked in the door right now."

The Dixie Cups' "Chapel of Love" was a phenomenon. "We were the first American group to take back the charts," says Rosa Lee. "Back then it was *Record World, Cash Box,* and *Billboard.* And your records were judged by how much play they got. Before 'Chapel' came out, the Beatles . . . had everything sewed up. Joe told us our chances of making a number one record was 150 million to one. And when 'Chapel' . . . went to number one, and we dethroned the Beatles, I must say, Danyel, had we been the Ronettes, or had we been any white group, we would have been made over a lot."

Arrangement for the Dixies' "Chapel" is credited to Joe Jones and Mike Stoller, with songwriting by Jeff Barry, Ellie Greenwich, and Phil Spector, and with production by Spector. These credits lead one to believe, and for compensation to reflect, that what the Dixies did was stand and sing, and that was it. But when the young women first heard "Chapel"—as sung to them by Jeff Barry and Ellie Greenwich—they didn't like it.

"It sounded," says Barbara Ann, "like a country and western song. We looked at each other, and I said, 'Well, do we have to sing it like *that?*'"

Barry and Greenwich were said to be "attuned to young America's hearts and minds, with a natural sense of teenage idiom." The Brooklyn-born Greenwich (an accordion player raised in all-white Levittown, Pennsylvania) asked them how they wanted to do it. Barbara asked Ellie to give them a minute. "So the three of us, Rosa, Joan, and myself, we went in a corner and we came up with 'Chapel' the way it is. Back then, we didn't know that we were actually producing."

The girls decided to come in a cappella for the first few bars. They decided on the finger snaps. They decided upon no drums until the end of the intro. Phil Spector, says Barbara, was never in the studio. "Ellie and her husband, Jeff, they were the ones that were working with us on sound. And after we sang it, Wardell Quezergue did the arrangement. . . . Joe brought him up to New York." Quezergue, known as "the Creole Beethoven," also worked with the Dixie Cups on their "Iko Iko."

"You will find, in this business," says Rosa Lee, "that a lot of times people's names will be on things. But when you start digging, they really didn't have anything to do with it. On our record, you might see it was 'arranged' by Joe Jones, but it wasn't." In 2000's *Girl Groups: Fabulous Females Who Rocked the World,* John Clemente writes: "Joe Jones received production credit for 'Chapel of Love,' [but] Ellie and Jeff actually produced and the Dixie Cups came up with the arrangement, with help from Wardell Quezergue."

Back home in Calliope, Rosa was dusting the living room when "all of a sudden, 'Chapel of Love' starts playing! And I'm listening, and I'm humming, and it hit me—that's me! I went flying up the stairs, calling my mom. She said, 'Inhale, exhale.'"

Rosa says they weren't really aware of "Chapel" moving up the *Billboard* charts. "We walked into the music business so blind," she says, "it was pathetic." Barbara Ann says they were paid "four hundred and eighty-six dollars, or something like that," for the session. For singing, and for vocal arrangement.

"Joe used to go to the record company once a week," says Barbara Ann, "saying, *We need this, we need that*—he was getting thousands of dollars from them, he was paying the hotel bill, and that's it." She pauses. "He wasn't passing us a dime. He was rebuilding his house in New Orleans. You see," she says, "when we met him, his house was laying down on its side. After 'Chapel of Love,' he rebuilt it."

"Joe took all the money," says Rosa Lee. "Because—you didn't get paid at that time; you had to fill out your forms and they mail you your check."

Barbara Ann adds: "And when we were on the road, on the Dick Clark Caravan of Stars tour, when all those checks came in, Joe took all our money." Asked where he is now, the sisters, in unison and without sorrow, say, "Dead."

When they were at Harlem's Apollo Theater with the Shirelles (Beverly Lee, Micki Harris, Doris Coley, and Shirley Owens), the Dixies received advice. "The Shirelles became," says Rosa Lee, "like our leaders. They called us on the set and said, *Look, ladies. You do five shows a day. You wear this kind of thing for the first show, and then when you get to the last show you wear this kind of thing. This is how you do your hair, let's go buy some wigs.* They were the first that took time to help us and teach us. We became good friends with them."

After the Apollo, the Dixies were on their way to *American Bandstand,* to selling more than a million copies, to becoming a staple at oldies stations around the world. The Dixie Cups, by Barbara's word, are broke. And have been so for years.

So much of the culture and money created by American music during this era is the product of Black female creative energy. Yet the dollars paid for this energy and labor are unfairly distributed. Monies paid in rights fees on big pop records are annuity-like and wealth-building. Thousands blossom quickly to multimillions. So those "credits" that appear between parentheses under song titles reflect decisions about who basks in halls of fame, and about who gets paid. Credits are claims, as the Dixie Cups' manager put it, to gold mines.

Eternal songs emerged from partnerships between Black women, and men and women of other races and ethnicities. But the politics of caste overlaid and overlay the democracy of creation. In a more equitable world, these projects could stand out as examples of ungendered, interracial synergy. But in the 1940s through the early 1970s, when receipts were typed out with who wrote what, who arranged what, who produced what—whiter was way righter, and the males were even tighter.

In 2003, the Dixie Cups sued Joe Jones and his Melder Publishing. The claim: that Jones had collected royalties without paying them their share, including a foreign interest derived from the use of "Iko Iko" in 2000's *Mission: Impossible II*. "A jury awarded the Dixie Cups $409,507.89 in damages and ordered Jones to relinquish his copyright claims and license."

In 2017, there was another dispute—about the portion of "Iko" royalties going to Joan Marie Johnson's heir, Jerri Jones. She'd stopped paying the Artists Rights Enforcement Corporation, which had wrangled Johnson's fees from Windswept Holdings (later acquired by EMI Music Publishing). For his services, per the deal with Johnson, Artists Rights proprietor Chuck Rubin had been deducting 50 percent from Johnson's "Iko" payments. Rubin, a reinvented 1960s agent and business manager, was characterized by *The New York Times* in 1986 as "a kind of modern-day white knight jousting with corporations to return lost honor and royalties to rock-and-roll pioneers." The 2017 suit was Artists Rights demanding back its half of Joan Marie Johnson's payments.

While it's not known how much in fees Artists Rights deducted from a list of over two hundred clients, including the Marvelettes, the Shirelles, the Silhouettes (who hit number one with 1957's "Get a Job"), and Frankie Lymon and the Teenagers (1956's "Why Do Fools Fall in Love"), what is known is that Black pop is forever. Words and phrases like "fairness" and "generational wealth" and "intellectual property" can seem abstract until you pick up your mobile or glance at a television. In 2019, "Iko Iko" leads a Samsung campaign for their Galaxy Tab S6. The tablet apparently allows one to "Create. Work. Anywhere."

LEONTYNE + DIONNE + CISSY
The Drinkard Family Dynasty

Since fifteen in my stilettos
Been strutting in this game
"What's yo age?"
Was the question they asked when I hit the stage
I'm a diva, best believe her
You see how she getting paid?

—FROM BEYONCÉ'S 2009 "DIVA," CO-WRITTEN AND CO-PRODUCED BY
  BEYONCÉ KNOWLES, SHONDRAE CRAWFORD, AND SEAN GARRETT

Through the year 1860, Black adult human beings in Mississippi—having been purchased at about $1,300 each—often sang as they labored through the bloodiest parts of planting, picking, and processing more cotton than in any other state. As in the other fourteen slave states, and throughout the Union, crimes against these shoeless and unpaid workers, who were mostly living on pig intestines and corn, were systematic and profound.

Leontyne Price, the first Black woman to gain international fame as an opera singer—a true diva—was born in February of 1927, and so, missed being born into soul-slaughtering, cotton-picking Mississippi slavery by sixty-three years. But it was in her blood.

The associations I have with opera include dozens of viewings of Julia Roberts as Vivian Ward in 1990's *Pretty Woman,* and Cher as Loretta Castorini in 1987's *Moonstruck*. In both fairy tales, opera—*La Traviata* in *Pretty Woman, La Bohème* in *Moonstruck*—is a reason for dressing up fancy, and for being moved to tears. Even though there are only quick shots of opera scenes, I am usually intrigued by the wigs, props, and soaring voices. But not intrigued enough to search for hidden doors into the art form.

In 1997, as part of an arts journalism fellowship, I toured the massive

stages and backstages of New York City's Metropolitan Opera. It's the setting for Nicolas Cage and Cher's big date in *Moonstruck*. All bayonets and shelves sagging with costumes, the mazy dreamland was off-limits to Black performers until Marian Anderson was allowed to sing there in 1955. The stages smelled of glue and hummed with the creation and hoarding of culture. I relaxed my shoulders and nodded appreciatively. I didn't want to seem tense before my fellow fellows. In 2015, the Met, capital of the global opera community, would decide to discontinue blackface. For a time, Leontyne Price had made this beloved and plodding institution her kingdom.

Drowning in magnolia. Teeming with catfish. Poor, secluded, and swampy Jones County is Leontyne Price's beloved home. One of the most brilliant artists in the history of American music, she has won thirteen Grammy Awards, was presented with the Presidential Medal of Freedom in 1964, and was honored by the Kennedy Center for lifetime achievement in 1980.

Her catalog is vast. Her version of Francis Poulenc's "C'est ainsi que tu es" haunts. Her "He's Got the Whole World in His Hands" admonishes as it celebrates. She wrings wretched truths from Gershwin's "Summertime." All casual splendor and serene strength, Price wore Afros and tiaras and shimmering press 'n' curls.

By the time Mary Violet Leontyne Price came into her own as a professional, the United States was headed to Vietnam. Opera—redolent with posh whiteness and European excess—was experiencing an American boom. The United States was awash in opera-length dresses, opera-length pearls, opera-length cigarette holders, and jeweled opera glasses. The pomp and vividly non-American melodrama of the art form—onstage, on television, and via radio and recorded albums—provided distraction for the middle- and upper-class masses: Dame Joan Sutherland, Maria Callas, and Luciano Pavarotti were among the most admired pop stars of the era.

And it wasn't just the big names who made a lasting impact. Patricia Hickey, Mariah Carey's mother, was a part of New York City's opera scene in the 1960s and '70s. ("It's in my genes," Carey has said. "My mother was an opera singer. I'm clearly dramatic.") When Hickey, who is white, was rehearsing at home for the small role of Maddalena in Verdi's *Rigoletto*, young Mariah apparently mimicked her mother perfectly. It was then that the recently divorced Patricia Hickey Carey began coaching her daughter, a light-lyric coloratura soprano and five-octave prodigy.

Leontyne Price, a lirico-spinto soprano with a three-and-a-half-octave range, had her soles on the shoulders of women like soprano Sissieretta "Black Patti" Jones (1868–1933), who toured Europe, South America, and the Caribbean with the Fisk Jubilee Singers, and Mississippi's own Elizabeth Taylor Greenfield (1819–76). And with her thick and shapely body, lustrous coffee skin, and profound cheekbones, Price was every inch a diva—in the way the word was originally meant.

"Diva" is an honorific often applied derisively to modern women pop stars. Sometimes, that title is taken on as an empowered self-identification. The word itself is traced to opera's prima donnas: white lady leads of operatic companies. "I never sit on my laurels," Price said in 1985. "The thing that's been misunderstood is that I don't give a lot of rhetoric before I say, 'No.' I just say, 'No.' It saves everybody time, and maybe because I don't give a reason, it's taken in a negative way." These white lady sopranos were the best of those allowed to compete to be the best. Until Leontyne.

The relationship between the heights of opera and the heights of pop is straight and strong. "Something that few people are aware of is that the legendary opera star Leontyne Price is my cousin," Dionne Warwick says in her 2010 memoir, *My Life, as I See It*. "Her relationship to me is from my mother's side of the family. Leontyne lived in the south and was not a constant in my life. But when we see each other at functions, we acknowledge each other with 'Hey, Cuz.'"

So, Warwick, born Marie Dionne Warrick in December 1940 in East Orange, New Jersey, is thirteen years younger than her cousin Leontyne Price. Warwick's aunt Emily "Cissy" Drinkard Houston was born in September 1933 in Newark, New Jersey. Cissy's daughter, Whitney Elizabeth Houston, was born in August 1963, also in Newark. All are pop-cultural royalty. Women who kicked down doors and influenced generations. All are of the Drinkard family bloodline.

Hey, Cuz, indeed.

Jones County, apparently, was weird. Full of forest, and the farmland was terrible. So, relative to much of the rest of Mississippi, it had few slaves. Led by farmer and Southern Unionist Newton Knight, Jones County's free townspeople—muzzleloaders and rocks in hand—rebelled against the Confederacy, and it became a haven for grayback deserters. The area was known as the Free State of Jones—subject of books, and of a swashbuckling 2016 film starring Matthew McConaughey.

Jones's tiny society acquiesced to, if it didn't promote, cross-racial marriages and families. It often shrugged at Jim Crow customs. Leontyne Price's hometown of Laurel was in Jones and was known until the 1930s as a "city in a bubble."

"My earliest musical memory," Price said in 2010, "was hearing my mother sing in the backyard." Kate Baker Price was a soprano and sang at nearby St. Paul's Methodist, along with both of Leontyne's grandfathers. Kate was a licensed practical nurse and, as her daughter calls her, champion midwife of Jones County. "[My mother is a] very strong, dramatic, beautiful, wonderful lady. The last of that type, really. And very feminine, also, at the same time."

Mississippi's 1890 constitution erased Black men's Reconstruction-era right to vote and placed "segregation" in bold caps. But many Black men of Jones labored next to whites—some rising even to foreman—as they massacred acres of spruce and loblolly for northern lumber companies. Leontyne's father, James Anthony Price, was a sawmill worker and carpenter. He could also play the tuba, and she loved him dearly, down to how he moved through the world. "His pacing is all," Leontyne said of her poppa in 1981. "This strong, but gentle, but very definite quality that I think a lot of black men in the South have . . . it's tempered with this *going-on* kind of thing. And lasting."

By the 1940s, more than half of Mississippi's population was Black.

And the state was the sizzling kernel of the burgeoning Civil Rights Movement. Black families were being terrorized by white gangs. There were beatings, kidnappings, and the hanging of people from trees. Blacks, before white crowds big and small, were being doused in gasoline and burned alive.

Leontyne was raised in a quivering bubble, but the bubble was still in Mississippi, and Mississippi had the highest number of lynchings in the country from the 1880s through the late 1960s. To the cheers of white people, tongues were sliced from Black peoples' mouths. The organs themselves were kept in white families' homes and businesses as trophies. Amid this violent messaging, to be quiet and stay small, the Prices kept on toward excellence. "[Our parents] never told us we couldn't succeed," Price says in Rosalyn M. Story's 1990 *And So I Sing: African-American Divas of Opera and Concert*. "The word 'failure' never entered their conversations with us. The words 'do your best' was the constant echo we heard. And that was all we did."

Laurel had a middle-class colored section of small, neat frame houses, and this is where the Price family lived. From the time she was three, Leontyne took piano and voice lessons from Laurel's Hattie V. J. McInnis, the one Black music teacher in Laurel. At a time when Mississippi law stated that textbooks for white children and Black children had to be kept in separate storehouses, McInnis was one of the few Black American music teachers to study with German composer and music educator Carl Orff.

Leontyne attended the segregated high school in Laurel. Organized by the wife of a wealthy white lumber boss and Black families of Jones County who matched her funds, the school was officially termed a "vocational institution," in order to appease and fool white supremacists. But according to Mississippi novelist Jonathan Odell, the committees "set about creating an institution that attracted and paid for the best Black teaching talent from around the country.

"Oak Park [High] launched surgeons, lawyers, political scientists, college professors, star athletes, army generals, concert pianists, and operatic superstars." Price's younger brother George also attended Oak

Park, and became a brigadier general in the U.S. Army. "The education," Leontyne Price said in a 2012 interview with the City University of New York, "was extremely well-rounded." She said the teachers found in each child "bulwarks of strength to build on."

Young Leontyne was a drum majorette. She sang at funerals for money. She sang at weddings. She sang Tchaikovsky, she sang "Boogie Woogie Bugle Boy," she sang "Deep River." Leontyne sang in St. Paul's choir alongside her mother, and she recalls, only half joking, that the Laurel neighbors would close their windows when they saw her mother walking along. "'Here comes Kate,' they'd murmur. 'She's going to brag about those kids as if no one else has ever had children.'"

Kate wasn't the only one who doted on Leontyne and George. They also had their mother's sister, "Big Auntie" Everline Greer. Greer, who sometimes lived with the Prices, had a small house in the backyard of pianist and lumber heiress Elizabeth Chisholm and banker Alexander Chisholm, a white family for whom she did laundry, cooking, and home-keeping for forty-five years. The prominent Chisholms, like so many affluent whites in the 1950s, were opera buffs.

Leontyne became friends with the Chisholm daughters, Jean and Margaret Ann (aka Peggy). As *Life* put it in a reductive 1961 photo caption, "As a singing maid, Leontyne wears a uniform while performing in the Laurel home of her benefactors . . . at a wedding reception held in 1951 for their daughter Peggy."

It's work to comprehend authentic friendship between Black and white women at a time of brutally and legally enforced white supremacy. In the bubble of Laurel, relationships were knotted and multiform. "Mrs. Chisholm," Price said in 1961, "taught me how to be a lady. The right manners, the right clothes, the right small talk." The Chisholms made available to Leontyne their "recording machine." From it was the first time she heard opera.

Funds were tight in 1948 as scholarship student Leontyne was finishing her degree in music education at Ohio's historically Black Central State University. While there, she sang with Paul Robeson at a recital. He encouraged her, and contributed to the Leontyne Price Fund, which had been established by Central to support Leontyne at a music school. There was a benefit concert that raised $1,000, but that wasn't going to pay for Juilliard, and living expenses, in New York City.

In Laurel, brother George was completing coursework at Oak Park High. Both of them: talented, focused, ambitious. Kate and James mortgaged the house. They took in extra work. "Somehow," Leontyne said in 2012, "with this focus on their kids being even better than they were in Laurel . . . that sacrifice was augmented in my case at least by [the Chisholms, who] were most interested in my pursuing an advanced career in music. . . . Because for extra fun, I would sing and play [piano] when they had parties. And one of my lasting friendships of my whole life is [with] one of their daughters. We were friends all our lives."

The Chisholms paid for the majority of Price's graduate education. And by 1976, in the week before opening in the title role of the Metropolitan Opera's new production of Verdi's *Aida*—the second Black woman to do so (after the great Gloria Davy)—Price was perturbed by white reporters' willful misunderstanding of the complex relationship between her family and the Chisholms.

"The press has made too much of that legend," she said (*People* magazine characterized her tone as "insisting"). "I love Miss Chisholm; she was here only last month. Her daughter Margaret Ann and I are best friends. But the Chisholms got exposure because of the racial angle. I guess it makes me angry because it denies the sacrifices my parents made for me."

Decades later, in the 2012 interview, Leontyne Price states what she did appreciate: "To their credit, [the Chisholms] asked permission from my parents—*would it be alright* if they subsidized my advanced study at Juilliard." It's this lack of paternalism that means everything to Price. What she insists upon in the interview is the true strangeness of real relationships between Blacks and whites in the American South in the first century after slavery. In the accompanying *People* photos—backstage at the opera, especially—Peggy and Leontyne look thrilled to see each other. Each radiates happiness. And so, the cross-caste and cross-race circumstance of their friendship is even more tragic.

———

During strictly segregated times, Leontyne Price and her husband, Arkansas native William Warfield, were both deeply creative and determined to win in white art forms. Yet most of the success was Leontyne's, and while the marriage was short, the relationship was long, snarly, and sophisticated.

Warfield, a baritone, was raised in Rochester, New York, performed with Price for many years, and is most famous for his rendition of "Ol' Man River" in the 1951 Technicolor adaptation of the problematic musical *Show Boat*. He and Leontyne were married August 31, 1952—"Porgy Marries Bess" is how the *Jet* notice went—and it says by the pastor and congressman Adam Clayton Powell at New York City's historic Abyssinian Baptist. In reality, Powell was stuck on Long Island, and his assistant, Dr. David Licorish, officiated.

It was a scary time for Black couples who pushed past the status quo. Just eight months before Leontyne and William tied the knot, crowds were protesting the assassinations of Florida NAACP activists Harry T. Moore and his wife, Harriette Moore. Fury was still in the air. The Christmas attack on Black protest and Black love made headlines nationwide.

The bomb, placed with diabolical precision under floor joists beneath the couple's bed, exploded at 10:21 p.m. "When those lights went out," scholar Sonya Mallard said in 2020, "the Klansman who was hiding in the grove waited, and then they crawled under the house, just like a snake." Mallard is coordinator of the Harry T. and Harriette V. Moore Memorial Park and Museum, which sits on twelve acres in Mims, Florida.

Harry died that night. Harriette lasted nine more days. After years of working with her husband at the battlefronts—lynching protests, voter registration, and standing up for Black people falsely accused of crimes—Harriette was tired. "There isn't much left to fight for," she is reported to have said from her deathbed. "My home is wrecked. My children are grown up. They don't need me. Others can carry on."

Harry was a school principal. Harriette was a teacher and insurance agent. They meet over a game of bid whist. The 1951 Christmas that ended their lives was also the twenty-fifth anniversary of their wedding. In 2006, law enforcement finally named the Moores' four killers.

In 1952, Leontyne and William headed for Washington, D.C. Still touring domestically as the stars of *Porgy and Bess,* they played the newly desegregated National Theatre (President Truman attended) and then flew to what was still Allied-occupied Vienna to reprise their roles. How might this young Black couple have felt—so glamorous, so accomplished, and on the run, at least for a while, from a homeland entrenched in pre–Civil Rights Era oppression?

Classical music magazine *Musical America* reviewed the couple's opening performance at the Vienna Volksoper. "William Warfield [as Porgy] . . . made DuBose Heyward's character extraordinarily vivid with his warm personality and superb voice," said the impressed reviewer. "Leontyne Price imbued the figure of Bess with fascinating feminine charm. Not only did her voice sound beautiful, but she exerted an erotic spell that gripped the audience." This praise from home must have been a salve.

Nineteen-fifty-two was the year Congressman Powell of Harlem withdrew in protest from the National Council of Churches in Christ after its board voted to take no action on the apartheid in their worship communities. As for the whites in Price's home state, according to historian Pete Daniel, they "stood out as the most obstinate and violent [in the United States] in the protection of segregation."

This was also the year Random House published Ralph Ellison's *Invisible Man.* Throughout the 1950s, '60s, '70s, and '80s, it was difficult for Warfield to find work in opera. He made his living as a recitalist, an occasional actor, and in 1984 won a Grammy in the Spoken Word category. Warfield would never escape "Ol' Man River," though—a Jerome Kern/Oscar Hammerstein blues, made famous by Paul Robeson and ostensibly about the hope and sadness of Black life in the 1920s around the Mississippi River.

It's almost a dirge. *Let me go 'way from the Mississippi / Let me go 'way from de white man boss / Show me dat stream called de river Jordan / Dat's de ol' stream dat I long to cross*. Even when it rises to beauty, it's an awful song to sing soulfully in front of white people, over and over and over again.

"There's a sadness to it," Warfield said in 2000. "Sometimes it's . . . laid-back, and sometimes it's even angry. The most difficult time I had with it was singing it just four days after Martin Luther King's assassination. . . . I had to hold back my emotion . . . to keep from breaking down altogether." It was especially cruel, as Warfield was rarely allowed to work in opera, the profession he loved, had trained for, and at which he excelled.

Price and Warfield divorced in 1972, having been legally separated since 1967—and actually separated since 1959. There were no children, and the duo apparently worked together cordially over the course of those years. Warfield, it is said, blamed "career issues." Almost everything written about their divorce, if it warrants more than a mention of the date, says it was the couple's "busy careers" that led to the end of the marriage. Perhaps it was.

On January 3, 1985, Price stood onstage at the New York City Metropolitan Opera amid "cheering, bouquet throwing, and confetti strewing," enjoying an ovation that lasted twenty-five minutes. This after a final, soaring performance of *Aida,* broadcast via public television to millions. Among the guests in Price's box that night were her brother and his wife, Georgina, and her friend Peggy Chisholm, from Jones County, Mississippi.

In the week ahead of her performance Price told *The New York Times* that she was close to fifty-eight, and that about her age she could not care less. The writer describes her as being "turbaned and be-pearled, muffled in a turtleneck sweater and dramatically long tartan scarf . . . dewily luscious as a ripe peach." "But at fifty-eight, I've got to steal some time for myself," Leontyne Price said. "I'd like to give the woman in me a bit of attention."

Price's conversation was described as a mélange of "French and Italian words, and American slang." The *prima donna assoluta* talked of taking on students. And of living her life. Ground zero in a musical dynasty of women who would literally change the face of American and global pop, Leontyne Price said, "I come from the stage, warmed in the light of center stage. This is the beginning of a virgin voyage. I want to know how to pass something on."

Nineteen eighty-five. The world was about to be tilted for decades by AIDS, but—as the journalist Randy Shilts would say of the sociopolitical response to the disease that took his life—the band was playing on. Though blood banks had started screening for the virus, by October closeted film star Rock Hudson was dead from AIDS at age fifty-nine. A month before he died, Hudson left a quarter million dollars for the launch of the American Foundation for AIDS Research (amfAR).

I was living in the Bay Area, and people were afraid to touch one another. *Can you get it from toilet seats? From sharing a drinking straw?* T-shirts screamed SEX = DEATH. It was a terrifying time to desire the body of a stranger—or to lick a cotton swab in order to smooth a client's brows. "We were losing hair people, and makeup people, designers, and not knowing why," Dionne Warwick said to *The Advocate* in 2015. "I was wondering, What is this thing? We have to pay some attention to it."

March 1985's "We Are the World" and its predecessor, 1984's "Do They Know It's Christmas?" set the stage for "That's What Friends Are For," a November 1985 benefit recording for AIDS research featuring Elton John, Gladys Knight, Stevie Wonder, and Warwick, and billed as "Dionne & Friends." In addition to raising millions and becoming the "unofficial anthem of those trying to stamp out AIDS," the song was a number-one pop hit. A phenomenon on radio. A television special.

Billboard named it the biggest song of 1986. It won two huge Grammys—Song of the Year for songwriters Burt Bacharach and Carole Bayer Sager and Best Pop Performance by a Duo or Group with Vocals for the singers. In 1987, Dionne was named United States Ambassador of Health by Ronald Reagan, whose administration cruelly and infamously both mocked and ignored AIDS.

Warwick spent the next decade in a dungeon of ridicule. She was hazed for being a money-hungry opportunist, for taking lowbrow gigs, and for hosting a popular syndicated television show deemed cheesy by white critics and Black influencers. Relegated to kitsch, and perhaps even in search of answers (and money), Warwick became spokesperson for the Psychic Friends Network. Hilarious, right? An actual and particularly operatic headline? "The Dizzying Downfall of a Bankrupt Diva."

Warwick was a late-night-monologue whipping girl back when jabs from white and Black male comedians mattered more to culture. Even as Warwick sat, in 2018, on millions in tax debt, those same laugh-track junkies, showing off Harley-Davidsons and scrambling for streaming deals, had less grace in their personas than the ash falling from Warwick's menthols.

Don't make me over.
—LYRICS BY HAL DAVID, AS RECORDED IN 1962 BY DIONNE WARWICK

Dionne Warwick was born in 1940 and raised in an integrated lower-working-class neighborhood in East Orange, New Jersey. She loved it. "Sterling Street was like living within the United Nations," she said in 2010 to *New Jersey Monthly*. "Every race, creed, and color lived on that street. We rode bicycles, skated. We played . . . all the ballgames you could play."

Her grandfather was minister at East Orange's St. Mark's Methodist. "He was my biggest fan," she said. "I was six when he discovered me, but really I've been singing all my life." Gospel music even taught her, like a dictionary, the meaning of words. "Gospel," she's said, "is basically the Bible in song."

Marie Dionne Warrick was part of an ambitious family relentlessly involved not just in the singing of gospel music but in the business of gospel music. Something often left out of the conversations about the correlation of Blacks with sport and music is that, however problematic the compensation and advancement structures, these were and remain two of the few avenues in which Black people were allowed to create, in one generation, the generations of wealth they'd been denied pursuing both while in slavery and after Emancipation.

Dionne's father, Mancel, worked at an electrical plant in Newark, and concurrently as a Pullman porter, and as a cook. Into all this Mancel squeezed being director of gospel promotions for the blues label Chess Records. Dionne's mother, Lee, was a court reporter, worked at a light-bulb manufacturer, and also managed the Drinkard Singers. In the 1950s, the Drinkards recorded for Verve Records, Savoy Records, and RCA Victor Records. They were the first gospel group to release an album on a major label. "It was a musical family," Dionne said in 2012. "It's what we did."

As a young woman, Dionne had a supermodel's long face. Chiseled cheekbones hovered above angular cheeks, and sharp jawbones bent into a crisp chin. When Dionne wore a high bouffant bun with bangs sweeping bold brows, her face seemed exaggerated to make a point. And with her palette of blasé expressions, Dionne looked like she'd rarely been surprised by anything. "At a very young age," Warwick said in 2012, "I was influenced by the style of stars such as Marlene Dietrich, Lena Horne, and Loretta Young—as soon as I saw them, I knew those were the looks I wanted to emulate."

Warwick attended the Hartt School, a performing arts conservatory affiliated with the University of Hartford, where she studied music education and piano—which she'd been playing since she was seven. As Dionne told *The Wall Street Journal* in 2018, "I often accompanied voice and opera students." By 1962, Dionne was ready to move beyond the Gospelaires, the successful group she'd formed with her sister Dee Dee. And she was ready to leave behind the background singing she was really good at. Warwick was ready to pop, and she might have heard about another "Dionne" who was making noise.

Philadelphia's Dione "Dee Dee Sharp" LaRue, who had been a background singer for Chubby Checker, Frankie Avalon, and Fabian, had her only hit pop single with 1962's "Mashed Potato Time" (Cameo-Parkway). On the pop charts she was kept from number one by the Shirelles' "Soldier Boy," but overall, "Mashed" was the number-three song of 1962. Sharp recorded it at the age of sixteen.

A regular on *American Bandstand,* Sharp also went on the road in the Deep South with the Supremes, the doo-wopping Dovells, and the Dixie

Cups as part of Dick Clark's Caravan of Stars. "We saw . . . burning crosses," says Sharp. "Dick Clark . . . made it comfortable for us, being African American . . . he never, ever allowed us to stay anywhere other than the finest hotels. If we couldn't stay there, then we didn't do the show. . . . They threw paint bottles at the bus. They started throwing stones, and one of the Dovells, [a white guy named] Len Barry . . . pushed my mother and I to the ground and covered us. . . . I never will forget Lenny for that." Her job was to go daily from terrorism victim to dancing the mashed potato before rare integrated audiences.

Sharp married writer and producer Kenny Gamble in 1967. The Gamble and Leon Huff songwriting and production team were inducted into the Rock & Roll Hall of Fame in 2008. Among their records: "I Love Music," "Back Stabbers," "You'll Never Find Another Love Like Mine," and "Me and Mrs. Jones." Big R&B records. Big pop records.

Dee Dee recorded for Gamble Records, and worked with Gamble and Huff behind the scenes at the various iterations of TSOP (The Sound of Philadelphia) Records. "When I got married, I decided I didn't want to sing anymore," Sharp told journalist Gary James in an interview for ClassicBands.com. "I wanted to take care of Gamble's recording artists. I was able to procure Jerry Butler for Gamble. To do the Blue Notes for Gamble. The O'Jays for Gamble. Lou Rawls for Gamble. And Billy Paul. So I was too busy taking care of the artists to deal with anything else." Sharp and Gamble divorced in 1980. At seventy-two, Sharp was finally honored in her hometown: the World Cafe Live hosted "A Night of Musical Celebration Featuring Philly Legend Dee Dee Sharp in Concert."

"I do Europe a lot," Sharp told James, echoing so many Black women in pop. "Spain, Brazil, England . . . I've never done [my show with my band] in Philadelphia. It's been a very long, long, long, long time. Long time. Long time. I work Philadelphia, but I don't *work* in Philadelphia [italics mine]. That's strange, but okay. It is what it is."

Perhaps it was the steely sophistication of a tall, talented, post-teen stick-ball player that Burt Bacharach responded to in an early 1960s Drifters session.

"One day we got the call to come to New York's Bell Sound studios," Warwick told *Mojo* in 2012. "We were told we'd be providing background vocals on [a song called] 'Mexican Divorce.' I didn't know who Burt Bacharach was. Or that he'd written the song, but he was at the session. We heard the song through twice and then *came up with the background*. It wasn't hard. My mother said I came out [of the womb] singing." Italics mine.

Dionne Warwick was singing background that day with younger sister Delia Mae, aka Dee Dee. Dee Dee Warwick was considered more beautiful than Dionne, and her tones were described as "dulcet." Dionne's aunt Cissy was there—in seven years she'd begin singing backup for Elvis Presley. And Doris Troy was in the session. She co-wrote and recorded 1963's indelible "Just One Look," and signed in 1969 to the Beatles' Apple label. The long-running 1980s off-Broadway musical *Mama, I Want to Sing!* is based on Doris Troy's life.

So, in terms of talent, this was a big room. But Burt wanted to work more with Dionne. "After the session ended," Warwick said in 2012, "Burt . . . came over and introduced himself. . . . He said he liked my voice, and he asked me if I'd be interested in doing some demonstration records with him and his new songwriting partner, Hal David. I said yes."

"Don't Make Me Over," the first song she recorded with Bacharach and David—her solo recording debut—begins with twenty seconds of quivery strings. The song's lyrics are based on a terse conversation between Burt and Dionne. Some say the conversation happened after he critiqued her work. Some say she was angry because the song she wanted to record, "Make It Easy on Yourself," had already been recorded by Jerry Butler. In an interview for his *Biography* special Burt Bacharach says that Warwick burst out with "Don't make me over, man . . . (you have to) accept me for what I am."

And *accept me for what I am* is what she sings, reaching concurrently for both primness and gospel release. *Accept me for the things that I do.* Like new and faltering love, the song is raw. It lingers in the valley between what you wanted and what you got. *Don't make me over / Now*

that I can't make it without you. The song dips and floats in the churn of
Blacks and whites creating together. It's heartbreaking.

In an oddly flat paragraph listing her achievements, Warwick says in
her autobiography, "[The song] was the first indication that my style
would appeal to a wide audience." Dionne has no writer's credit on the
1962 record, and Lord knows official credit has been assigned for less
input. Her family name, Warrick, is apparently misspelled as Warwick
on the single. So she kept it. The record, awkward and desperate in its
declarations, has only become more loved by radio audiences over the
years and was inducted (the second of three Warwick hits) into the
Grammy Hall of Fame in 2000.

That the Grammy Hall of Fame honors "recordings of lasting quali-
tative or historical significance" is appropriate, as the song is the first of
thirty-eight charting singles the accidentally christened Warwick created with Bacharach and David. A quarter of those were top-ten hits.
There's the muted sexiness of "Reach Out for Me," the devastation of
"Walk on By," and the Grammy-winning, at-loose-ends antics of 1968's
"Do You Know the Way to San Jose."

Known as "the triangle marriage that worked," Warwick, Bacharach, and David were an insanely successful creative team. "Burt and Hal
wrote specifically for me," Warwick said in 2010. "I simply had to listen
to the songs they had written for me and record them in my special way."

By 1972, the triangle stopped ringing. Creative and personal differences surfaced. Contracts signed in the optimism of youth curdled with
age. By the midseventies, the trio's constrained brand of pop was giving
way to vibrant tendrils of disco. By most accounts, Warwick wasn't interested in it. She was having a tough time finding a space for her sound.
But as one from a music biz family—promotions, management—
Warwick was pragmatic.

She wanted to work. And the truth is, while they'd come close, Dionne Warwick, who had sold thirty-five million records by the end of
1971, never scored a number-one hit with Hal David and Burt Bacharach. For that she had to wait for 1974's "Then Came You," a spring
poem produced by Thom Bell, from Warwick and the Spinners' leads

Bobbie Smith and Philippé Wynne. "Then Came You" is a miraculous groove that lays the foundation for Peaches & Herb and Marilyn McCoo & Billy Davis, Jr.'s buoyant late-seventies runs.

Dionne didn't think "Then Came You" was going to work, but it was a new day. Many of the new clubs and discothèques featured DJs of various races and cultures who played music of their own and local tastes. In the field, club DJs were change agents and were often not held to the segregated customs and playlists of their radio counterparts.

"Disco developed . . . underground," says singer and actor Melba Moore, who had R&B, disco, and pop hits in the 1970s, '80s, and '90s. "DJs . . . were more in the foreground, becoming the stars. It [was] music you [didn't] necessarily hear on the radio. . . . You [had] to make an effort to go out and hear it." This underground was surging. Nixon was re-signing. *Vogue* finally put Black model Beverly Johnson on its cover. And these disco DJs played Dionne and the Spinners' "Then Came You" to appreciative Black, mixed, and white audiences, over and over again.

"Then Came You" wins because of the naturalistic ecstasy—vocal and instrumental—being batted around, especially in the ending ad libs. Listeners wait for them every time. Know them by heart. Warwick—like Diana Ross on "Love Hangover," Amii Stewart on her "Knock on Wood," and Cynthia Johnson of Lipps Inc. on their "Funky Town"—sounds free.

While disco was an imperfect space that thrived on exclusivity emblems like velvet ropes and VIP sections, once inside the club, where people were wearing the fresh fashions and doing the new dances, rock and the musical religion built up around the sanctity of the guitar was rendered just another vibrant movement, and not automatically everlasting, or better, or more deep than anything else. If you were a tween or a teen during these times, and *not* a rock fan, it was like your heroes had suddenly been given superpowers.

Disco didn't just happen in white spaces on Saturday nights in New York City. It happened in Black spaces like John Daniels's Maverick's Flat nightclub and restaurant in Los Angeles's Leimert Park. L.A. also had Lonnie Simmons's Total Experience nightclub, and the Memory

Lane Supper Club (purchased in 1980 by Marla Gibbs of *The Jeffersons* and *227*).

Everyone from Ike and Tina Turner to Parliament-Funkadelic played Maverick's, and it was a hot spot for my mother, my aunt, and their friends. They were all in a club called Kids & Company. It functioned like a less moneyed version of a Jack and Jill of America chapter (bringing Black kids together for social and cultural events). Along with Easter-egg hunts and day trips to the San Diego Zoo, there were afternoon dress-up dances, and the one Kids & Company threw at Maverick's had a real DJ booth, and the biggest speakers—blasting Cheryl Lynn's "Got to Be Real"—I had ever seen.

"It was the kind of high-energy scene that was relaxed enough to attract the Hollywood elite," John Daniels has said. "It was word of mouth. Muhammad Ali would come in and work as the disc jockey, doing his rhymes. [Film producer] Jon Peters would come in. The Rolling Stones, the Mamas and the Papas. Marlon Brando came in and was almost put out because he wasn't wearing any shoes."

I remember the DISCO SUCKS bumper stickers. They shouted at me. It was worse, though, when the stickers (and T-shirts) came to life. In 1979, between the games of a Chicago White Sox doubleheader, fifty thousand people at Comiskey Field chanted "disco sucks" while crates of disco records were blown up and burned on the field. A huge media event, this was called Disco Demolition Night, and it was widely covered on Los Angeles radio.

The host, a recently fired rock DJ, broke vinyl records by slamming them on his head. As Eve Barlow wrote in 2016, "Some have argued that the Death to Disco movement by rock fans was blind idiocy. Others have alluded to a more sinister attempt at ethnic cleansing of the charts, as disco's origins were found predominantly in the Black, Latino, and gay communities." Yes, and yes. And disco is thick with the voices and energy of Black women: Donna Summer, Gloria Gaynor, Thelma Houston, Amii Stewart, the Pointer Sisters, A Taste of Honey, Sister Sledge, Anita Ward, Diana Ross, the Gwen Dickie–led Rose Royce, the Cynthia Johnson–led Lipps Inc., Norma Jean Wright, Alfa Anderson, and Luci Martin of Chic, Warwick, and more. A corps d'elite of pop music.

And meanwhile, there was a riot at Comiskey during the "Disco Demolition." Seats were ripped from rows by angry and drunk white people. Urinals were pulled from walls. Major League Baseball teams were shut in their clubhouses for safety's sake as twenty thousand more people outside the ballpark chanted "disco sucks!" and damaged property. For many older Blacks in Chicago, the violent whiteness was familiar. The White Sox had to forfeit the game to the Tigers. All this because the emerging American culture—with Black women as its spine—had shifted beneath white peoples' feet.

Dionne in particular was headed into a segment of her career as potent as her emergence. "[Producer and executive Clive Davis] asked was I recording," says Warwick, "and I said, 'No, I've . . . had it with recording at this point in time.' And he says, 'Well, let me tell you something young lady . . . you may be ready to give the industry up, but the industry's not ready to give you up.'"

The 1979 *Dionne* was produced by Barry Manilow for Davis's Arista Records, which in four short years would be the label home of Warwick's cousin, Whitney Houston. Featuring production and songwriting from Isaac Hayes, Adrienne Anderson, and Cissy Houston, the romantic bombast of *Dionne* is precursor to Houston's 1985 debut.

Dionne boasted two lush Grammy winners in "I'll Never Love This Way Again" and "Déjà Vu." Though it was called "mush" by one of the most prominent rock critics in the country, *Dionne* was Warwick's first platinum album—the biggest selling album of her career. It set the tone for classic Black female pop breakthroughs like Patti LaBelle's 1983 *I'm in Love Again* and Anita Baker's 1986 *Rapture,* as well as Cyndi Lauper's radiant 1986 *True Colors* and Cher's 1989 *Heart of Stone*. And after *Dionne* came "That's What Friends Are For," which functions as a collaborative capstone atop a genius career.

As recently as 2017, with just a trio of musicians, Warwick appeared at the B.B. King Blues Club & Grill. People picked at spicy corn and catfish as she walked onstage in a medical walking boot and proceeded to talk about her life in Brazil. But when she breezed through hits with the semi-bored elegance that has had fans at her feet since the 1960s, not a fork clinked against a plate. If people sipped vodka tonics, they did so quietly.

Every sequin of Dionne Warwick's tunic twinkles in time. Even wearing the boot, in her seventh decade, she is graceful. And if you stare long enough, it's easy to see how Whitney Houston might have set her shoulders, and her jaw, as an elder. How Whitney might have held herself in the kind of esteem that one cannot fully model for another, even if that other is your brilliant baby cousin.

Because, as Leontyne Price's cousin Dionne sang for that small 2015 crowd in New York City, Warwick's aunt, Cissy Houston—leader of the Sweet Inspirations and mom of Whitney—was still grieving the deaths of both her daughter, who died in 2012, and her granddaughter Bobbi Kristina, who died earlier in 2015. Both women were silently intoxicated and had much living to do as they drowned behind closed doors in deep tubs of marble.

When people have said to me, "You are serving two Gods," I look at them like they have a problem, because I know there isn't but one.

—CISSY HOUSTON

The idea of the Sweet Inspirations as "background" vocalists is beyond unfortunate. The group, in its varying incarnations, are under-credited and unheralded partners in the deep creative work and necessary creative mischief that makes musical history. Since 1967, Houston and her cohort—known as "Cissy's girls" before producer Jerry Wexler apparently named them the Sweet Inspirations—have provided vocal heft and authenticity to the brightest stars of American music.

Though it would be enough, it's not just that the Inspirations have functioned as advisors, influencers, and co-conspirators to everyone from Elvis Presley to Aretha Franklin to Paul Simon to Mahalia Jackson to Dionne Warwick to Donny Hathaway to Linda Ronstadt to Van Morrison to Gladys Knight to Whitney Houston. It's that these artists are among the most emulated and revered in American music. It's that the Sweet Inspirations' voices, vocal arrangements, style, and energy are in the very genes of popular American soul, R&B, and rock 'n' roll.

The Sweets had their own hit in 1968, an Elvis Presley favorite called "Sweet Inspiration." Asked how it was to have a top-twenty pop hit, Cissy answered, "Hard."

Cissy Houston was born Emily Drinkard in 1933 in Newark, New Jersey, to parents who had migrated from the "prejudice," as she calls it, of Blakely, Georgia. "I'm the youngest of eight," Houston said in a 2008 interview. "I had to get all my information from my sisters and my . . . [youngest] aunt. . . . She introduced us to everyone. . . . We knew, if anyone was named Drinkard, they were related."

In the early 1900s, the Drinkard family owned land. This was a rare situation, and it didn't last. "There was a cousin who was a drinker," Houston says in '08. Speaking about the whites of Blakely, she says, "They took every opportunity to get what they wanted. He lost half . . . of the farmland. . . . Every time he landed in jail, there was . . . not a lot of money to get him out. . . . [The family would] sell some of the land to get him out." So the cousin was arrested a lot. And the reason the Drinkards were able to own land in the first place was because, as Cissy puts it, her grandmother was Dutch and "she probably fronted, you know, the deal."

Cissy is a woman with a tendency to laugh in stressful situations— she's been dealing with cold realities since she was a child: "Get out the window," an unnamed "mean aunt" said to young Cissy as she awaited news of her ill mother, "Your Ma is dead." Cissy recounts this story of death notification with a chuckle, and it's painful to witness.

"[My mother] miscarried three sets of twins," Cissy continues. "She was mid miscarriage when she died. . . . There really were fourteen of us. My father wasn't taking noooooo pity." More choked chuckle. Cissy had already been singing professionally for three years when her mother, Delia Mae Drinkard, died. She was a soft-spoken woman, who loved Pepsi-Cola. "I have a picture of her," Cissy says, deadpan, "when she was not cripple, but it's from when I was a very little girl."

That little girl grew up to lead the Inspirations, a singing group and background vocals crew so in demand, they were flown on private jets to concerts and to recording studios around the world. The Inspirations' musical roots are in a 1950s gospel group called the Drinkard Singers. They started out performing around the Northeast's tristate area for a few dollars a show, and to Cissy, it was a chore. "Daddy would say, 'Come upstairs and sing me a song.' That's the kind of dad he was. We [grumbled], but when we got up there, we knew that's what we had to do," she says.

They made it work for them, though. "We'd . . . take that time to rehearse." The group was soon noticed by Mahalia Jackson, whose gospel-soul genius had been and would continue to be purposefully overlooked by white show bookers and major record labels for years. Jackson had been performing urgent and bluesy spirituals before grateful Black crowds for decades, making less money and performing at less prestigious venues than white Southern gospel counterparts like the Statesmen Quartet and the Blackwood Brothers. By 1954, Jackson finally signed with a major label. She was on her way—to rising as high as a Black woman could in the segregated United States—and in the segregated universe of American popular music.

Born in 1911 in New Orleans, Mahalia had been singing at Baptist churches since the age of four. Her mother died when she was five. Mahalia spent most of her youth living with an aunt, who raised her near the levee that burst in 2005 under Katrina's gales. Mahalia often set out Mississippi River driftwood to dry, as fuel for cooking. Many of the elders of her community had worked while up to their shoulders in animal shit, hacking sugarcane with machetes. *Lawdy, Capt'n, I's not a singin'* goes one of the plantation workaday songs. *I's a jes hollerin' for help.* The elders had toiled in boiling rooms, testing molasses temperatures with their elbows, claying mounds of muscovado into cones, all for free. So, yes, the aspiration—the ambition—was intense.

Mahalia snuck in her creative sustenance. "I never let people know I listened to [Bessie Smith]," she said. "She dug right down and kept it in you. Her music haunted you even when she stopped singing. . . . I don't sing the blues myself. . . . But you've got to know what the blues meant to us then. . . . The Negroes all over the South kept those blues playing to give us relief from our burdens and to give us courage."

Courage was required. "You could be in the house and you could see the sun outside, through the roof," Jackson has said of her childhood home. "If it rained, it rained inside." She went to school through the eighth grade but had few illusions about her postacademic prospects in the South. "What was I going to try to learn for, down there? It wasn't no work for me," Jackson said to historian Studs Terkel in 1963, two years after she sang at John F. Kennedy's inaugural ball. "If I woulda got a chance to go to college, it wasn't nothing for me to do but still push the white peoples' buggy . . . clean their babies . . . clean their house." As a teen, Mahalia worked as launderer, maid, and laborer in a logging camp.

Jackson moved from her Carrollton 'hood to Chicago—as part of the great migration from the sugar plantations and racial terrorism of Louisiana and other slave states toward the fuzzy hope of Northern industrial jobs. Mahalia, whose goal at the time was to become a nurse, was part of the huge human waves rolling from hot Jim Crow towns to cold ones. By most accounts she arrived in the Chi in 1927, at sweet sixteen.

But Mahalia's desire to become a nurse was not to be. Soon she was relegated to (among other jobs) nursemaid and hotel maid, and to packing dried fruit at a factory. At the same time, she not only performed as a stomping and shouting soloist around the South and West Sides of Chicago, but also as the only female member of the Prince Johnson Singers. Jackson then spent years touring with composer and "father of gospel music" Thomas A. Dorsey, who had been Ma Rainey's accompanist.

Dorsey, a gifted depressive who by most accounts was guilt-ridden by his love of the secular, is credited with "discovering" Mahalia. So often forgotten in the narrative of Jackson's life is gospel pianist Mildred Falls, Mahalia's accompanist and long-suffering creative partner for over twenty years.

In 1958, Ralph Ellison reviewed Mahalia's Newport Jazz Festival performance: "[She] and Mildred Falls . . . create a rhythmical drive such as is expected of the entire [Count] Basie band. It is all joy and exultation and swing, but it is nonetheless religious music." Cissy Houston performed at the same festival a year before as part of the Drinkards, who wowed the audience with their harmonies.

Broadcast internationally on the government-funded Voice of America Radio, the prestigious and influential Rhode Island festival was still new, and something of a youth movement in the 1950s. Mahalia's hair was in pinned curls, which from afar could seem like the bantu knots that originated in southern Africa and were famously worn by Lauryn Hill at the height of her success, as well by Rihanna and the Spice Girls' Mel B in videos and on red carpets around the world.

I made it over, the style seems to state, *and I am bringing my slave family and all of the homelands with me.* Mahalia showed up to Newport in glamorously modest church-lady gear, a crisp ivory frock worthy of praise dance and holy sweat. In her puffed eyelet sleeves, she could have been an usher on any given First Sunday. Subtext: We 'bout to have this come-to-Jesus moment for real, and right here in front of all these thirteen thousand white folks.

Because in Mahalia's soul, the surging NOLA blues had already gelled with the sacred. *When I get to heaven / Going to sing and shout / Be nobody there to put me out.* She's talked about her relationship to "the drum, the cymbal, the tambourine, the steel triangle," and Jackson brought with her to Chicago—and so to the world—the ceremonial relief of New Orleans funeral processions, and the hard beats of poor peoples' organless and pianoless churches. Jackson sang to and for the Lord. Jackson sang all her life to get people out of their seats, and to be paid fairly for it. "The only thing we are interested in," she said to Terkel, "is equal rights where we can make a living. To survive! You understand?" Divorced twice. No children. Known to carry as much as $15,000 in her bra. And Jackson's reputation for penny-pinching is fairly etched in stone.

In 1959, she both opened at Chicago's Orchestral Hall and appeared in Douglas Sirk's successful and subversive *Imitation of Life*. In 1963, at the request of Martin Luther King, Jr., Jackson sang—*You know my soul look back and wonder / How did we make it over*—as direct prelude to his "I Have a Dream" speech at the March on Washington. Gospel and its cousin, folk music, ruled that day. And Black women—including Odetta Holmes and Bernice Johnson Reagon's Freedom Singers—were in the majority.

Jackson was booked often during the 1950s at Carnegie Hall, and the

Drinkards were often onstage with her, singing. As author Tony Heil-but plainly says in his *New York Times* obituary: "Singing these [sacred songs in a 'soul' style] . . . to black audiences, Miss Jackson was a woman on fire, whose combs flew out of her hair as she performed. She moved her listeners to dancing, to shouting, to ecstasy. . . . By contrast . . . Miss Jackson's television style and her conduct before white audiences was far more placid and staid."

Jackson was not just a soaring contralto but also a rebellious rock 'n' soul persona. In the 1950s, she integrated Chicago's Chatham neighbor-hood, and soon after, her windows were shot out. Then Jackson posed for a newspaper photo, glamorously mowing her front lawn. "I hadn't intended to start a crusade," Jackson said. "All I wanted was a quiet, pretty home to live in." So she might not be surprised by the fact that even in 2021, "Black gospel" and "white gospel," like the many churches that remain segregated along racial lines, would still have distinct fan bases and award systems.

Mahalia's rise was no accident. She was clear on her mission to be deeply relevant to Black and to the broader population, and to be a prag-matic servant of God. Cissy Houston was a sponge for this formula, which enabled a poor Black woman of 1950s America to become known to wide audiences as the greatest gospel singer of either sex, any race, and of any era.

Connections abound. Cissy Houston sang as a teen onstage with Ma-halia Jackson, one of Elvis's favorite gospel singers. As an adult, Cissy, with her group the Sweet Inspirations, became a background singer for Elvis's bejeweled, ivory-collared Vegas era. Though the devout Cissy came off the road as a singer after just a few months—the vibe was sev-enties bacchanalia—the Inspirations worked with Elvis not only in Ne-vada but on his national concert tours and on recordings, and were down with Elvis's "Memphis Mafia" until his death in 1977.

Prior to getting down with the King, the Sweets were pop's most wanted. Cissy, Estelle Brown, Sylvia Shemwell, and Myrna Smith ap-pear on more classic records and in more influential sessions than can be counted. British music writer David Nathan lays it out in his liner notes for 2014's *The Sweet Inspirations: The Complete Atlantic Singles Plus:*

While no full documentation exists of which records they sang on, "The Group" (as they became known) were heard on hits by The Drifters, Wilson Pickett, Solomon Burke, Garnet Mimms, Esther Phillips, Lou Johnson, and . . . Aretha Franklin. The ladies worked consistently with all manner of up-and-coming writers and producers including Carole King and Gerry Goffin, and Burt Bacharach and Hal David. It was a safe bet that if you needed real tight gospel harmonies on a demo or a final recording, you called The Group.

The Group became the Sweet Inspirations, and the Sweet Inspirations appear prominently on Dusty Springfield's Grammy-winning, Wexler-produced 1968 "Son of a Preacher Man." Dusty Springfield is the most beloved woman pop singer of Britain's pre-Sade, pre-Adele era. Springfield's hit "Preacher" was introduced to a new generation via Quentin Tarantino's 1994 *Pulp Fiction*.

"Preacher" is never not on the radio. Never not being streamed. And the Sweets are there, owning the vibe, being the prototypes. As *Rolling Stone* says in the capsule that explains why "Preacher" is on its definitive list of the five hundred best songs of all time, Springfield "was white and English but sang as if born with Black American soul. . . . Her deep, heated voice captured the carnal fire of the [American] South." Not a hint of irony or self-awareness—nor a mention of the Sweets.

The Sweets are there with Jimi Hendrix on "Burning of the Midnight Lamp" from 1968's *Electric Ladyland,* too. But one of their most incandescent and authoritative performances is with Irish singer-songwriter Van Morrison. Morrison is hailed by the Rock & Roll Hall of Fame as "a model of artistic consistency and workmanlike devotion." He is noted as an influencer of such pop-rock icons as Bruce Springsteen, Sinéad O'Connor, and U2.

And that is Cissy Houston and her girls on his Summer of Love anthem "Brown Eyed Girl." Originally titled "Brown-Skinned Girl," in 2015 the song was number five on Spotify's list of five hundred "greatest songs"—ranked by overall popularity of streaming play.

As of 2018, "Brown Eyed Girl" had been streamed at Spotify over 248 million times—and Spotify has only been in business since 2006.

The 248 million does not include streaming numbers from TIDAL, Apple Music, and other streaming companies. The song is emblematic of the classic rock radio format, and a foundational brick in the rock 'n' roll canon. It's been covered by over a hundred bands since its release.

The song, like so many pop hits, is about a magical chorus, or hook. And each time Morrison sings, *Do you remember when we used to sing,* it's the Inspirations who lay down the resplendent, ultrachantable *Sha-la-la, la-la, la-la, la-la, la-la-tee-dah!*

Bay Area rock band Counting Crows, one of the most popular bands of the 1990s, launched their major-label recording career with a song called "Mr. Jones." Big radio hit. Huge. It launches with what *Rolling Stone* calls a "willfully 'Brown Eyed Girl'–like 'sha-la-la' passage" from lead singer Adam Duritz. Whether they're mentioned or not, it is inspired by the Inspirations. *Sha-la-la, la-la, la-la, la-la, la-la-tee-dah.*

Then: *Ooo. Ooo. Ooo.* That's the Sweets—along with Aretha's sisters Carolyn and Erma Franklin—on Aretha's 1967 "Chain of Fools," the Grammy Hall of Fame song that went to number one on *Billboard*'s R&B chart, and number two on the pop chart. They are right there, in deep, shooting the song through with melodrama, from the third vocal note of the single. What even is the song without the churning instigation of the "background" singing?

> *You told me to leave you alone*
> *(Ooo, ooo, ooo, ooo . . .)*
> *My father said, "Come on home"*
> *(Ooo, ooo, ooo, ooo . . .)*

They don't ease into Aretha's 1967 "I Never Loved a Man (The Way I Love You)" until the fifty-fifth second of the two-and-a-half-minute song, but it's with the most empathetic and richest of whispers, an inch away from a voice you might use when speaking directly to God.

"We used to sit and say, 'You know, people never mention us,'" Cissy said in 1995. "But Aretha never would have had all those hits if the background wasn't so good." The amount of sales of the records they have helped shape is in the billions. The Grammy Awards of the artists they have influenced would fill a hangar.

Along with the Sweets, Elvis drafted a group of all-white, male background singers, the Imperials, onto his crew. Out of Atlanta, with personnel from the aforementioned Statesmen Quartet and Blackwood Brothers as well as the Oak Ridge Boys, the Imperials joined up with Presley in 1969 and added their voices to the Inspirations. Both groups were billed on the marquee. The Sweets' song "Sweet Inspiration" was in the set, with Elvis on lead.

Add to that: rock and roll musicians, and behind them, a whole orchestra. The Sweets' Myrna Smith recalls the sound as "magic." As in-demand as the girls were as background singers, The Sweets' Estelle Brown says things were rarely as solid with their own bookings. Elvis was a sure thing. "A definite. We knew that whenever he worked, we were working. We knew we were coming to Vegas twice a year. Whatever shows he does, wherever, we knew we would be a part of it."

And when they were, Cissy, Myrna, Estelle, and Portia Griffin didn't have to fight promoters for fees or pay for their own airfare or gasoline. Myrna is clear: "Have you ever heard of the chitlin circuit? We're R&B. We're not playing the Copacabana, we're playing, like, Gus' Road Stop, or the Howard Theater. . . . You're a headliner, but sometimes being a headliner isn't as lucrative as being a background singer. . . . Elvis paid us very well. He allowed us . . . we brought our own band with us. We *opened* the show . . . twenty-two minutes . . . He paid for us to get our charts done. . . . He was very generous."

In the 1972 *Elvis on Tour* documentary, one of the interviewers says that everyone onstage seems to be a friend of everybody else onstage. And whether that person is alluding to the gender mix or the racial mix of the band and singers at that particular point in history (or both), the interviewer then tiptoes up to saying, "That's something very rare."

Then: "I think it's because we enjoy it," Elvis says unselfconsciously. "We *constantly* enjoy it . . . it never ceases."

In 1969, Presley recorded the iconic and strings-laden "Suspicious Minds" in his first sessions at American Sound. It was to be his last number-one record. He also recorded "In the Ghetto," perhaps the only song about generational poverty (set in Chicago!) that the King of Rock 'n' Roll ever recorded.

It's not a stretch to imagine Elvis as indelibly influenced by the Inspirations, since he was influenced by pretty much every Black artist he ever encountered—from the performers in Memphis's sanctified churches to B. B. King and Ivory Joe Hunter. Nary a time is a woman's name mentioned among his influences—even though, when Elvis needed to come back from nine years of irrelevance, the Inspirations were among those he sought out for collaboration.

When Team Elvis first called, though, the Inspirations were confused. Cissy mimics her Inspirations as incredulous: *Why? For what?* Estelle Brown was clear: "I said, 'No way. What in the name of God are we going to sing with Elvis?'" Because Elvis was known as a racist.

Elvis / Was a hero to most / But he never meant shit to me / Straight-out racist that sucker was / Simple and plain / Motherfuck him and John Wayne are iconic bars from Chuck D in Public Enemy's 1987 "Fight the Power." They are perhaps the group's most remembered and most quoted lines. A particularly lasting—yet never verified—Elvis quote is "The only thing a Black woman/a Black man/a nigger can do for me is buy my records and shine my shoes."

The line was actually chased down by *Jet* reporter Louis Robinson, who heard many versions of its origins, including one that had Presley saying it on Edward R. Murrow's *See It Now,* a show on which Elvis never appeared. Robinson, who died in 2016, interviewed Elvis himself on the set of 1957's *Jailhouse Rock.* "I never said anything like that," Presley told him, "and people who know me, know I wouldn't have said it."

I am the daughter of a Black Elvis fan. I listen to Presley's "Blue Christmas" as often as the Temptations' "Silent Night." The grisly conundrum of being a pop fan is that I want for those who concurrently partied with us and benefited from white supremacy to at least not have gone to the Klan meetings. It's because I like Elvis's music—which is Black music—that I entertain the notion that Presley's manager, Colonel Tom Parker, may have outright molded or further sharpened an already racist Elvis, to make the star safe for white girls to fall in love with in the 1950s. I am doing that thing: trying to make my white friend A-OK by making him a victim.

Parker, who by time of Elvis's death was raking in 50 percent of Presley's income, sculpted him into a teen-dream matinee idol, when (based on his performance in 1956's *Love Me Tender*) Elvis could have been a dramatic film star. *It's easy as cake*, Marshall "Eminem" Mathers rhymes two generations later. *Simple as whistling "Dixie"* to ease the fears of anti-Black white parents and radio jocks by aligning Elvis with the terms and conditions of white racism.

But when whites—due to their status and regardless of class—get the cultural credit and actual money, it's a nuclear attack on Black wealth and creativity. And the definition of privilege. That's why no one can forget the unverified Elvis quote (and truly, it's not the only one of its kind attributed to Elvis). It reads American. And even if it was never said by him, Presley benefited so much from Black artists who got nothing in return that it is his quote, whether he said it or not. It's Elvis Presley's legacy, to be emblematic of that larceny.

God bless, for example, the talents and the tribulations of Janis Joplin, but in life and in her afterlife, she—in a country that produced Bessie Smith and Billie Holiday and Ma Rainey and Mahalia Jackson and Etta James—is the most popular and famous blues singer in American history. "I just want to feel as much as I can," Joplin has said, words that will be emblazoned sixty years later on photos of her Instagram. "That's what 'soul' is all about."

Soul is actually about a universe of things, most of which revolve around the transmogrification of Black oppression to fleeting and inclusive Black joy. But Joplin's thoughts on the topic, however sincere, are elevated by her whiteness to objective truth. All while women like Mahalia Jackson and Dionne Warwick and Cissy Houston were struggling to get booked in integrated settings, and rarely being asked by mainstream newspapers and magazines to define for fans what they were creating.

In the rearview mirror, American culture looks more "Black Is Beautiful" and "Summer of Love" than it was. What dominated were trends around cultural supernovas like *Bewitched, Cool Hand Luke,* and

The Andy Griffith Show. Straight white men and women were U.S. pop culture. American stories, even as the Supremes and the Dixie Cups played on the radio over and over again, were by and for white people. Life was white life. Women were white women.

"When we finished rehearsing for [Elvis], we'd just sing gospel, all of us," says Cissy. "We . . . had a good time," she says about her time in Vegas. "Good money." Various incarnations of the Inspirations continued as a part of Team Presley even after Cissy left to raise her children, Michael and Whitney, and to figure out the music she'd record for her 1970 solo debut, *Cissy Houston*. Cissy had a top-twenty R&B hit with a cover of Bobby Darin's 1964 "I'll Be There," and she covered the Beatles' 1970 "Long and Winding Road." *Cissy* also includes "Midnight Train to Georgia," which was originally "Midnight Plane to Houston."

"It was a country ballad," Cissy said in 2013 *to The Wall Street Journal*, "that told a good story—about two people in love. But I wanted to change the title. My people are originally from Georgia, and they didn't take planes to Houston or anywhere else. They took trains. We recorded the single in Memphis in 1972 with a country-gospel thing going, and I arranged the background singers. But Janus, my label, didn't do much to promote it, and we moved on."

In '73, Gladys Knight & the Pips made music history with the record. Gladys loved Cissy's version, but for her it was a jumping-off point. As she said in 2013, she wanted "something moody, with a little ride to it . . . horns, keyboards . . . to create texture and spark something in me." It sparked something, all right. The number-one pop hit is one of the most crystalline in R&B and pop history.

Cissy may not have been into the pop-star drag—the clinging dresses and bare midriffs. She's alluded to the idea that, at a certain point, she just didn't want to wear revealing clothes onstage—didn't want to embarrass her church, or her family. In so many of her interviews, it's clear: Cissy attributes her musical life, her indelible influence, and her very survival to her relationship with Jesus Christ. It's a relationship steeped in faith, love, and unforgiving conservatism. Oprah Winfrey, in 2013 asked Cissy Houston if she would have been bothered if her daughter, Whitney, were a lesbian—as has been rumored for years.

"Absolutely" is how Cissy responded, without so much as a pause.

Cissy Houston has long had the flat affect of a woman born too soon. Her gaze reminds me of the blank-eyed photos of even the most celebrated players of baseball's Negro Leagues. *I'm as good as or better than the white guys in the majors,* the look reads. *But because I'm Black, I must play for pennies on the dollar, on dilapidated fields.* Imagine the Black *women* ball players, who (but for a notable three who played in the Negroes) were not allowed in the 1940s all-white All-American Girls Professional Baseball League. Whites in power wanted things separate, separate, separate—in sport, in song, in everything.

To allow oneself to feel this abject unfairness for long moments, to stare into the abyss of hatred—can be a slope into existential agony. So we fight the power. We keep it moving: like Leontyne, and Dionne Warwick, and Cissy Houston. The "going-on kind of thing" modeled by Price's father and billions of Black people requires discipline and sublimation. It requires management of the violent pruning of one's legacy.

There are a zillion ways to quantify such things, but the Drinkard women are right there with, if not hovering above, heralded clans such as the Marsalis family; the Cash/Carter tribe; the Beach Boys' Brian Wilson and his daughters Carnie and Wendy; the Bob Marley and Rita Marley clan; Frank Sinatra and his children; Julio Iglesias and Enrique Iglesias; and Nat "King" Cole and his daughter Natalie Cole. All of these systems have males at center. The discourse spinning around the Drinkards is mostly about fun facts: *Did you know Whitney Houston was related to that opera singer Leontyne? And Dionne Warwick? Oh wow.* When in fact they exploded racist and sexist cultural norms, and tilted the world.

And, in the Drinkard dynasty, last is first. Whitney is sun. "[She] taught me how to sing," Whitney Houston said of her mother in 1996. Cissy is far more than Whitney's mother. But—their problematic relationship notwithstanding—Cissy's training of Whitney Houston is one of the most important accomplishments in the history of American music. "[She] taught me . . . where it comes from," said Whitney. "How to control it. How to command it." It shows.

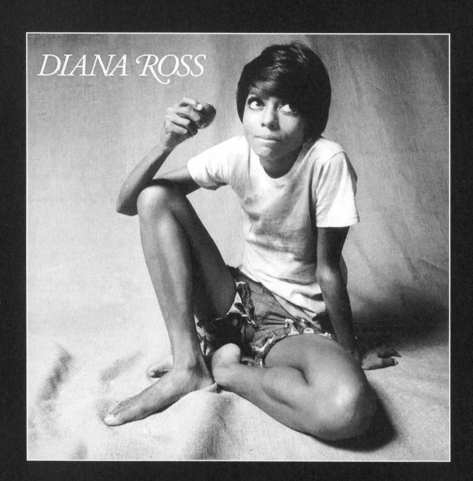

MISS ROSS

I have all different sides of me. Just like everybody else.
—DIANA ROSS

The goal is to discuss Diana Ross's solo career. To let the Supremes be. But it's hard. Because the Supremes are the model for every girl group that comes after, and even those that came before. If you don't believe that, ask Miss Ross. In 1997, she dismissed the Dixie Cups, the Ronettes, the Chiffons, Martha and the Vandellas, and other groups that recorded big hits before (and at the same time as) the Supremes.

"We actually created an image for girl groups," Diana Ross said to Jill Hamilton of *Rolling Stone*. The Supremes went from sweating through chitlin circuit gigs to London's Talk of the Town. The sequin budget was top-line. It's how you become the prototype when you aren't the first—all systems go, all the time.

At the Beatles, at the Kinks, at the Rolling Stones, at the Who—the Supremes flung number-one pearls, including "Back in My Arms Again," "Where Did Our Love Go," "Baby Love," "Come See about Me," and the hallowed "Stop! In the Name of Love." The Supremes were Motown's flagship, and one of the top-five musical acts of the 1960s. Because they modeled glamorous freedom for a Black population denied equitable wages and unmolested travel, the scandal of Diana Ross leaving the Supremes in 1970 has never quite cooled. And there are several other reasons Ross's solo career goes underscrutinized.

One, her solo hits were very often labeled "disco."

Two, Ross's biggest post-Supremes hit, "Endless Love," was created with the former leader of the Commodores, and the song's vast success seemed to many a pairing of ringers and the work of traitors.

Three, there's a massive amount of disdain, across race and gender lines, for Black women who not only know their worth but revel in it, ideate from it, and have expectations—of themselves and everyone else—of flawless production.

Four, Diana only occasionally performs graciousness with her fellow Supremes, or other women singers.

Reasons five, six, seven, eight, and nine? Ross married and created a family with a white man in the Black Power 1970s. She kept private her love affair with Berry Gordy, and the paternity of her eldest daughter. And she refused to be all tragic about it. Prom queen of Motown's charm school, Diana Ross made it a lifestyle.

1989's *Call Her Miss Ross,* an unauthorized book by J. Randy Taraborrelli, is one of the bestselling books of its era. It came to define Ross's post-Supremes life. Noted by *The Washington Post* as "one of the most heavily documented pop bios of all time," the *Post* also called it "one of the meanest, portraying Ross as egotistical, insecure, mean-spirited, paranoid, devious, [and] arrogant." Taraborrelli, who went on to write bestselling biographies of Michael Jackson, Marilyn Monroe, Frank Sinatra, and Madonna, got his start establishing a Supremes fan club out of Philadelphia. The title of the Diana bio worked because, for years, a rumor persisted that Diana insisted everyone address her as "Miss Ross." Ross's alleged dictate apparently symbolized a confidence and haughtiness unbecoming of her status. It was said that she was "not Black in her mind." It was said that Ross was not to be looked in the eye. So the "Miss Ross" phenomenon is the weighted number-ten reason her solo career is minimized.

In 2011, Ross told Oprah Winfrey that she in fact has never asked to be called Miss Ross. That's wild, because "Ms. Ross" is the name on her official Twitter account (@dianaross). "Ms Ross" is the entirety of Diana Ross's Instagram bio.

In the eighteen-acre Black-city-within-a-white-city known as Brewster-Douglass Homes, Diane is the gangly one, a saucer-eyed standout with a ruthless, wide smile, the teen smelling of focus and drive that, back then, was rarely called focus and drive. Like millions of others, her family had migrated north toward rumor of livable social norms.

Fred Ross, Sr., was born in Bluefield, West Virginia. By the age of two his mother was dead, and by the age of 17, he'd moved to Detroit to board with a paternal aunt there. The Rosses had been owned by the Reverend Frederick Augustus Ross, and descended from an Eastern Tennessee plantation said to be haunted to this day by the reverend's daughter. Fred's biological family, in the 1880 census, were listed as "mulattoes." Ross's mother, Ernestine Moten, was born in 1916 in Hale County, Alabama. As recently as 2009, Hale County's largest town featured grocery stores informally segregated by race, and a legally integrated but actually and completely segregated high school. The Motens were listed in the 1920 census as "mulattoes."

Ernestine gave birth to Diana Ross in segregated 1944 Detroit. At Hutzel Women's Hospital, though her parents named her Diane, the clerk wrote "Diana" on her birth certificate. Hutzel Women's Hospital had a colored ward until 1956. Family and close friends have always referred to Ross as Diane.

Fred—former U.S. Army—and schoolteacher Ernestine ran a tight household. "We were poor," Ross said in 1981. "But not without. Everything we had was smaller than what normal people had. We had a car, we had a house, we had beds. Things were smaller, and less of it." All over Detroit, there were posters featuring white families with slogans like "Veterans: If Buying a Farm, Home or Business: GUARANTEED LOANS." There was one of a pensive white PFC with the caption, "Shall I Go Back to School?" Diane's soldier father would have had little if any access to the provisions of the GI Bill that transformed the white American middle class.

Yet as a Supreme and as a solo artist, Diana's posture rarely curves with world-weariness, or humility. Her gaze is bright with dare. "I guess [it's] being a second child and always wanting attention," Diana Ross said in 1978. "Whatever reasons I'm in show business today, I've always wanted everyone to care about me. You can't get everybody to love you, I guess. You know? And I try very hard. Just, like, *lovemeloveme loveme,* please."

For a girl who wanted to be loved, and wanted to rise, Detroit was cold year-round. The picturesque neighborhoods were off-limits. In the two decades after 1945, whites attacked at least 250 Black families—usually those who were the first or second to move into all-white neighborhoods: "breaking windows, burning crosses and vandalizing homes." In 1978, when describing what she felt like the "perfect life" would be, Ross said, "I picture myself in some beautiful home, with a lot of land around me. I want some space . . . where there's grass, and trees." Classic raisin-in-the-sun desires. "Picket fence," she added. "Horses, and things like that."

Diane wasn't content to just dream. In 1960, she became the first Black bus girl at Detroit's now-defunct Hudson's—known locally as "the Big Store." She was sixteen and must have seen the sheet music and the pianos and organs on the thirteenth floor. She had to have seen Better Coats on the seventh, and the Deb Shop on the sixth. "I was very influenced by windows and fashion magazines," Ross said in 1997. "I went to Cass Technical High and majored in costume design and fashion illustration." Cass, a magnet school, accepted achievers from all over Detroit. Alums recall it as a space where the city's usual lines of segregation tended to blur.

My mother and aunt attended majority-Black high schools in East Oakland, California, a city like most, where educational desegregation never happened. A place where even if you were accepted to college or trade school, the means were often not there. Situations—pregnancy, early marriage, self-sabotage, sabotage by family members or from institutions—did not allow for a lot of continuing education. My mother tells the story of being accepted to the California College of Arts and Crafts, and of being, due to my 1965 birth, unable to attend.

But by 1975 we had, like the new sitcom *The Jeffersons,* moved on up: to Los Angeles's Hi Point Street from Oakland's East Thirty-First. Hi

Point had a full stereo system in the long, sunken living room. We weren't allowed to fool with the stereo, or the albums. 1976's *Songs in the Key of Life,* Diana Ross's 1972 soundtrack to *Lady Sings the Blues,* Barbra Streisand's 1974 *The Way We Were*. Natalie Cole's 1976 *Natalie,* with its iridescent "Mr. Melody."

I don't remember seeing my mother's Elvis Presley and Hues Corporation 45s in that living room with the louvered windows. Albums, on the other hand, were sophisticated. And on Hi Point, for the year before alcohol became top tenant, a mood of sophistication was key.

For my mother and Alvin's dazzling midseventies get-togethers, my sister and I, for an hour or so, would act as little servers. Before the parties, at Alvin's direction, I was cleaning the fireplace, polishing tables with Brasso, and scrubbing floors on all fours. I still don't know for sure that this kind of kid-cleaning wasn't normal in the 1970s. I was ten or eleven, and my sister was two years behind me. Then my mother smoothed our hair into long pigtails, and we got to wear our pinafore dresses with the strawberry print that were hemmed at the ankle. I pride myself, even now, for knowing what clean actually is.

I balance trembling drinks. We are beaming and careful in our dresses—my mother made them herself. I'm a year away from fearing joy, so the sound of ice-filled bags crashing into a bathtub, the loudness of Ross and Wonder and Streisand on the stereo, the clove-scented chaos of arrival after arrival—this is all pure possibility. I watch merlot fingernails and the embroidered cuffs of velvet blazers. Fringed and ginned, party people sway above us like trees.

The debates unfurling in the sunken living room were about whether Diana Ross had cheated the other Supremes out of money and legacy. And about whether or not Ross had basically killed Florence Ballard. Ballard, a Detroit-born mother of three, had given interviews about being on public assistance. She was the eighth of thirteen children. Her father died of cancer when she was a teenager. In 1976, Ballard herself died of cardiac arrest, at the age of thirty-two.

"The bitch died of a broken heart!" So went the hollers on Hi Point. *Diana and Gordy snaked her! Flo started the Supremes! If Flo did drink everybody's drinks, so what? All of them doing way more than drinking, any-*

way. They might as well have shot her. The Supremes' breakup was likely locked in near the beginning, when roles were cemented. Flo the Talented Addict. Mary the True-Hearted. Diana the Machiavellian. Diana the Least Talented. Diana the Dream Girl. "We," says Diana Ross, "started very young."

I sucked cream cheese from rolled salami slices. *Diana is a diva, that's her problem.* "Diva" was new for me. "Diva" was hawked like "tramp," like it ended the ostensibly decent part of a girl's life. But what caused the loudest hooting was when someone spit out, like it was blasphemy, "Miss Ross?!?" I weaved through the revelry, offering artichoke hearts. It seemed everyone was saying different versions of *We gotta call her Miss Ross, now?*

Ross spoke to Oprah Winfrey about the everlasting Miss Ross phenomenon in 2011.

Oprah: I don't even know if you know this, but people say that you demand to be called Miss Ross all the time.

Diana: [Smiling] Nobody says that.

Oprah: Yeah they do!

Diana: When I was growing up, anybody . . . who worked at Motown, who cared for us and supported us . . . we called them by Miss This and Miss That. But . . . at first I wasn't accepting of people calling me Miss Ross because it made me feel much older than I was at the time. But then . . . when you get on the phone with an operator or some service or something, and they say, "Hey Diana," that doesn't feel like it's correct. Like, first of all, wait a minute, I'm so much older than you, and you don't really know me [laughs]. But the thing you said—"demand"—no, I do not demand. I think it does come out of . . . and by the way, you earn respect. And . . . when you earn it, people call you that naturally. It's not a forced thing. I've never told anyone that they had to call me that. I like it, though.

I'm pretty satisfied with who I am, and I think that shows.

—DIANA ROSS

In 1970, the waif look was in, and Ross appeared on the cover of her first solo album, *Diana Ross,* looking boyish and bashful. Only Ross's heavily lined eyes were reminders of her previous life. In cutoff denim shorts, a plain T-shirt, and bare feet, Team Diana stated clearly that she was set to perform a different kind of supreme.

And it went beyond style, with Valerie Simpson on music, Nickolas Ashford on lyrics, and both of them on melody. Future Songwriters Hall of Fame inductees, they had written defining hits and American classics for Motown—"Ain't Nothing Like the Real Thing," "You're All I Need to Get By," and "Ain't No Mountain High Enough" among them. Their rare and prolific partnership would impact culture for decades to come. But in the game of thrones that was America's most influential label, to land a whole album was huge. And Diana was still queen of Hitsville U.S.A.

"It was a coup," Simpson told music historian Bruce Pollock in 2009. "Most people only got to contribute a song or two to a [Motown] album, so for [Gordy] to give us a whole important project was one of the biggest things we did as a production team. Creatively, he left it all in our hands."

That creative power included the creation of "Reach Out and Touch (Somebody's Hand)" as well as Ross's six-minute version of "Ain't No Mountain High Enough," which went to number one. Simpson recalled the Diana sessions for the *Chicago Tribune* in 2011: "She came in prepared, she knew the songs, knew her lyrics. When you work with someone who knows what they want, even if she is a diva, we knew how to finesse it."

Ross married music manager Robert Ellis Silberstein in 1971. He helped guide the careers of Rufus and Chaka Khan, among others. That same year, with an assist from guests the Jackson 5, Ross starred in the ABC special *Diana!* and was busy with principal shooting for *Lady Sings the Blues*. Produced by Motown for Paramount and costarring Billy Dee Williams, the Billie Holiday biopic also featured *The Jeffersons'* Isabel Sanford and Richard Pryor.

The Oscar-nominated screenplay for *Lady Sings* was co-written by Motown executive and label wunderkind Suzanne de Passe. De Passe,

born in New York City, started at Motown in 1968 as assistant and pro-
tégé to Berry Gordy. By 1989, she had Motown producing the Emmy-
winning western *Lonesome Dove,* which had a mostly white cast. When
pressed by the *Los Angeles Times* to account for this move, de Passe spoke
for generations of Black creatives:

> I don't think we've broken the Motown mold . . . we've expanded
> it. . . . I think people should be free to do and create anything that
> turns them on, and I think Motown Productions would be accom-
> plishing a great deal if what our mold became was great entertain-
> ment. What I think is interesting . . . is why no one asks Carsey/
> Werner [the white producers of *The Cosby Show*] why they're in
> business with Bill Cosby, and nobody asks Simpson and Bruck-
> heimer [the white producers of the *Beverly Hills Cop* films] why
> they're in business with Eddie Murphy. It's very interesting that I
> have to answer for the black company that does projects [starring
> white actors]. I guess it's because the people who are asking me the
> questions are more fascinated with what appears to be an encroach-
> ment on what has heretofore been pretty much their domain—
> rather than in any way to think they may have encroached on
> someone else's domain.

However far it strays from the facts of Holiday's life, *Lady Sings the
Blues* thrilled me to my bones. I must have been eight or nine when it
made its network television debut. The scene in which Ross cowers in an
actual padded cell, crazy from heroin, or from the lack of it, is tatted on
my brain. These were the pre-Alvin years. Guinea pigs and hamsters
and a parakeet named Cochise. Mustard and margarine on pigs in blan-
kets. Pancakes for dinner. My mother gave us context throughout the
whole movie.

"It's a true story. That lady really lived. That's Diana Ross, from the
Supremes, playing her."

"Playing her" was confusing to me. I thought the "Lady" in the
movie was herself, "Billie." And that "TV" somehow had known to follow and film her, over her whole life.

"How did they know to pick her, Mom?"

"That's not her. That's Diana Ross. Just watch the movie."

I faced the same confusion over James Caan and Billy Dee Williams in 1971's *Brian's Song*. For my whole childhood, whenever the real Chicago Bears running back Gale Sayers showed up on television, I blinked, because he was not Billy Dee. What we had in the *Lady Sings the Blues* era was *Julia* and *The Flip Wilson Show*. Denise Nicholas and Eric Laneuville of *Room 222*. I saw 1972's *Sounder* in the theater—a double feature with the original *Walking Tall*. I thought all of it was real.

Billy Dee enters the padded cell, and Diana kind of recognizes him, but she's in a straitjacket.

My mother: "A straitjacket is for the crazy people so they don't hurt themselves. Or hurt the people that work at the hospital."

Terrifying, the way the Lady can't move her arms. The Lady is hugging her own body so hard she must be suffocating. Then handsome Billy Dee speaks to Ross with intensity. He wants her. He offers the Lady, in her lowest moment, a diamond ring. I'm like, eight, and feeling the joy of rescue.

My mother, not missing a beat: "That man is not that nice in real life."

Lady Sings the Blues was a sensation, and it was nominated for five Academy Awards, including Best Actress in a Leading Role. Roger Ebert in 1972: "The opening scene is one of total and unrelieved anguish; Billie Holiday is locked into prison, destitute and nearly friendless, and desperately needing a fix of heroin. The high, lonely shriek which escapes from Ross in this scene is a call from the soul, and we know this isn't any 'screen debut' by a Top 40 star. This is acting."

All I knew was, I had not seen a lady on screen like that before: brown, close-up, and for long stretches of emotional time. "Diana Ross really went to the woodshed to become Billie Holiday," de Passe said in 2005. "She was not just showing up on the set every day. She immersed herself."

The *Lady Sings the Blues* soundtrack (produced by former Supremes musical director Gil Askey) is a double album with an iconic matte-brown cover. It went to number one on *Billboard*'s pop albums chart.

Perhaps because so many had decried her being cast as Holiday, the album contains some of the best work of Ross's career. It's easy to forget that Holiday died in 1959, at the age of forty-four, when Diana was fourteen. Billie was a huge star in Ross's formative years.

"The drug problem, even if you're not in show business, is a big problem," Ross said in 1981. "It will destroy any career. . . . Billie Holiday's life is like, if you're on a road, and you decide to go in one direction or another, for whatever reason." Then she talks about herself. "It is a lonely life. Yet a very glamorous life. I can perform for a wonderful audience, and sometimes you can go home and spend many hours alone. It can be dangerous because you think a lot. Probably think not always positive thoughts."

Ross was not to follow in the Lady's footsteps. By 1978, Diana was coming off the international tour of her Tony Award–winning one-woman show, *An Evening with Diana Ross*. With 1975's *Mahogany* she won hearts and minds in A Melodramatic Love Story Starring Black People (and Anthony Perkins). She had four solo number-one hits—the gossamer "Touch Me in the Morning," the urgent "Theme from Mahogany (Do You Know Where You're Going To)," and the morning-after "Love Hangover." Still ahead of her was the 1980 number-one hit "Upside Down," as well as "I'm Coming Out." The iconic 1983 Central Park performance lay in Diana Ross's future, like miles of buried bulbs.

Barbara Walters, in one of her powerhouse ABC specials, asked Ross in '78 about being "cold, or difficult, or testy." Ross, in silky, wide-sleeved pajamas at her Beverly Hills home, was all flawless skin and gleaming chignon. "When you're wanting everything to be right," Diana said, "you make a lot of mistakes." Ross added, without apology or hesitation: "And you are quite rough on people."

In the 1970s, disco—a building block and precursor to the rap revolutions of the 1980s, '90s, and 2000s—was simultaneously peaking and transmogrifying. Diana Ross and other icons of R&B and Black pop were figuring out their place in a genre music critics were calling "soulless." White stars of American and British rock were trying to do the same.

Even I, at fourteen, knew that nightlife was suddenly less about bands and more about DJs. I was into the Knack's "My Sharona" as much as everyone else, but the other biggest pop songs of 1979 were by the Village People, Donna Summer, Gloria Gaynor, Rod Stewart, and Chic. At Los Angeles's integrated John Burroughs Junior High School, the final vote for class song was between Chic's "Good Times" and the Led Zeppelin staple "Stairway to Heaven," which had been released in '71 and was still played relentlessly on "classic" rock stations. I voted for Chic. Zeppelin won, but it was a last stand.

Disco was denigrated by most of the white rock–critic community, and by many straight white males who wanted their Kiss, and Blue Öyster Cult, and Clapton. "Disco music was black music, basically," music historian John-Manuel Andriote said in 2017. "It was mostly recorded by black artists until the mid to late 1970s, when white artists realized how popular the music had become."

Millions of Americans, of many races and cultures, embraced disco's multihued glam. They bought the songs, danced at their new local discothèques, and called in to their local radio stations and requested it. And disco culture—in *People* magazine, in explanatory television specials—looked like a never-ending and integrated bash. Cary Grant and Grace Jones knock back Dom Pérignon, boobs pop from halter tops, and Diana Ross, in a feathered lemon minidress, affects boredom while standing with Cher and Elton John.

Though she was busy being a mom ("We were not raised by nannies," daughter Rhonda said in 2015), in the late 1970s, Ross was partying hard at New York City's famed Studio 54. All the cool kids were in the house: Debbie Allen and Michael Jackson. Diane von Fürstenberg and Lionel Richie. James Brown, Andy Warhol, Eartha Kitt, Chaka Khan. Brooke Shields and Mariel Hemingway looked too young to be there. Janet Jackson recalls being at Studio 54 as a tween.

With bobbed hair, and in red taffeta, Diana chills with Studio 54 co-owner Steve Rubell. Cross-legged and barefoot on the DJ booth, she's lost in music. The magic of Black music culture springs as much from carefree and luxuriant moments as it does from the torturous truths of field hollers. But some thought disco was thin and fake—too much rhythm, not enough blues. Deeply influential Black creators like *Soul Train*'s Don Cornelius and New York radio DJ/executive Frankie Crocker only reluctantly embraced Black disco. Yet, as with so much Black and outsider art, disco lost cultural battles during its lifetime but won the war of everlasting influence.

"I'm Coming Out"—written and produced by Chic disco architects Nile Rodgers and Bernard Edwards—is all bright joy, long strut, and renewed love of self. A year after the song's release, Ross said to Dutch television host Mies Bouwman, "Some of the teenagers buying these records don't know the Supremes. They don't know," Ross said, pinching her own jaw, "that I'm real."

The deep imprint of "I'm Coming Out" was even more clear eighteen years later, when Christopher "The Notorious B.I.G." Wallace's "Mo Money Mo Problems" was posthumously released on July 15, 1997. Built on a chiming sample from just after the sax break on "Coming Out," the Bad Boy production was nominated for a Grammy, spent two weeks as a number-one pop record in the United States, and was pretty much a top-ten pop around the world.

"It's a perfect record," says author, host, and TIDAL chief content officer Elliott Wilson. Wilson, who is my husband, first heard "Mo Money" in an Arista Records office when Sean "Puffy" Combs and Biggie presented *Life After Death* to the editorial staff of *The Source* magazine, of which he was then music editor. The meeting was prerelease, but Puff and Big knew what they had. "The song is so well done it deaded all the talk about how it wasn't authentic to use pop-music samples. 'Mo Money' is one of hip hop's signature songs. I can make the argument that it is one of the top twenty hip hop songs ever. I can also make the argument that it is number one."

"Mo" was a collaboration across eras. A snatch of Ross's vocals—*I'm / Coming / Out*—is laid, mantra-like throughout. The ecstatic quip functioned in the nineties as an announcement of hip hop emerging from the shock and grief over the twin murders of Biggie and of Tupac. It functioned also as the parade music for hip hop's march toward cultural dominance. Mase's opening, *Who's hot / Who's not,* sets off one of the most swaggeringly flippant verses of his career. Christopher Wallace's verse, which includes *Player, please / Lyrically / Niggas see / B.I.G.,* is a diamond among his pearls.

But the epic chorus of "Mo Money Mo Problems" is where the money is. It rises to the glory of Diana Ross's "Coming Out" vocals, and it belongs to a middle child named Kelly Cherelle Price of Queens, New York.

When Biggie and Tupac died, many of us thought hip hop might go to the grave with them. Gatekeepers had been saying since rap's beginnings that it wasn't real art, that it was a fad, that it wasn't worthy of documentation, let alone praise or respectful critique. In the face of that mourning and fear, singer/songwriter Price helped keep hip hop alive as much as Big, Puff, or Mase.

Her *I don't know / What they / Want from me / It's like the more money / We come across / The more problems / We see* is the kind of sure, glossed blues that makes pop *pop*. Price braids lament, panic, and celebration—but it's the slant thrill regarding new status that seduces.

In addition to background work on Mariah Carey's 1995 number-one hit "Fantasy" and on hits from Aretha Franklin, Elton John, SWV, and more, Price went on to a vibrant solo career that earned her nine Grammy nominations. It was an uphill climb. "[The record executives said] I had one of the greatest voices they'd ever heard," Price said in 2006 to the Christian Broadcast Network. "But no one wanted to look at a fat girl sing." Price's body is not featured in the video for "Mo Money Mo Problems"—her head and shoulders appear on a monitor floating above Puffy and Mase.

1980's "I'm Coming Out" is the signature song and epilogue of Diana Ross's solo recording career. But in August 1981, she and Lionel Richie released a duet that stayed in the number-one pop slot for nine weeks. Diana Ross's taffy soprano is stretched to glowing. Richie delivers melodrama and sincerity. "Endless Love" is dewy eyes, the slow dance, the wedding. "Endless Love" remains, as of 2020, the most successful duet in *Billboard* history. It's the hope for a forever companion made melodic and real.

So, at sixteen, while the song was not my absolute fave, I was fascinated by the hostility it inspired. You couldn't pull up to a Los Angeles stoplight without hearing "Endless Love," so, from the back seat of my mother's Monte Carlo, I heard people calling in to Black stations like KJLH accusing Ross and Richie of racial disloyalty, and of having no soul. They were accused of selfishness, outsized ambition, and, to my ears, plain old disruption of the status quo. On stations like K-Earth 101, white disc jockeys bemoaned having to play the song at all. "Endless Love" was usually framed as "cheesy" and "schmaltzy."

I get that not every pop song works. Rehearsed earnestness can smell of gas. But Larry Graham's huge 1980 "When We Get Married" isn't awful because of its ambition, or because Graham split from the beloved Sly and the Family Stone as well as his own Graham Central Station. The song grates because Graham, even with his one-in-a-million voice, makes a walk down the aisle sound like a march to entombment. Roberta Flack's "Killing Me Softly" doesn't stir me because—unlike Nancy Wilson's definitive 1960 recording of "Guess Who I Saw Today," or Diana Ross's swirly 1973 "Touch Me in the Morning"—there's more story in the "Softly" lyrics than in the vocals.

And with regard to the departure "Endless Love" marks from the bluesy grind of songs like the Commodores' 1974 "Machine Gun" and the straight-out-the-projects ecstasy of the Supremes' 1964 "Baby Love," there's a response to be found in Jay-Z's 2009 "On to the Next One." Shawn Carter rages against a culture that demands he remain the same guy from the Brooklyn housing projects where childhoods barely exist: *Niggas want my old shit / Buy my old albums,* he raps. Or at least wait until the streaming era, right? When pop is a less dirty word. *World can't hold me,* Jay-Z says in the song. *Too much ambition.*

I used to think that fans and critics overlooked Black pop as big, radical art steeped in the spirit of reparations for the cultural theft upon which much of the music business is built. But over the years I have to believe people see quite clearly that Black pop shakes the foundation of white-is-right American music culture. And that's why Black "crossover" artists, murderers of biz as usual, were flogged so relentlessly.

On the *Lady Sings the Blues* soundtrack, Ross sings with a glassine strength in her voice that sets it apart from any work she did with the Supremes. And though the album was a favorite at the parties with the shag rug and the quivering cocktails, folks weren't loving on the lives of women like Diana Ross back then. A diva was not yet a female version of a hustla.

But the lives of Black women who excelled in traditionally feminine roles were often placed squarely on pedestals. We swayed to hit songs like the Spinners' 1974 tribute to the self-sacrificing "Sadie." From the opening monologue:

> *But they live on in memory to quite a few of us*
> *And this song is dedicated to those who cherish that memory.*

As culture mourned the passing of Sadies, and the dynamic Black women with "Grandma's Hands" whom Bill Withers wrote about in 1971, it stared—in fear, with hate, with desire—at the rise of the Dianas.

GLADYS

My questions have never changed. Been asking since L.A. was new to me. Since my first eighty-degree Christmas. Since my first paychecks from the 'hood pool where I swabbed concrete with chlorine.

Why does Gladys have to go back to Georgia if she's doing okay in Los Angeles? He's the one, after all, who pawned all his hopes. Why are the Pips so certain of Knight's decision to climb aboard Amtrak? They nearly step on her mournful *I'll be with him* with their unified *I know you will*. My questions have never changed.

The 1973 song, a huge R&B hit and the group's only number-one pop single, is the stunning and succinct story of a woman torn. One of the most forlorn and perfect songs ever recorded, "Midnight Train to Georgia" is my favorite song of all time.

Why? Because though Knight is forthright—*I got to go / I got to go*—about leaving, she also sounds like she's convincing herself. Even when I was a kid, Gladys Knight sounded to me like she was singing one thing and wanting another. In my mind, she gets him to the station, but when the train pulls off, Knight is still on the platform.

I was into two emotions in one. Loved the joyous regret in the O'Jays' "Use ta Be My Girl." I live for when lead singer Walter Williams, Sr., sings that the girl is "so smart." I didn't know how bad I needed that line until I heard it and, when I heard it, I had to hear it over and over again. I took my home-taped version of the song to Salvation Army away camp, and the contraband was a hit, even with the counselors.

We had a great time at Camp Mt. Crags. Raquel and I had gone to Adventist vacation Bible school in Oakland, so we were used to low-key Christian enthusiasms. Two weeks away from Alvin, in the wilderness of Malibu Canyon. There was a shimmering pool and hikes and moths like mad white butterflies. I thanked God at every meal prayer for my freedom, and for Quel's and my space on the sliding scale. My mother was likely footing our fees alone. Because home on Hi Point Street— with its roots, via Alvin, in the slim society of 1950s upper-middle-class Black San Francisco—was still raging.

I was told that Alvin's father beat him. Alvin's father was both a sky-cap and a proprietor of two or three liquor stores. I was told about Alvin being hit by his father because I asked my mother: "Why is he this mean? Why does he hate us? Why do we stay?" My questions have never changed.

Even in her glowing, tiny-waisted, full-throated prime, Gladys Knight was underrated. She is often underappreciated even now. Part of this is because she came of age in the shadow of Diana Ross, whose anime eyes had seduced the world. But it is equally because—though she has sold millions of records, toured globally, been nominated by her peers for twenty-two Grammys, and won seven, and was inducted in 1996 into the Rock & Roll Hall of Fame—Gladys is almost always a part of a group or collaboration.

One of the most transcendent pop records of all time, 1985's "That's What Friends Are For," stars Dionne Warwick, and features Stevie Wonder (on harmonica as well as vocals) and Elton John. But it's Knight who rolls into its last third, infused with the holiness of giving back (the song raised near $2 million for AIDS research) and the convergence of talent by which she is surrounded. The earnest emotional surge of

Knight's voice and body language give John permission to get grimy. In the video he looks as if he might come out from under that bolero.

Knight did the same for the Pips—led by example. Of the many Black R&B pop groups to come out of the Motown era—the Supremes, the Shirelles, the Temptations, Smokey Robinson and the Miracles, the Four Tops, the Stylistics, Martha and the Vandellas, the Marvelettes, the Isley Brothers, the Drifters, the Jackson 5, and the O'Jays among them— Gladys Knight, along with Ruby Nash of Ruby and the Romantics, are the only Black women lead singers with an all-male vocal backup.

The energy around Gladys Knight & the Pips is radical. Electric. It's like an all-boys treehouse is infiltrated and a brilliant girl emerges as its charismatic leader. Gladys Knight and her Pips' chemistry is powerful in part because, within the harmonies, there is tension. It contributes to the kind of wildly earnest vocal conversation that makes 1970's "If I Were Your Woman" emerge from swarms of Motown slow jams as a royal offering.

The singularity of her leadership did not go uncommented upon by the all-male writers' room of Richard Pryor's 1977 *The Richard Pryor Special?* (NBC). There's a skit featuring comedian Shirley Hemphill. Her character suggests to a tuxedoed Pryor that he should host her favorite group—"the Pips"—on his show. "I didn't," Hemphill's character reminds, "say nothing about no Gladys." Pryor wonders how Gladys might feel about that. He's told that Gladys can take care of herself. Cut to an announcer saying that *The Richard Pryor Show* is proud to present "& the Pips."

The funny is in the ampersand, right? In the precision with which Knight is clipped. The real Bubba, William, and Edward, in high spirits, go into a couple of GK&TP songs, beautifully doing absolutely only their background vocals. One camera breaks wide to capture costumes and choreography, and another focuses closely on what would be Gladys—a standing microphone. The joke is on who? The woman who led her crew into immortality?

The fact is, Knight makes songs bigger. Take, for example, her 1974 live recording of "The Way We Were/Try to Remember," when she remakes Barbra Streisand's Academy Award–winning version. *Why don't we try to remember / That kind of September / When life was sloooooow:* so goes Knight's introduction, elocuted with Sunday-grace pacing. And then, blues: *Come to think about it / As bad as we think they are / These will become the good old days of our children.* She goes on to convey the complexity of "the way" so many Black people in America "were" forced to be, and our complex relationship with the past. On her way—unofficially by herself—to a number-three pop hit, Gladys Knight sings out all that misty dissonance. Can it be that it was all so simple then? No.

The song is so fluid in its urgency that, even sampled and sped up over three decades later for 2007's "When They Remember" (produced by Roosevelt "Bink" Harrell III for the Philadelphia rapper Freeway), Knight's vocals—*Sooooo it's the laughter / We will remember*—lose none of their Gladysness. In the original and shimmering "The Way We Were," Streisand sings about the love between two. Knight sings about Black people in the scattered pictures of American history. Her dismay is mistaken for and embraced by the masses as Black joy.

Despite Alvin's collegiate accolades, and Mission High School football feats that stand to this day, his father, William, apparently favored his older brother. Another recurring explanatory montage is about Alvin having been in a car accident while in college. It hurled him through the front windshield from the back seat. Beautiful Alvin, scarred on his face and back and arms by The Accident. When I came to know him, he already had the keloids, and everyone seemed to think Alvin—with his coffee skin and silky jet hair—was good-looking.

My questions have never changed. And in the Monte Carlo, with Gladys Knight or Elvis in the background, my mother answered us with the fables she would tell us our entire lives. The guy driving the Accident Car is supposed to have been Alvin's white law school friend "Arlen." The supple details include Arlen cheating on the state bar examination, and Alvin, for reasons unclear, taking the rap.

Alvin was disbarred before being barred. I was told that Arlen became a lawyer. And as a kind of payment, Arlen's (powerful and rich?) father—who I pictured as looking like Ken Howard in *The White Shadow* and who was apparently deep into California politics, offered Alvin a deal. For giving up his law career, and for the scars, Alvin was granted a position in the governor's office, when the governor was Jerry Brown. The move from the Bay Area to Los Angeles was spurred by this position.

All of the above were stories told to a confused and angry child. No doubt, details were enlarged and abbreviated for effect. But since I even now feel an obligation—like on some never-ending episode of *Law & Order: SVU*—to prove that my life actually happened, I will say that I have answered the Hi Point phone and it was Gray Davis, who was chief of staff in Brown's office from 1975 to '81. Alvin was likely what's referred to as an "aide." I always remember his business card, with "Special Assistant to the Governor" next to the great seal of California.

I have been told that Alvin's job was to go to every cocktail party and political event. Go, drink, glad-hand. Maybe that's why he was assigned to glamorous Los Angeles instead of Sacramento aka the Big Tomato. Before these professional soirées, Alvin pressed Vitalis into his scalp as brutally as he bragged about his "fifteen hundred dollar" suits. In his bathroom mirror he watched his thickest facial scars—on his chin, on his neck, across the bridge of his nose—like they were worms that might slither away.

Alvin was "bitter" is what I was told. That's why he drank. He got his life stolen by "Arlen." By the age of eleven, my main question was "Why can't we just leave?" I was told that when you love someone you don't leave them at the first sign of trouble. My mother said that Alvin hated happiness in general, but specifically—"yours." I was told, "It's hard for him."

So I made myself scarce. My sister and I learned real quick that joy put a target on your back. Finding delight in anything—a flavor of jelly, a pair of jeans—meant it was snatched away by the kind of person who had placed my sister in his army duffel bag when we still lived in Oakland. This was when she was small enough to be tricked into getting in.

He spun her around over his head like a helicopter blade. I'm not saying Alvin didn't carry Quel in his arms to the emergency room that time she had a fishbone in her throat. But he was an evil fuck. To us and to our mother. And once we got to Hi Point, we were locked in.

My questions never changed. Do people live up here at Mt. Crag's summer camp the whole summer? Can we stay that whole time? Can I work here? That's what I asked of the Salvation Army counselors, who appeared to me fearless—of the pitch-dark, and of moths big as sparrows. How old do I have to be to apply?

In 1944, Gladys Maria was born to Merald Woodrow Knight and the former Sarah Elizabeth Woods. Elizabeth, as she was called, was admitted to Wing C or D, one of the colored areas of Atlanta's Grady Memorial Hospital. Wings A and B, which faced the opposite direction, and toward the city, were for whites only. Blacks in Atlanta at that time often referred to the place as the two hospitals it was: the Gradys.

This was Black suffrage now Atlanta. *Gone with the Wind* premiere—with no Hattie McDaniel or Butterfly McQueen in attendance—Atlanta. In this city, infant Gladys Maria lived in the Gray Street projects with her parents and her older toddler siblings, Brenda and Merald, Jr. (also known as Bubba). The family was growing, and soon they moved into a small house. Another brother, David, was born. "We didn't know we were poor," Gladys has said. "If you want to call it poor. I thought we were pretty rich, myself. Because we had a home. We polished them floors every weekend." William Guest, Gladys's cousin and one of the Pips, recalls Atlanta as the New York of the South. "It was segregated," says Guest, "but . . . in the business I'm in—show business . . . it never was as segregated as the rest of the people were."

Gladys remembers herself singing at two years old. At four, as part of the children's Sunbeam Choir at Atlanta's Mount Moriah Baptist, she sang "Ave Maria" in Latin. When she was seven, in 1952, Gladys appeared by herself on Ted Mack's *Original Amateur Hour*—the *American Idol* of its day. She won $2,000 covering Nat "King" Cole's 1951 "Too

Young." It was a windfall, the equivalent of over $19,000 in 2021. Young Gladys wore a white dress with spaghetti straps, white bobby socks, and black Mary Janes. *And then some day they may recall,* Gladys sang, *We were not too young at all.* The microphones were almost as large as her head.

Cole's "Too Young" sold a million copies and was number one on the *Billboard* pop chart for five weeks. Gladys was just out of second grade and already following in the footsteps of a Black man who had managed, after leading an adored jazz trio, to become (behind Frank Sinatra) one of the most successful pop singers of his generation. As Knight has said of her life before there was an official Gladys Knight & the Pips: "We were youngsters . . . we were familiar with the pop music."

Compared to the decades to come, there weren't as many recorded songs from which to choose during the 1950s. The pop music then was Dinah Shore's pristine version of "Buttons and Bows." With its complex rhymes and exacting enunciation, the 1948 song was *still* popular at the top of the 1950s. Crooners Perry Como, Bing Crosby, and Tony Bennett—all constantly called "smooth"—were among the leading white male pop stars of the era. They did novelty songs and show tunes in front of big bands and girls called "swooners." This, in addition to King Cole, was part of Gladys's education in pop.

It also included the Ink Spots, led by tenor William "Bill" Kenny, Jr., who pioneered Black male pop with ballads like the heartbreakingly restrained "I Don't Want to Set the World on Fire." Kenny died in 1978, and his *New York Times* obituary states, "The quartet had a smooth pop-harmony sound. This is credited with having helped them to be among the early crossover groups—blacks making money in white markets before the mid-1950s." That definition of "crossover" is too succinct.

Crossover artists managed via creative work, everyday protest, and genius to depart from vibrant Negro circuits unable to pay market rates due to customary and legally sanctioned racism, in the form of segregation. Crossover artists did this so they could be paid much closer to what their white counterparts were paid for like work. They did this so they could claim their destinies—to matter, as much as possible, as artists.

One of the best lies the devil ever told is that this kind of ambition and desire for fairness is equal to "sappy" music and the concept of "selling out." The ambitious Black pop of Gladys Knight's youth, when the requirement for something closer to fair pay was evenness and predictability, is a miracle mix of precision and emotion. This did not kill the soul in the sound. And every generation gets a little more free.

Gladys loved Lena Horne, Sarah Vaughan, and Dinah Washington, but her favorite was Ella Fitzgerald. "Miss Fitzgerald is the epitome of not only a musician, but of her craft," Knight said in 2011. "She was the most unassuming woman for the supergiant talent that she had. She . . . had a sweetness about her that I aspired to embrace in my life. She had to know how great she was, she had to know she was a legend. But . . . she was so cool and unassuming and so humble in it. Even if she was performing with another artist, she just did her part. That was my lady. That was my girl."

Fitzgerald, who appeared on some of the Ink Spots' biggest hits ("Into Each Life Some Rain Must Fall," "I'm Beginning to See the Light") released *Ella Sings Gershwin* (Decca) in 1951. The smooth sound of her epic "Someone to Watch Over Me" is a Trojan horse for messy truths. Fitzgerald sings *I hope that he / Turns out to be / Someone to watch over me* with a spectacular and meticulous melancholy. Like a pressing comb, Fitzgerald's pleas for companionship sear and soothe. "Someone" is one of Knight's all-time favorites. "I lived that [song]," she's said. "This business takes so much out of your personal life. . . . There was . . . that wish of saying, 'There's somebody I'm longing to see, someone to watch over me,' so I'm not carrying the load all the time. I've lived these songs."

While the road to Ella's success was paved with albums like 1956's *Ella Sings the Cole Porter Songbook,* she was also apparently drug free, and presented as maternal—the anti–Billie Holiday. Fitzgerald's sound was tightly curated. "The trick," said Ella's manager, Norman Granz, "was to change the backing enough so that, here and there, there would be signs of jazz." And according to *The New York Times,* the reasons for Fitzgerald's impact included her "equanimity and her clear pronunciation, which transcended race, ethnicity, class and age [and] made her a voice of profound reassurance and hope." Ella as a human, with a life that didn't in every moment exist to be in the service of people's moods and fan worship, was, in her time, rarely explored.

It should have been. If not to reveal the soul that informed her art, then so we could better understand the mechanics of how she invented the jazz vocal. Instead, Fitzgerald often endured with forlorn grace the kinds of questions that Black women in pop would be subjected to for decades to come.

In a 1980 CBC interview, the host asks Fitzgerald, "What kind of standards do you set for your own behavior?"

He notes that there have been "no great scandals" about Ella Fitzgerald. Three decades later, in an era of #melaninpoppin and #blackgirl-magic, Fitzgerald might have responded with "What kind of standards do you set for yours? The list must include rudeness."

But Fitzgerald immediately and sincerely answers Mr. CBC. She begins speaking about having fallen in love, "In Norway, with a Norwegian. It was not a scandal," she says with what looks like a wince. "It was just at that time people did not accept the fact of . . . the racial . . . situation. So it became like a little headline." Fitzgerald's is a detailed and personal answer to a condescendingly delivered personal question. Hers is the kind of answer hosts dream of: a door opening into a celebrity's actual life.

But he doesn't leap over this tantalizing threshold. Instead of acknowledging Fitzgerald's statement, he becomes as animated as a Dr. Seuss character and alludes to her famous Memorex campaign: "'Ask her,'" he says, mimicking his kids' thrilled faces, "'if she can break a glass!'"

Fitzgerald is wearing large eyeglasses, and she wipes at something in the corner of her right eye. "Your blues ain't like mine" would be an appropriate thing to scream in response. *I get that my polished pain makes you feel whole and human, but show me the courtesy of acknowledging that I could not be with a man I loved for no good reason at all.* You *asked the* question. *Note my humanity, please. And the breaking of my heart.*

Fitzgerald was all over the radio during Gladys Maria's childhood, and really, her entire life. Fitzgerald's "A-Tisket, A-Tasket" (which she recorded with Chick Webb and co-wrote with Van Alexander) went to number one on *The Hit Parade* in 1938 and into the Grammy Hall of Fame in 1986. She recorded over one hundred albums and sold more than twenty-five million—by some counts it's forty million. In the United States, Fitzgerald's success at normally all-white venues helped usher in the opening of integrated nightclubs and ballrooms.

Her philanthropy was often in support of children who had suffered abuse, and who managed cognitive disabilities. She adopted her half-sister's son and raised a niece. Having lost both of her lower legs to diabetes, the genius Ella Jane Fitzgerald died June 15, 1996, at her estate on N. Whittier Drive in Beverly Hills. In the spare poetry of her death certificate, she is "Black," and a singer in the business of entertainment.

The month after Fitzgerald's death was a big one for Gladys Knight. She sang "Georgia on My Mind," alone, at the opening ceremony of the 1996 summer Olympics. And Mariah Carey inducted Knight & the Pips into the Rock & Roll Hall of Fame. Carey, at the time, was sitting on "Always Be My Baby," her eleventh number-one pop song.

First, Carey jokes about Knight having made her debut at the Mount "Mariah" Baptist church. "But that's not the only reason I feel a special attachment to this extraordinary singer," Carey says. "When I was a little girl . . . I used to sneak out of my room, steal a portable radio from the kitchen, hide under the covers, and sing along with 'Midnight Train to Georgia,' 'Neither One of Us,' and 'The Best Thing That Ever Happened to Me.' The voice of Gladys Knight pulled me through a lot of lonely times. And I just wanted to thank her for that tonight."

Carey's remarks are rich with affection. "Gladys is a singer's singer," she continues. "It's all about that voice, her incredible gift from God. If you have the desire to sing, and you love R&B, she's like a textbook you learn from. You hear her delivery, and you wish that you could communicate with as much honesty and genuine emotion." That night, Mariah Carey said that even on Gladys Knight's earliest records, her voice was so filled with experience that Gladys sounded like she'd already seen, and lived through, everything.

The concept of a group was baked into the idea of Gladys as performer from early on. The idea began at a bologna-sandwich-and-Kool-Aid tenth birthday party for Knight's brother and future Pip, Bubba. It was 1952, and a neighbor brought over his record player. Another future Pip, William Guest, recalls the event as a Labor Day party—which makes sense, as Bubba was born in the first week of September.

"Our families," Gladys said, "were believers in us not being idle." So when the neighbor, angry that a record he wanted to hear wasn't being played, left—and took his player with him—in place of the recorded music, an impromptu talent show was staged. Jokes were told, tricks performed. "And that's when," says Guest, "we started singing." By all reports, folks at the birthday party went wild.

Some report that cousin (Elizabeth's nephew) James "Pip" Woods suggested the kids sing together professionally. Gladys recalls her mother formalizing, for her, the formation of the little crew.

"Later on," Gladys said, "after most had gone home, my mom said to me, 'You look like you're bored.'"

"I 'look bored'?"

"Mom said, 'Yeah. Why don't you do something?' Mom said, 'You all should start a group. Do you want to do that?' Bubba was there and was like 'Yeah, we want to do that!'"

Elizabeth Knight, according to Gladys, asked Pip to manage them. He is, of course, the man whom the group is named for. Their first booking was at a YWCA. "We played for a ladies' social," said Gladys. "We did a tea and they paid us ten dollars. And it was five of us then [laughs]. Two dollars apiece. That was the beginning of Gladys Knight & the Pips."

Called just "the Pips" at that time, the young crew was busy. "We'd had our little church group before we had the Pips," says Knight, "and that was the same group that went down to the Royal Peacock [nightclub] and performed on Sunday nights. The church [folks] would just migrate from Moriah down to the Peacock. They were there to support their little Sunbeams, their little Youth for Christ children. They were proud of us, even though we were . . . singing popular music."

The nightclub had opened in 1937 in Atlanta's Sweet Auburn district as the Top Hat and was considered one of the finest clubs "for African Americans" in the country. When it became the Peacock in 1948, new owner and former circus performer Carrie B. "Mama" Cunningham, a Black woman who employed Egyptian revival as a motif, hung white peacock feathers from rafters. The Supremes came through the Peacock for their first Atlanta appearances. Aretha Franklin played the sweaty 350-person room, as did Bessie Smith, Louis Armstrong, Cab Calloway, Otis Redding, and more.

Pip Will Guest told me the audience fell in love with the youthful group for specific reasons. "Because it was just more than Gladys Knight as the singer and us as a regular background group. The people couldn't tell whether to watch her or us, because we both was interesting. And each of the boys—we knew Gladys was our lead singer, but we didn't want to be looked at like part two, you know? We wanted to be just as good as her, and so I think that's what made the group really grow. People wouldn't know who to look at."

The "people," on Wednesdays and Saturdays, were white patrons only. Mama Cunningham also ran the nearby Royal Hotel & Restaurant. It was a home away from home for Black artists on the road, as they were not legally or customarily welcome in Atlanta's hotels until after a 1964 Supreme Court case (*Heart of Atlanta Motel, Inc. v. United States*) that challenged the Civil Rights Act of that same year.

Locked in the big linen closet for the crime of not having turned off its light. Chased around the big apartment on Hi Point with a belt. Chased with a hunting rifle. Beat and poked at with hangers. Me and Quel crouched deep in our clothes closet hoping to be forgotten, amid the stinking alcoholic fits.

I'd read thick books like *Roots: The Saga of An American Family* and *The Glass Inferno* by the time I was eleven, but I didn't have to read 1976's *The Great Santini*. From what I overheard on grown-folks' talk radio, I was living it. I threw a peppermill at this motherfucker when I was in sixth grade. Surprised everyone. Alvin looked at me and laughed with some kind of respect for my finally returning fire.

He waited, though, like a snake in tall grass. Until the week of dress rehearsals for *The Music Man*. Joy and jitters were everywhere. Hems needed raising. Feathers needed pinning. One of my jobs in the play was to say the names "Chaucer" and "Rabelais" with snobby zeal, and I still could not get down the unselfconscious correct pronunciation of "Rabelais." The whole of Carthay Center was light with musical energy. We were sold out for all five performances.

I was so tired. And so happy. Alvin told me, drunk and hissing, that I would not be performing. "You're out of that play." The cast had been practicing for four months. I was in the chorus and had my five little lines in the "Pick-a-Little, Talk-a-Little" scene. I can't recall my precise response to Alvin's statement. I can't remember where I was in the Hi Point duplex. I do know that I took him at his word.

"That's what you get" is what he said.

My memory of the few days before opening night has no shape or order. In Alvin's lunges, he referred often to the peppermill—which I'd thrown because he'd been in a vicious, taunting rage against everyone in the duplex. I hoped, when I threw it, that the peppermill would kill him. I think he knew that. I also think I told my teacher, the director of the musical, that Alvin was holding me out of the play. She knew some about my home situation, and she called my mother.

In my memory, the peppermill flew by Alvin so close he could feel the wind. I hope it's true. It has gotten me through many a miserable night, believing I was near to at least knocking Alvin out.

Things were compounded by the fact that during that dress-rehearsal week of *The Music Man*, Alvin searched for and located my diary, with its decorative lock, and he read aloud my detailed daily weather reports and my detailed descriptions of hate for him. He ripped out pages and threw them, literally, into a burning fire. "You want to write something?" He pointed at the sun coming through the louvered windows. "Describe that, then. You can't. Describe the fucking sunlight."

My diary was a jam-packed ballpoint-inked indictment. I quoted him. I described him. I described his and my mother's relationship. I called him all kinds of names. I was glad he read it. *At least you read that shit. And you wanted to read it*. I wrote out my hate, hate, hate. I wrote dozens of times: "KEEL OVER AND DIE." He told me that nothing was mine. Not the diary, not anything. And he told me to stop going to dress rehearsals.

There was nothing going on at school *but* dress rehearsals. That was literally the whole, entire day for all of the fifth and sixth graders.

I was exhausted from lying, from faking, from begging my mother to say *something* to Alvin, from asking my teacher, "What did my mom say?" From saying my lines well and good in practice, knowing I was banished. I was ashamed on levels that have stayed with me, and when I think I have managed that curdling shame, it is back.

I'd had so much fun. I don't look back on any of it very often. I don't sing *The Music Man* songs. I try to watch the movie. Our multicultural production featured a Black Professor Harold Hill. Sometimes I get through the film, because Robert Preston does almost as great a job as my friend D.B., who played Hill at Carthay. I watch it, also, to know that I can.

"Describe the sunlight"? I counted dust particles between the glass louvers in the window frame. They floated in the bright air, lazy and calm. I got dizzy from calculating, and from asking God to just kill him. With each passing second I lost more respect for all adults, including my mother and my grandmother and my aunts and our family friends, for their secrecies and tequila sunrises and complicity.

I performed in all five shows, that I do know. *Just melt her down and you'll reveal / A lump of lead as cold as steel / Here! / Where a woman's heart should be.* Those were some of my lines from the "Pick-a-Little, Talk-a-Little" scene. How I must have screamed them.

The teenage Gladys Maria Knight—whether with the Lloyd Terry Professional Jazz Band (Terry was band director at Knight's high school) or with the Pips—was *the* local Atlanta act. At that time, the Pips consisted of Gladys's sister, Brenda, her cousins Eleanor Guest and William Guest, and her brother Bubba Knight. By 1957, Gladys's father had left home, and the family. Water was running cold. Electricity was spotty. The pantry lean. Though Elizabeth Knight often worked more than one job, the kids were very much helping pay bills.

The children being a group was as much an economic decision as the achievement of a creative ambition. They'd already toured—billed as the Pips—with Sam Cooke, Jackie Wilson, B. B. King, and others. "This music," says Gladys Knight, "helped me to help my mom feed our family during my high school years. . . . That's how, actually, I got introduced to it. It's not something I just came up with."

Gigs could be difficult. In 2006, Gladys told Tavis Smiley about her first encounter with racism, at a gas-station stop on the way to a gig in Alabama. "We fueled up the tank, and I said, 'Oh, I gotta find a bathroom.'" She squirms with the memory. "[The Pips] looked at me funny, but I walked right in the thing and said, 'Can you tell me where your bathroom is, sir?' You know. And he looked at me, and he said, 'We don't allow niggers to use our bathroom.' I said, 'What'd you say?' And I was getting ready to get indignant. You have to understand. I'm only nine, ten [years old]."

This story is one Knight tells often. The details sometimes change. But there is usually a key required to pee. Always there is the word "nigger." Always, there is the statement of her age at the time.

The Pips came in and grabbed her. "By both of my arms," she told Smiley. "Because I didn't even realize the *extent* of it. These are African American *men,* traveling in the *South*. They lynched people. . . . I didn't know about the severity of all of that, at the time. . . . We were not brought up," Knight has said, "to know racism. . . . We lived in segregated communities. . . . We didn't feel it."

In 1961, the Pips flew to New York City to record the Johnny Otis–penned "Every Beat of My Heart" for the tiny Huntom label. It went to number one on *Billboard*'s R&B chart, bumping out Ben E. King's "Stand by Me"—no small feat—and was a number-six pop hit.

Record man Morgan Clyde "Bobby" Robinson produced the song. And after apparently asking, "What the hell is a Pip?" he said, "Since Gladys is the leader of the group, the group should change its name. Let's call the group Gladys Knight & the Pips."

Robinson, who died in 2011 at age ninety-three, is an unsung personality in music, from the blues to R&B to hip hop and American pop. In addition to producing records, he was proprietor of Bobby's Happy House, an influential Harlem record store. "Gladys Knight & the Pips" is how the group is billed on the single—and has been, of course, ever after.

Recording, getting gigs, yes. But the crew was in transition. Founding members Brenda Knight and Eleanor Guest were moving on. "The two ladies," Gladys said, "got fed up. . . . Then they started dating and stuff. I was one of the boys. . . . [The women] opted to go on to . . . college, and get married. That just left me."

Edward Patten—another cousin—and Langston George got involved. "We got intricate with our dream," Gladys has said. "Our dream was to be the best group in the world. Not just in Atlanta. In the *world*. Okay, so how do we go about doing that? We gotta have some hit records. And we have to be entertaining. . . . We want to be a *performing* group. Right? We'd been watching people for a long time, and fortunately, we had the people around us that directed us in that path."

The group had rules. "People might think they're silly now," said Knight, "but for me, it just set the base . . . for other things that came later. We had a silly rule that you couldn't sit down in your uniform . . . because we had to be *pressed* when we were onstage. So that means you get dressed *right* before you go. And if you did sit in your uniform? You got a fine. Okay? Because we couldn't be slovenly. We couldn't be sloppy."

Another rule was that the lead singer often had to be on lockdown. "We always protected Gladys," says Will Guest. "The men and boys be at the women. We would come to rehearsal . . . we would sing on the show, and we'd take Gladys right back to her room, and make sure she'd be in her room for the night. And then the boys would go out and have the fun night all the rest of the people did."

After *The Music Man,* Alvin could feel me changing. Shit got increasingly ugly over the next three years. One time, so drunk, and so pissed at me for staring into his forehead as he lectured, he pointed at me hard enough to cut the bridge of my nose with the nail of his index finger. Right between the eyes. I stayed standing. Blood trickling down the side of a nostril. I flinched. I stared.

"Look at me!"

I was trying to see through him to the other side of his body and outside of the Hi Point duplex, to my yellow Huffy bike, to Venice Beach—to freedom. In Roald Dahl's "The Wonderful Story of Henry Sugar," Henry teaches himself to see through playing cards by staring into the center of a candle's flame. This was my inspiration. Well into my teens, I believed.

People wonder why I have been able to stand up to men in this business of music. To go to shows—glamorous and grimy—by myself. To negotiate with the worst of the promoters, the performers, publicists, security guards, police officers. To, on behalf of any given media organization, but mostly on behalf of *Vibe,* and on behalf of myself, not stand down. I just wasn't that scared of men, not for a long time. "Step to me" was my front. "If you want this smoke." A motherfucker had already hit bone.

A famous artist-executive told me once, because one of his artists was not on *Vibe*'s cover in a month that most helped his company, that he would "see me dead in the trunk of a car." Not missing a beat, I told him he needed to take that threat back. "Take it back." Like I was ten.

"Take what back?" Then, with a shit laugh, he said, "Fuck you."

I said something to the effect of "You need to take it back now. Or I'm calling my lawyer, and you're going to jail."

He said, "I know where you are right now. Right on Lexington."

I called my personal lawyer. Within two hours, the artist-executive faxed over an apology. My male boss was upset that I had not involved him. Because the artist-executive had called my male boss to complain that I had sicced my lawyer on him, as if I somehow wasn't playing fair. Also, the artist told my male boss that he needed to have me under better control.

My boss adored and resented me. It was his way to put his own interests, and the interests of the magazine, far ahead of my safety and sanity.

This was an era in hip hop in which artists occasionally stormed the offices of magazines. In which artists were fighting one another. In which artists occasionally threatened culture journalists with guns. Hip hop, as a movement, was also a part of a larger culture war. So I handled it myself.

So many photos exist of the artist-executive and me smiling from red carpets. So many exist of me and the male boss. I partied with them over the years so many times. It wore me out. It's the music, man. Fucked up, yes, but the surge and strength of Black pop is why I could stand up to fools who came at me. That and the fact I'd known since the days of Carthay Center and Hi Point that I was pretty much on my own.

Gladys had long been crushing on the attractive Jimmy Newman, a fellow high school student, and a saxman in the Lloyd Terry Band. At fifteen, Gladys found herself with even more serious feelings for Newman after she fought off a stranger who climbed into her Atlanta bedroom and tried to rape her. Newman, Gladys has said, was there for her in the aftermath of this terror.

By the time she was sixteen, Gladys had another hit, "Letter Full of Tears," and her high school diploma—and she was pregnant with Newman's child. Elizabeth Knight gave Gladys legal permission to marry, and after a wedding in the family home, Knight was back on the road with the Pips. Though he didn't play with the Pips, her husband was a part of the larger tour. Three months into the pregnancy, her husband out for the evening, Gladys Knight miscarried.

"By the time he got there," Knight has said, "I was getting up. I was getting ready to go to work." Sweet sixteen. "It wasn't like they could go to work without my going. And we needed the check. So I got up and I got dressed and I went to work."

She was soon pregnant again, and this time she came off the road. In August 1962, Little Jimmy was born. A year later, her daughter Kenya arrived. "In order to utilize that gift I was given," said Gladys, "I was going to have to leave home, be away from my kids." She went back to touring. She and Newman placed their children in the care of Elizabeth.

Things were not going well with Jimmy. Addicted to drugs, he was acting out. Gladys was the toast of Atlanta—a taffeta-clad debutante of the chitlin circuit. Newman kind of hated Gladys's leading role. "Some of the pressure," said Bubba in 1984, "of Gladys being 'Gladys Knight' may have come into play with my brother-in-law." One night in South Carolina, Bubba was called upon to pull an intoxicated and violent Newman off of his sister. "[Jimmy] just couldn't deal with some of the pressures," said Bubba. "We got into it physically."

According to Gladys, Newman left the tour the next day. "I can't save everybody," Gladys has said. "Sometimes I gotta save me. Let me save me. And . . . I got two kids now, so I gotta save them, too."

Knight and the Pips were soon being managed by Margherite Wendell Mays, the ex-wife of Major League Baseball's Willie Mays, Jr. A two-time MVP, Mays began his Hall of Fame career in the Negro Leagues on teams like the Chattanooga Choo-Choos, and went to the majors four years after Jackie Robinson, in 1947, crossing into baseball's all-white ranks.

Often named as Mays's widow, Margherite was married to him from 1956 to 1962. She is just the kind of Black woman whose existence and influence goes unrecorded and uncelebrated. At a time when a woman as artist manager or A&R rep was rare, at a time the segregated worlds of professional sport and pop music were being disrupted by people of color, Margherite married (twice, actually) into the business of a new Black culture.

Called a "café-society beauty," she was born Scarlett Margherite Wendell. She was also known as Marti Marciano, and was also the ex-wife of the Ink Spots' Bill Kenny. Her and Kenny's marriage ended in scandal, as Kenny proved that a daughter that she said was his, was in fact, not. Margherite's moves were regularly chronicled in *Jet*—whether it was about her ten trunks of clothes, her lustrous baby hair, or her fights with her boyfriends.

Margherite was a kind of Shaunie O'Neal (successful television executive producer/ex-wife of NBA Hall of Famer Shaquille O'Neal) or a Mona Scott-Young (Scott-Young managed the careers of Missy Elliott, Busta Rhymes, Mariah Carey, and more before expanding to film and television), before Monas and Shaunies were allowed. Margherite Mays knew about new Black stars. Both of her husbands crossed over from the Negro Leagues.

Draped in mink, she stood on tarmacs before TWA jets while Mays held her boxy and expensive luggage. In the kind of gracious everyday wear Michelle Obama brought to the fore decades later, Margherite managed the moving men as she and Mays furnished their splendid San Francisco home. Margherite moved with confidence in the newly integrating universes of pro sports and show business. It's hard to assess the mix of business and emotion in loving partnerships, but many believe Margherite even functionally managed the Ink Spots for a time.

"I used to go with her niece," says Pip Will Guest—an example of the kinds of connections that make the music world go around. "She said, 'Oh, you're one of them boys that sing with that group with that girl in it.' I said, 'Yeah.' And she said, 'You're a good group . . . but you need to polish up a little for places like the [New York City nightclub] Copacabana.' "

Guest says he brought Gladys and the other two Pips to meet Mays. "She said, 'You need that professional touch.' From that point, we . . . started going to the Copa, [Philadelphia's] Latin Casino, big places. . . . When we got with that lady, she . . . introduced us to the next level of people." Mays even put Knight in her own couture gowns.

The polish paid off. In 1966, Gladys Knight & the Pips signed a seven-year contract with Motown Records. The move was against Gladys's better judgment. "She was outvoted," her brother Bubba has said, in a foreshadowing of more tense group politics to come. Gladys was the youngest, she was female, and an all-male majority ruled.

"She went to Motown hollering and screaming," Bubba said. " 'I don't want to go to Motown and get put on the shelf.' "

In 1967, Gladys Knight & the Pips released *Everybody Needs Love*. The Motown album featured Norman Whitfield and Barrett Strong's "I Heard It Through the Grapevine." The first recording of the song to be released, it sold over 2.5 million copies and went to number two on the pop charts. There was "If I Were Your Woman" and "Friendship Train" before the monster hit and moody prequel to "Midnight Train" that was

"Neither One of Us (Wants to Be the First to Say Goodbye)." It went to number one on the R&B chart, and number six for pop, and won the Grammy for Best Pop Vocal Performance by a Group.

Still, says Gladys of Motown: "We were never, in my opinion, a part of the in crowd. The new acts would get the hand-me-down stuff . . . like, from the Temptations, or from Diana and the Supremes. You can do so much to make it yours," she explains. "But it's already been worn." Gladys had had it. "Motown wanted everything from you, and I didn't like that," she said in 2017, alluding as well to conflicts of interest: "They wanted to manage you, they wanted to record you. . . . I didn't feel like we'd get our due."

So it was off to join Buddah Records, who had the Isley Brothers, the Edwin Hawkins Singers, the Five Stairsteps, Bill Withers, Curtis Mayfield, and fellow Motown expatriates Honey Cone. Gladys & the Pips were signed to Buddah by Neil Bogart, who would sign Donna Summer to his next venture, the disco powerhouse Casablanca Records.

It was the late '60s, and songwriter Jim Weatherly, known for penning great country records, was on the phone with pre–*Charlie's Angels* Farrah Fawcett. Fawcett was married to Lee Majors, who was on a flag football team with Weatherly. This was about five years before he became the TV astronaut Steve Austin, and Majors was starring as moody Heath Barkley on *The Big Valley*. Fawcett told Weatherly that Lee wasn't in. This conversation is the origin of Gladys Knight & the Pips' definitive song. What was Farrah doing? Packing to visit her parents, she said. About to get on a midnight plane to Houston.

Weatherly says he jumped off the phone and wrote the music and lyrics to "Midnight Plane to Houston" in about forty-five minutes. Then, he said in 2013, "I filed away the song." Two years later, he sent a recorded version to Cissy Houston. Cissy recorded Weatherly's song, but changed "plane" to "train." The destination was changed, by Houston, to "Georgia," and Cissy says she recorded the song with "a country-gospel thing going." But there was no buzz on it. Weatherly then sent the song to Gladys and the Pips. They'd already recorded his "Neither One of Us," to much success. According to Weatherly, Neil Bogart called in producer Tony Camillo to record and arrange. Camillo looked to Ed Stasium to mix and engineer "Midnight Train." Stasium was twenty-two, and his tastes back then ran to Sinatra, Ella, Basie, Bing Crosby, and Nat Cole. "I didn't know what I was doing. . . . But I had an idea," he says. "Everything was 'Get it on the tape.'"

The tape's cold open is a crisp Andrew Smith snare-drum call to attention. Horns jump in right on top. The sax and trumpet are the Brecker brothers, Michael and Randy. This was when the siblings were living in New York City and doing, by Randy's count, ten to fifteen sessions per week—James Brown to Funkadelic to James Taylor. Randy Brecker, winner of seven Grammys, was in the first iteration of Blood, Sweat & Tears. Before Michael Brecker died of leukemia in 2007, he was awarded fifteen Grammys, as composer and as performer. So, the joint was jumpin'.

"I do remember," Randy told me in 2014, "that Gladys Knight was there at the session—in the booth, which . . . 95 percent of the time, the artist wasn't there."

Knight was there because it was her record and she wanted to see who was making it. The energy was tingly—a hit was on the way. "The place was jammed," Knight has said. "Managers, label executives, Tony's crew." She recorded her scratch vocal—something the Pips could hear in their headsets while they recorded their parts. Knight and the Pips laid the final vocals later, in a small Detroit studio.

While the song functions as a conversation between Knight and the Pips, for Knight, it was tied up in her real life. She and Jimmy Newman didn't formally divorce until 1973. And while she married three other men, in her 1997 memoir, *Between Each Line of Pain and Glory,* she calls Newman the love of her life. "I was thinking about my own situation," Knight said in 2013. "My husband at the time was a beautiful saxophonist, and so gifted. But he was unhappy that we didn't have a more traditional marriage, because I was often on the road, or recording. Ultimately it all proved too much for him, like the song said. . . . I was going through the exact same thing that I was singing about when recording—which is probably why it sounds so personal."

The talk around Gladys Knight & the Pips so often centers the idea of them being equal entities that, even when it's true, it feels didactic. "She was lead," William Guest told me, "and we would hear the lead words—and what we would do . . . [was] sort of answer her . . . so we could be, like they say, Gladys Knight *and* the Pips. We always were proud of that name—*and* the Pips, you know? Because we were just as much as she was. You'll listen to her, but you'll watch us. We'll make sure of that."

The kernel of my love for "Midnight Train to Georgia" is its actual setting, which is not Georgia.

Gladys*: Mmmmm / L.A. / Proved too much for the man.*

Pips: *Too much for the man / He couldn't make it.*

I know that Los Angeles. In the 1970s, I lived on its outskirts. The vibe was very Marlena Shaw and her winds-at-high-tide "California Soul" (1969). The Ashford & Simpson composition has lived long as a component of rap songs, soundtracks, and commercials, but when I was twelve-going-on-twenty, "California Soul"—a B side, and not a hit— seemed always to be playing on L.A.'s Black radio.

Stars like Diahann Carroll lived in Los Angeles. Redd Foxx, too. Marvin Gaye and Diana Ross and what felt like all of Motown had moved to L.A. The son of Texas sharecroppers and UCLA classmate of Jackie Robinson, Tom Bradley was rallying a multiracial coalition to become the first Black mayor of a big American city with a majority-white population. My sister's friend Dawn was the daughter of Don Mitchell, who starred with Raymond Burr in *Ironside*. Running toward the pool at his home, I crashed right through a sliding screen door. I was eleven, with *The Music Man* on my mind.

He couldn't make it. He couldn't make it. I got that so early. The failure. His failure. I got that the nameless "he" in "Midnight Train to Georgia" knew when he was beaten and had the decency to leave.

He couldn't make it. Even with his job at the governor's office, and the navy Armani and the Vitalis, Alvin could not hang with the puka-shell pleighboys barbecuing snapper on the nearby lip of the Pacific. With the Spelman and Howard and Harvard cliques in the manicured enclaves of Ladera Heights. Tangerine sun setting heavy over Santa Monica. Play a weekend right and you could, without much effort, avoid white folks' condescension entirely. It was a wild time, a surging time.

Black folks migrated to the City of Angels for creative freedom, and for plain old freedom. They moved to L.A. streets with optimistic names like Hi Point after a bad time elsewhere. They came to make music and politics and movies and money and to be front and center in the American machine. Or to just send their kids to good public schools. And trim hedges in whatever shape they chose. Play music loud in their Monte Carlos, holding back the tears, relieved they're not in the places left behind.

On February 20, 1996, a story with relevance for me was on page four of the *San Francisco Examiner,* at that time the city's afternoon paper. At the time I was living in New York and was music editor of *Vibe.* On newsstands was the "Live from Death Row" cover featuring Snoop Dogg, Dr. Dre, Suge Knight, and Tupac Shakur.

I knew most of the people in the *Chronicle* story. The setting was a meticulously beautiful home in the Diamond Heights neighborhood. As a kid, I was occasionally in that house on Ora Way. From most any window there, San Francisco looked like stacks of Legos.

William Raine, 73, critically injured his son, Alvin, is the lede. As it says:

Raine ordered his son, Alvin, to leave the house . . . because the younger Raine had been drinking. Alvin . . . refused to leave and armed himself with a golf club . . . prompting his mother, 71, to run into a bedroom to get away from her son. Alvin knocked down the door to his mother's room, and then knocked her down. He then went after his father who had armed himself with a kitchen knife. "Yeah, you're too old to do anything," the son allegedly told his father as he knocked him down and threatened to kill him. As the younger Raine bent over his father, the elder Raine plunged the knife twice into his son's back, police said.

Everybody survived. No arrests were made. My questions have never changed.

DONNA

I'm always slightly depressive. My whole life is work, and it's always been work. Even when I'm home relaxing, I'm playing the piano or singing. I've always got to be doing something creative, or constructive. I hate the feeling of doing nothing.

—DONNA SUMMER, 1979

At St. Mary's Academy I was cranky and high-achieving and literally Most Involved in School Activities.

September 13, 1982

Hazy, warm. School was okay today. Seems like I have a zillion things to do and worry about. Firstly, I have schoolwork—so much reading. Then I have Yearbook—taking pictures plus after-school meetings. I'm now co-editor of the newspaper, "The Belle Vine." I'm Section president and have to go to Associated Student Body meetings every Monday. I'm on Senior Control [and] Senior Advisory Board. I have to work three days a week. I have to do that volunteer work for Delta's Head Start Center and on Saturdays at St. Joseph's Help Center. Am I bogged down or what? Please let me handle everything without messing up.

"Section" is equal to homeroom. I have no memory of Senior Control or what it was. I almost made salutatorian (at SMA you had to be in the top 10 percent of the class and win a speech contest). But my speech was an inch less than upbeat and had too many song lyrics. Most of it is lost to history, but I used Donna Summer and Barbra Streisand as inspirations, so I must have outlined why enough was enough.

My sister and I were in maybe the most hostile years of our relationship. Teenage girls sharing a room. Too much freedom. Money was
tight. I was falling in like with girls, and with boys, but really I had not
been the same since breaking up with my boyfriend, a cornet-playing
boy I met in junior high school. Lee and I were so in love, he convinced
his mother to send him to Serra High, SMA's brother school.

Toward the end of our tenth-grade year, because I was "holding
out," Lee had sex with another girl. Who I was on the track team with.
It was a scandal. Lee was by this point a friend of the family. Even
though I was "holding out," the betrayal was a punch I didn't see coming. So, even in senior year, I mostly wanted to be hugged up and loved
on by someone at a place not my home.

Six days after my graduation, I walk onto the University of California, Berkeley, campus for what was called the Summer Bridge program.
Alvin, who has picked me up from the Oakland Airport in a car I can't
remember, drives into an empty parking lot at Cal's Stern Hall. The
place looks deserted. "Let me go see," I say to him, and jog into the
dorm. I'm embarrassed and feel that maybe I haven't actually been accepted, or maybe Alvin will think I'm lying about having been accepted.
I forged my mother's signature on my application. Maybe the university
has found me out.

Deep inside Stern, I find a resident assistant, who tells me I am in fact
a day early. But not a problem, he says, and he walks me back out to the
lot to help with my luggage. I don't see the car. My luggage is sitting on
the asphalt. The RA is confused. Alvin is gone.

The RA's mood moves quickly from sleepy to awkward to jaunty.
He feels sorry for me. I can see on his face that he knows I do not belong,
and that I will not succeed. He carries the two cases to my room. I swal-
low the cupful of saliva in my mouth. Once alone, I say aloud that I will
forget all of this, because none of it matters. I speak this aloud because I
want it on record, if only to the stinking eucalyptus trees, that I hate
everyone.

If it wasn't for DeBarge's "All This Love" (sung in falsetto by El
DeBarge) and New Edition's carbonated "Candy Girl" (sung in the true
adolescent falsetto of Ralph Tresvant), I would not have survived that

summer, or freshman year. If it wasn't for Donna Summer's "State of Independence," there would have been no anthem of my life. I stood up when I heard that song. I remembered myself, and got through shit.

The third of an eventual seven children, LaDonna Adrian Gaines was born on the literal eve of 1949. Influential firsts were playing out in *Ebony*. Black newspapers (supported in part by ads for records by blues-women and Black vaudevillians like Ethel Waters, Clara Smith, and Hazel Meyers) covered boycotts and lynchings, children reciting, and neighborhood leaders. Communities like LaDonna's were charmed by Black debutantes in white tulle. In satin gloves, they balanced bouquets and an abundance of luck.

Donna Summer was sixteen in 1965, the year I was born, and lived in the Mission Hill neighborhood of Boston. Her father, Andrew, a soft-spoken butcher, had served in Germany during World War II. Her mother, Mary, a schoolteacher, was known for her chatty personality. "I came from a lower-middle-class black family," Summer told *Penthouse* in 1979. "My mother and father worked real hard. My father worked three jobs. He struggled like hell to keep our house."

In a 1980s interview on a BET news show, Mary, who also joked about the challenges of getting herself plus seven children dressed, fed, and out of the house by seven in the morning, said of LaDonna, "You knew she was gifted . . . it had to come from God . . . because from the time she was small, all she talked about was what she was gonna do, what she was gonna be. She was going to be on *Johnny Carson*. . . . Who-ever were the young ladies who were out singing at that time, [LaDonna] was gonna do it . . . I really believed her."

The young ladies who were out singing during LaDonna's mid-1960s youth include Mary Wells, the Supremes, Streisand, Martha and the Vandellas, the Dixie Cups, Dionne Warwick, Leslie Gore ("It's My Party"), and Betty Everett ("The Shoop Shoop Song [It's in His Kiss]").

There was also Millie Small, who won big with a ska cover of Barbie Gaye's "My Boy Lollipop" in 1964. It sold over seven million units world-wide, and "Lollipop" went to number two on both *Billboard*'s pop chart and the UK pop chart. The song made history—five years before Desmond Dekker and the Aces' hit "Israelites," and eleven years before Bob Marley's "No Woman, No Cry" breakthrough—as the first song from a Jamaican to sell over a million copies. Millie Small's vocals, charisma, and work paved the road for all that reggae would become.

Millie's father is described as an overseer on a sugar plantation. Her mother was a dressmaker. One of the few girl singers on Jamaica's early ska scenes, Millie made a name for herself first as a talent-show winner, and then as a duet specialist, with mostly male singers. Enter Chris Blackwell, who—according to *Men's Journal,* but really, according to umpteen media outlets—would transform reggae "from a niche, fairly provincial music into a full-fledged international pop genre." Eventually home to Marley and the Wailers, Jimmy Cliff, Marianne Faithful, and U2, Blackwell's Island Records was newish when Small was on the rise as half of Roy and Millie.

Blackwell's family was one of the richest in Jamaica—sugar, rum, horses, chutney, and more. He grew up on his parents' banana-and-coconut plantation while Jamaica was still a British colony. Blackwell hung out with Miles Davis, John Coltrane, and Cannonball Adderley in their early 1960s heyday, and then tried without success to get a ska swell going in England, where he came of age. He was still back and forth to Jamaica, though, and while there, Blackwell experienced the buzz around "We'll Meet," a duet led by Millie. He soon scooped Small from Kingston, took her to London, and became her legal guardian. Millie, the youngest of a dozen children, was headed for the big whiteness of Europe to get her life. "When I came to England it was . . . June 22, 1963," Small told *Goldmine* in a rare 2016 interview. At the age of 69, she recalls good times. "It was exciting. I wasn't afraid of anything. . . . I loved it, straight away."

According to Jamaica's *The Gleaner,* once there, Small was "given intensive dancing and diction training" at what was then called the Italia Conti Stage School; her accent was to be toned down. West Indians who had come to England to work were excluded from white society. And in the same year "Lollipop" was released, conservative candidate for Parliament Peter Griffiths triumphed with the slogan "If you want a nigger neighbour, vote liberal or Labour." But Blackwell thought Millie could appeal to Black and white audiences. He was right.

In the September 1964 issue of *Ebony,* a headline: "Exciting New Singer: Millie Small, 16, Challenges Beatlemania." The piece notes Blackwell as her "guardian angel-manager," and includes a series of explanations about why Small isn't making the money it seems she ought to be. Next to an ad for the skin-lightener Nadinola, Millie is pictured learning to properly curtsey due to an upcoming introduction to Princess Alexandra and Prince Philip.

The *Ebony* caption also notes that "through a mix-up, she was not presented." Millie Small appeared briefly in ABC's *Around the Beatles* special, and what an impression she must have made on any young Black girl who happened to see her—chocolate, in a mod pixie—and carefree.

Six years later, for the cover of her *Time Will Tell* (Trojan Records, in which Blackwell was a partner), Millie, with her bare back to the camera, straddles a giant plantain. She posed seminude for the UK's *Playboy*-inspired *Mayfair* in 1970 as well. Any lawyer will tell you that if you are an artist, and your manager is also your record label, that is a conflict of interest. And if you add to that having your manager as your guardian—responsible for and in charge of your person and your property interests? Where was Millicent Dolly May Small in all this? The lollipop kid from the scalding sugar works of Clarendon Parish who put Chris Blackwell's Island Records on the map?

In the 2016 interview, it's noted by author Tom Graves that in 1987, Small was featured on Thames TV as being "without money and living in a youth hostel with her toddler daughter." When asked about royalties from "My Boy Lollipop" and other songs, Small said, "I haven't received *any* royalties yet, my dear. I haven't received anything like that in my hand. I haven't received a check that said for 'Lollipop, here is one million.' But I hope one day I will."

Chris Blackwell had apparently bought Millie a house in Brixton after hearing of her financial situation. After quietly living there for decades, Millie Small died of a stroke on May 6, 2020, at the age of seventy-two. She is survived by her daughter, the singer Jaelee Small. At the time of Millie's death, "My Boy Lollipop" was still one of the bestselling reggae Jamaican songs of all time. "I told my parents," Millie said early on, "I was going to be a singer, or a movie star." Anything, but small.

In the shadow of hulking Catholic churches and dingy pubs with "Guinness Sold Here" signs. That's where LaDonna did her daydreaming. Six feet tall in heels. Neighborhood-famous in Mission Hill. She received local store credit based on the promise of her future fame. "I grew up with a very good outlook on who I was, who I was supposed to be," Summer has said. "I lived in a very mixed neighborhood—Irish, Italian, Catholic, doctors, teachers, students, regular families—a real melting pot."

Yet white people were actually in flight from Mission Hill/Roxbury and nearby Dorchester in the 1950s and early '60s. Flush with GI Bill funds not available to Black veterans like LaDonna's father, they flapped to all-white suburbs. In the wake of *Brown v. Board of Education* and *Brown II,* many of Boston's Blacks and some whites protested the inequalities of Massachusetts's education systems. In 1965, Martin Luther King, Jr., led fifty thousand people from Roxbury to Boston Commons— protesting residential and school segregation.

So, the blocks were hot as LaDonna Gaines attended segregated Jeremiah Burke High School in Dorchester. She was listening to Mahalia Jackson and doing breathing exercises and singing and working and exploring her immediate world. There was a lot of hooky-playing and boyfriend-having. But she remained true to her school, referring to it as "the Jerry," and recalled being a "permanent member of the glee club." Not everything was gleeful, though: "I went to school with some pretty violent people," Summer said in 1978. "And I was an outsider because I couldn't live on that black-and-white separatist premise. Racial? I didn't know what the word meant until I was older."

As she dramatized in a skit for her 1980 *Donna Summer Special,* the Gaines family spent a lot of time at Grant African Methodist Episcopal. Summer had been singing there since she was eight, and her range was well known. "I used to go to four or five churches every Sunday," Summer told *Ebony* in 1977, "and sing solos and appear with gospel groups." Her father didn't allow the girls to wear makeup or nail polish.

"He was a real dominating father," Summer said in 1979. "But a very good father." At times, they had nothing at all. "But my parents just never let us down. There were times when my girlfriends would all be going to school with new skirts, new this, new that, and I didn't have anything new. But I never envied them. I was always," she said, "a little different."

Maybe she didn't envy them because she was the lead singer of beloved local band Crow. "The 'crow,' being me," she told Craig McLean of *The Telegraph* in 2008, "because I was the only black member of the group." Crow held down Boston's Psychedelic Supermarket, and that's where Summer saw Big Brother and the Holding Company. Braless Janis Joplin drank whiskey from a porcelain keg. According to so many sources it's memeish, this blew LaDonna Gaines's mind.

With her parents' blessing, LaDonna left the Jerry a few months before graduation. Donna's moves around this time were back and forth between Mission Hill and New York City's Greenwich Village. She was singing and taking meetings, and she almost signed with RCA Records. Donna was cast in *Haare* (the German version of *Hair*) and was soon in Munich portraying the female lead, Sheila, in a massive Afro.

Donna learned German in record time. She lived in Germany fulltime and appeared in local productions of *Godspell, Porgy and Bess,* and *Showboat*. For a short time, Donna was a member of the Vienna Volksoper opera company. She was also busy doing session work. These were the days of experimental European electronic groups like Tangerine Dream and Kraftwerk. In 1973, Donna fell in with synth-pop producer/studio owner Giorgio Moroder, British songwriter-producer Pete Bellotte, and musician/songwriter Harold Faltermeyer. "Basically, Donna Summer was one of the girls in a backing band that we used on a record," Moroder said in 1998. "And we liked her voice and the way she looked."

Summer was a vibrant young Black woman making waves and making a whole life for herself in Europe. Donna Gaines the expat mar-

ried an Austrian actor named Helmuth Sommer. In 1973, when Donna
was twenty-four, they had baby Mimi. The German "Sommer" is the
English Summer. "I was a clean-cut, funny American girl who was in
Europe doing top European music," Donna told *Penthouse* in 1979.
"That was my image."

Boston was in the rearview. LaDonna was gone. But even with the
white husband and white creative partners and working in a world of
theatrical European whiteness, none of it was easy. LaDonna of Massachusetts had wanted her freedom from a strict but loving home, and
from the racial separatism of Boston. So she'd created it.

Freshman year. Banking on Love's Baby Soft. Jesse Jackson, on his presidential run, fills Sproul Plaza and registers voters himself on an ironing
board. I watch basketball from the bleachers at Cal's Harmon Gym. My
thrills are sandalwood incense and small earthquakes. In the dorm cafeteria, I can eat peanut butter Cap'n Crunch cereal for breakfast, lunch,
and dinner. I am obsessed with the sauerkraut and bratwurst at Top
Dog on Durant Avenue. At home I'm used to bright yellow on my Louisiana hots and my Hebrew Nationals. Spicy brown mustard is new.

I am familiar with the emergency loan line at the office of financial
aid. I take a massive U.S. history (1865–present) lecture class, maybe
300 students. Even though I tested out of freshman English, I'm out of
step, because my whole high school class had just 151 girls. We were
99 percent Black and 1 percent Latina. My junior high school in rich
Hancock Park was more integrated than Cal. I read all the lecture-class
readings in like three weeks. Then I sit in the back rows of a Dwinelle
Hall auditorium thinking, *These are too many years to learn about with
this large group of people*.

I realize that college requires me to have cool stories about myself. I
don't recall my affect, or much of what I said. But in pictures of myself
from 1983 and 1984, I look on the verge of requesting a map. I make
friends that last decades. I have sex with hazel-eyed Peter. I dance to
Evelyn "Champagne" King's "Betcha She Don't Love You." I dance to

Run-DMC's "Hard Times" in a pinstripe denim mini. I dance at clubs like Stargaze in nearby Fremont. Sweating through my clothes, sweating until my hair is dripping, on whatever night is Black night. I dance to Midnight Star's "Freak-A-Zoid," and Donna Summer's "She Works Hard for the Money." In drama class, the professor says, "Use real feelings to improvise your scenes." That's not just, like, life? Bye. I take ferries to Sausalito and back just for clam chowder and the cold wind.

At the end of freshman year I'm nineteen. Nothing in me wants any part of going back to Los Angeles. I move in with my great-grandmother's half sister, Vivian. She has an immaculate two-story brick house in North Oakland. Aunt Vivian is about slicing raw chicken for her cat, offering me afternoon brandy, and crisping clay platters in her kiln. Even though I see Luther Vandross on his *Night I Fell in Love* tour that summer, Aunt Vivian thinks I am not having enough fun. Lisa Fischer (1991's "How Can I Ease the Pain") is Luther's lead background vocalist. I am in love with a boy named Axel, we have lawn seats for the show, and the stars are shining—as Vandross sings, brighter than most of the time.

I'm working at a camera store in Richmond's Hilltop Mall. Axel is shaky, so when I meet a boy named David with a red MG, I let him take me to see *Purple Rain*. This was July 27, 1984, in downtown Berkeley— the night it opened. I liked boys with cool cars because I didn't know how to drive. But I did have money that summer. When I bought myself a flouncy gray-and-white sundress from The Limited, I just knew I was Apollonia.

My slow dropping out of Cal began with an accident.

During the first quarter of sophomore year, I'm in the passenger seat of a rental car on my way to the wedding of some people I don't know. My friend and roommate, Denise, slams on the brakes. There's a pileup ahead of us. My side of the car hits the cement center divider. I break the passenger-side window with my head.

Blood drips in my eyes, stinging. I have on a light dress, and I see the red on my outfit. Glass shaves the skin from the entire right side of my forehead, into my widow's peak, and takes off my right eyebrow. Slits my right eyelid. I have glass in both eyes. I recall no pain of any kind. With eyes closed in the ambulance, I ask a paramedic, "Am I going to be blind?" Rote and warm from habit, he says, "I'm sure it'll be fine."

"Don't tell her that!" This is the driver from up front, familiar and cold-blooded. "Don't tell her anything. You don't know what's happening with her." In the emergency room, with eyes still closed, I lie my way out of a tetanus shot. This is before mobile phones.

Everything about the accident, and the hospital, is like a dream. I am alone with men who have no responsibility for me.

I feel like my mother and new stepfather were not home in Los Angeles, and were unreachable. I feel like an Oakland friend of my grandmother's came to the hospital. He was nice. I'd dated his son for a short time. But this man and I, we really don't know each other. I am in the hospital for a day. Or two. Maybe Mr. Townes drove me from Vallejo General to Oakland International. Or it could have been my godfather, Bob. What feels closest to true is that it was Alvin, unemployed and living with his well-off parents in San Francisco, who picked me up from the hospital.

The ogre from my childhood is now my slurring and ashy chauffeur. Alvin tells mild jokes about my injuries, but all I want is for him to keep his yellow eyes on the road. I'm strong off hate and codeine and desertion, and I'll swerve his ugly car into another center divider if he tries me.

After the situation at Stern Hall, I expect nothing from this motherfucker. I have no luggage, so at the Pacific Southwest Airlines curb I say "thanks" and get out. The attendant at the gate asks if I've been in a skateboard accident. My forehead has literally been peeled. Yet for all the skin gone, there are relatively few bandages. I have tiny stitches on my right cheekbone and eyelid. I've been assured that after the healing, my vision will be the twenty-twenty it was before the crash, but at the gate, my eyes are swollen and my vision is off. The attendant asks if I am alone. Then she allows me on the flight early, with the senior citizens.

It's late. I have no memory of who picks me up from Los Angeles International. At their house, my stepfather tells me that it will be too much for my mother to see her daughter so injured. As per a nurse at

Vallejo General, I sleep with dry-cleaning plastic over a pillow so my face won't stick to the fabric. *In this life,* Prince screams on *Purple Rain*'s "Let's Go Crazy," *you're on your own.*

I miss half a quarter of school recuperating in Southern California. I fall in love with a boy from junior high school. He'd been nice to me, as I lived in shame of a beating Alvin gave me in front of a bunch of kids on our schoolyard one day. And Taylor again looks past my scars. With money he made repairing bikes, Taylor buys me giant ten-dollar sunglasses on Melrose. I feel understood—and incognito. We talk seriously about my transferring to UCLA, and about us getting married. I want to love Taylor. I never was quite fair to him.

On my first day back at Cal, my entire forehead is hot pink, and I wear my hair in a Sade ponytail. She's a new artist and, to my teen eyes, is even more sophisticated than Donna Summer. Sade's slicked-back look is what I need. I'm not trying to camouflage my injuries.

I had again escaped Los Angeles. Not even Taylor could convince me to stay. The Bay Area had always symbolized freedom and independence for me, and even with blurred vision, I could see that it still did.

I still can't get it together to learn to drive a car, though. Never had a license in my life.

In 1974 Netherlands, Donna Summer releases a folksy R&B album, *Lady of the Night*. A collaboration with Giorgio Moroder and Pete Bellotte, it's a moderately successful studio debut. In 1975, Summer brings her crew some lyrics for what will become "Love to Love You Baby."

Moroder recalls the moment: "I'd suggested doing a sexy song," he says. "One afternoon Donna came to the office and said she'd come up with the title 'Love to Love You Baby.' That sounded good to me. Back then I had a studio in the basement of my Munich apartment building, called Music Land . . . so I went straight down there and composed the song. A day or two later, Donna came in and we did a very rough demo."

> *I love to love you baby*
> *Do it to me again and again*

The notes lick out over and again in exactly the right place until, in the most shattering way: release. The lack of shame on the record is glorious. *Time* magazine, for just one of many examples, called the single "lubricous."

"I just made up the voice for that song," Summer said to *Penthouse* in 1979. "I found a hole in the market . . . a loophole, and that's how I got my foot in the door. That was a big foot . . . and it boosted me up a long, long way from my Boston roots." The song struggled in Europe, but when Casablanca Records released "Love to Love You Baby" in the United States, it was seventeen minutes long.

Made for DJs. Made for spinning. Made for kids used to recession and long lines at the gas station, kids high on neighborhood life and coke and integrated parties and same-sex kissing at the club. Made for those who, on sticky Saturday nights, imagined themselves high-stepping over velvet ropes and twirling under a mirrored ball. Donna's song went to number two on *Billboard*'s pop chart, and number three on the R&B chart.

"Brilliantly packaged aural sex," is what *Rolling Stone* said. "Donna became a servile vixen with a whispery voice, intoning and moaning over a metronomic beat that had all the intensity of a sex act between consenting androids." This was mild compared to other criticisms. Yet, to those of us weary of Queen and Glen Campbell, Summer sounded like a boozy booty call free of white male primal screams and Hallmarkian romance. Summer sounded like Blackness momentarily free of blues, and like a refusal to perform innocence. Besides, the Ohio Players had a hit with "Sweet Sticky Thing" in the summer of 1975 that left little to the imagination. B. T. Express's "Do It ('Til You're Satisfied)" was big as well. Summer, for all the fuss, was in the spirit of the times.

Nine years later I'm part of a busy girl crew. We in college or junior college or not at all. We tight roommates or we friends because our boyfriends are. We broke as fuck and we running from the landlords. We thin and thick and plump of lip. We go hard with the eyeliner. We have good posture and we talk loud on the bus. We get our acrylics done at the MacArthur-Broadway mall.

No more blushy Love's Baby Soft—now it's vials of gardenia oil from the man in the kufi at the flea market. My mother sends my sister, Raquel, to live with me after my sister graduates from high school. Like, in the nicest way, y'all on y'all own.

My great-grandparents help us some, and me and Quel are usually pissed at each other, and we also head on Thursday nights to Geoffrey's Inner Circle, where there's a DJ. Geoffrey Pete in a good double-breasted, standing outside of his spot in Jack London Square, moderating an unruly line. He gestures toward us: "Aren't you Janelle's daughters? Vicki's nieces? Miss Lottie's granddaughters?" Geoffrey went to high school with our mother and aunt. He waves us in past folks talking about "Who is them Berkeley bitches?" We these East Oakland bitches if it's a problem, sweetie, and we comped, too.

I am not enrolled at Cal. I find a fullish-time job at a real-estate fore-closure business. The manager of the place, Sharisse, is in her thirties, and divorced with two daughters. I babysit Alise and Alexis for money, and on the weekends, when Sharisse's ex-husband has their girls, I go with Sharisse to her boyfriend Mark's main gig—at Roland's, in San Francisco.

Mark's a drummer. Sharisse does some waitressing. No one knows me at Roland's. So a whole yoke of expectations is lifted. I'm still comped, because I'm Sharisse and Mark's "little sister." But no one knows me at Roland's. It's a dream.

I always sat down front at Roland's. I liked San Francisco in the mid-1980s. The historically Black Fillmore District had not yet been gentri-fied. Chinatown had not yet been gentrified. The historically Latinx Mission District had not yet been gentrified. And Roland's was where the races mixed. Where whites, even if they own the club, don't out-wardly act like they own the scene. Saxophonist Jules Broussard led the house band. He'd spent the seventies playing with Santana, and Boz Scaggs. At twenty, I was at Roland's pretty much every other Friday or Saturday night for a year. Sipping milky brandy and jamming to Tower of Power covers. Occasionally, Scaggs came through and had everybody finger-snapping to "Lowdown."

The nights Rosie Gaines dipped in were special. After an early set someplace else, Gaines peacocked on Roland's tiny stage, stretching out Chaka Khan ballads. All of us sweating in the hothouse of "Papillon." I had new people. No one knew to ask about my family, or my home situations. In a valley of cool olds I was young, could read music, and requested songs like Herb Alpert's "Rise." Never a plate of nachos did I pay for. Had I been doing coke, my lines would have been long and free.

I liked the DJs at Geoffrey's, and the boys my own age, but I lived for live music. There didn't have to be a flute onstage for me to understand the teamwork and the joyous trills. I'd stopped even thinking about getting back into Cal. I wanted money and music and to be away from what everyone expected of me in Oakland. Next up: I needed a job I actually liked.

> It was sort of like being in Times Square on New Year's Eve, you know? And you want to go home. You're in the middle, and you can't get out. So it's a very, very, very busy, very stressful, difficult time. There were good things about it. But I think that just the labor, what you have to do to succeed, is just really difficult.
>
> —DONNA SUMMER TO SOLEDAD O'BRIEN, 2003

Summer won her first Grammy in 1979 for "Last Dance," the most perfect song of her career. And woven into this big Donna era is a lexicon of sadness: "struggled with," divorce, antidepressants, valium. Contemplating versus attempting. Suicide. Two hours of sleep a day. Maybe three.

There were also the white male uprisings against the art form she led like Lady Godiva. The Disco Sucks movement was anti-Black, anti-gay, and anti-woman. It was pro–white rock, organized, and it was violent. Rock radio stations were switching to disco—and many in that community saw it not just as the loss of a job, or a staff, but as a scalpel to the belly of white culture. What swirled above all this was the idea that

Summer herself was not real. Even as millions purchased her records and danced to her voice at parties and at discos, the feedback from the cultural intelligentsia was that her art was pap. And that she was without a soul.

Mood on the day Summer tried to kill herself: "I was on my way out the window. I had one foot out, and the maid opened the door at the exact right moment. I was literally shifting my weight." Summer was eleven floors up. "I wasn't getting a feel," Summer told Soledad O'Brien. "I was jumping over. I was attempting to go. I didn't plan it. I just decided, I'm out of here."

I can only think of the terror in the eyes of Ingrid Bergman in 1944's *Gaslight*. The mistrust her character had in herself as her partner tells diabolical untruths and makes her doubt her (accurate) perceptions of the world around her. "I imagine things," says the tortured character, Paula Alquist. "I'm frightened . . . and of myself, too." In Summer's case, Charles Boyer's role is played by pop-music writers. She was gaslit by the gatekeepers.

So many of the words thrown at Summer—"disco," "pap-pop"— exist to make it clear that her creations are less than "rock." "Disco" is an epithet that means: no matter what you create and how well it performs and how much people love it, it remains art unworthy of respect. You and your art are fake. You discarded your Black soul as you chased your dreams. Your quest for success and for the payment that comes with it: that is bad. The messages were clear: be a Black woman in music—but stay in the R&B and soul tradition. There's nothing wrong with the chitlin circuit—we separate but we equal, yeah? Stay in the lane we made for you.

"There's more to me than meets the eye," Summer said in 1978. "I've sung gospel and Broadway musicals all my life, and you have to have a belting voice for that. And because my skin is black they categorize me as a Black act, which is not the truth. I'm not even a soul singer. I'm more a pop singer."

Summer was a new global citizen as much as Josephine Baker was, as James Baldwin had been, as Black World War II veterans were. People who, an ocean away, blossomed in an atmosphere of progressivism and racism lite. Back in America, Summer often slipped into German out of habit. "Going home to Boston was a shock," she said in 1978. "People couldn't understand me, a Black, speaking German."

She said this before the double album *Bad Girls* was flung on the world in the spring of 1979. It was to be a massive year for Summer. "I had three bodyguards," she said in 2003. "I was ushered in and out of everything. . . . I had little time for enjoyment. And when I did [have time] I needed to sleep, because it was like we were on one continual tour back then. I wonder now how on earth . . . I ever did it."

Bad Girls went to number one on the pop albums chart. Moroder and Bellotte were on board with Summer again, and as a team, they were ahead of the curve by infusing heavyish metal into Blackness. Three years later, Quincy Jones and Michael Jackson did the same for *Thriller*. Russell Simmons and Rick Rubin blended Aerosmith and Run-DMC for 1986's "Walk This Way."

All of these projects, with Summer's landing first, swerved the course of American music. And as goes music, so goes culture. This was nine years before Robyn Rihanna Fenty was born in Barbados, and a generation before Fenty recorded fourteen (one more than Michael Jackson) number-one hit songs and named herself @badgalriri on Instagram.

When Donna Summer won Favorite Pop/Rock Female Artist at the 1980 American Awards—she was up against Olivia Newton-John and Barbra Streisand—the award was presented by conservative Christian Pat Boone. Boone is notorious for having covered Black songs throughout the 1950s, marketing them to white audiences, and paying Black songwriters like Little Richard no royalties. "Well, I might as well say this, since Pat is here," Summer said cheekily before walking offstage with her trophy, "When God is for ya, *who* be against ya?" The phrase, from Romans 8, is the apostle Paul speaking to Christians who had been blamed for the burning of Rome.

Summer wrote 1979's "Dim All the Lights" herself, an update of "Last Dance," and it went to number two on *Billboard*'s pop chart. It was Summer all summer, and then came October's number-one duet with Barbra Streisand, "No More Tears (Enough Is Enough)." The song was written by Bruce Roberts and Paul Jabara, and Roberts, who has also written for Cher, k.d. lang, Dolly Parton, and Whitney Houston, talked about Summer after she died of lung cancer in 2012. "People don't give her enough credit for being such a brilliant writer, and changing pop music—which she did," he said. "Electronic dance music is based on what she did when she started. . . . She really started a whole genre. . . . She was always called the queen of disco, but it was so much broader than that." Summer left behind devastated husband and creative partner Bruce Charles Sudano, and a reported $75 million estate.

In 1994, Bruce and Donna appeared on *Live with Regis and Kathie Lee*. It's a joy to watch. The occasion was a new greatest hits package and a new song. "Melody of Love (Wanna Be Loved)" was number one on *Billboard*'s dance chart. On *Live,* Donna chose to sing "On the Radio," from 1979. She and her husband were seated on tall stools, and he played guitar. Donna looked like what she was: slightly melancholy, bizarrely effective, and beautiful.

All of her television appearances are movies in themselves. In 1978, Summer appeared on *The Tonight Show Starring Johnny Carson,* just as, when she was a little girl, she told her mother she would.

Donna looks the perfect disco princess—sleek black gown and heeled sandals with an ankle strap. She fans herself as she sits, and then blows kisses to an audience that doesn't want to stop screaming. Summer has just performed "Last Dance," and the surprise hit *Thank God It's Friday* was in theaters. Carson affects a finger snap and says how difficult it was to not want to "move" while listening to her perform.

"I always wanted to be on your show," Summer says, by way of an answer. She is sincere, and her Boston accent is intact. "As a child . . . I thought if you were really going to be a star, you had to be on the Johnny Carson show. It was always my biggest dream. . . . Today when I go home I'll look at myself and say, You know something? You made it."

She did make it, and that drive was rooted in unambiguous and very Black American desires. "[This all] comes from a sense of my desperately needing to be understood," Summer said in 1979. "And desiring to effect change through something that I have to say. I question myself all the time. Why am I doing this? It's not even the money. At some point it's just madness. I don't know why I have such a drastic need to be understood, but I do. The only specific thing . . . people need to understand, is that I need to be free."

For our 1983 St. Mary's Academy production of *The Wiz,* our director put us through rehearsal warm-ups to Summer's "State of Independence." Fairly new at the time, the song was produced by Quincy Jones, and among those singing on very forward background are Lionel Richie, Dionne Warwick, Michael Jackson, Brenda Russell, Christopher Cross, James Ingram, Kenny Loggins, and Stevie Wonder. The follow-up to the hit "Love Is in Control (Finger on the Trigger)," "Independence" was not a huge American hit, but it went to number one in the Netherlands, and in Summer's adopted home of Germany.

Back then, I didn't know what reggae, or calypso, was to recognize those rhythms. Ernie Watts is on sax, and the crisp gospelly claps took me straight back to my friend Dianita's Watts church, where if you weren't going to participate musically, you might as well go downstairs and help with the food. Donna's song mesmerized as we sweat through jumping jacks at St. Mary's.

> *This state of independence shall be*
> *This state of independence shall be*
> *This state of independence shall be*

Even if independence was just going to Berkeley. Even if it was getting dropped off like an orphan at my dorm. The grown woman known as "Danyel" was far off in the future, a blur. But I did hear her calling out, urging young Dany to pack lightly, and go.

MARILYN + PEACHES

At five . . . I announced to my family—this is thanks to film, TV, and just *Ebony* on the table with Josephine Baker— I announced, "I'm going to be either a star, or a nurse." And they all just kind of looked at me like, What makes you say that? What is a star?

—LINDA "PEACHES" GREENE

L inda "Peaches" Greene of Peaches & Herb and Marilyn McCoo of the 5th Dimension came of age on opposite sides of the United States. Neither singer had honed her skills in a church choir. Each in her own way had a feeling of being somehow different. Greene and McCoo are both middle-class girls from striving families. Like Donna Summer as Nicole Sims in 1978's *Thank God It's Friday,* Linda and Marilyn shared a "kinda free, kinda wow" mood. Linda and Marilyn carried themselves like they had their own money.

Thank God It's Friday, a 1978 Motown-Casablanca production, also featured the Commodores, Jeff Goldblum, and Ray Vitte. The film functioned as a West Coast, racially integrated response to 1977's all-white, Brooklyn-set *Saturday Night Fever*. When I was thirteen, I dressed up for a daytime day party at Osko's, near the time *Thank God* was filmed there. Called "the Zoo" in the film, it was walkable from the Hi Point duplex, and a block away from Ponyland. The nightclub sat on La Cienega like a coconut cake.

When I was eleven, Gramma stood smoking her Slims, watching us ride ponies in a circle. I can smell the green hay. My sister is bored. Gramma, fifty and looking not even forty, has shorter hair but presents as precise and as glamorous as Marilyn McCoo in her *American Band-*

stand interviews. At Ponyland we are Black and in public. There is little room for error. Boredom itself is a passive acting out. I can feel my sister straightening.

Inside Osko's, when I'm thirteen, I smell the lime rinds spoiling. I stand under speakers and let the bass tremble me. It's pitch-black in the daytime. My dress is a pretty ice-blue with a lace collar. My grandmother made it, and I don't feel like trying the Hustle. I picture Donna Summer singing "Last Dance," as she had in *Thank God It's Friday*. I conjure Ray Vitte as Bobby Speed—clinging trousers, half-buttoned shirt, jewelry, the champion's smile—deejaying in the booth above everyone. I'd quickly fallen in and out of love with Tim Reid as radio jock Venus Flytrap on CBS's *WKRP in Cincinnati*. Vitte's character is the first Black DJ I'd seen spinning records for a crowd.

> Danyel: There's all this sophistication that you guys are tagged with. "Champagne soul" and "sunshine pop" and—
>
> Marilyn McCoo: [unintelligible; feels like an expletive] champagne soul.

A first post–Civil Rights Movement cultural wave was rolling through. Pam Grier, Nichelle Nichols, and Vonetta McGee were on the big screen. Cicely Tyson, in cornrows, was on the cover of *Jet*. Elaine Brown was on her way to the top of the Black Panther Party. "Which Way, Black America?" asked the August 1970 *Ebony* cover. The choices offered were "Separation? Integration? Liberation?" The magazine might well have added, Individuality? Eccentricity?

Because Patti LaBelle and the Bluebelles, a 1960s vocal group in the style of the Supremes, was by 1971 the futuristic LaBelle, featured on the cover of *Rolling Stone*. LaBelle is the first Black vocal group to appear there. Forget sleeveless sheaths and flipped-up wigs: Nona Hendryx, Sarah Dash, and Patti are in silver bra tops and thigh-high platform boots.

LaBelle's sexy 1974 "Lady Marmalade" went to number one on the pop charts. The single's B side, written by Nona Hendryx, was called "Space Children." *You may be flying through the air / Wrapped up in how high you can go.* The song is daughter to the 5th Dimension's 1967 "Up, Up and Away."

Marilyn McCoo's serene vocals on "Up, Up" feel like fresh freedoms, and the dream that there must be someplace on planet Earth where things are gloriously fair.

The song was a top-ten pop hit. And by 1970, the 5th Dimension—McCoo, Billy Davis, Jr., Florence LaRue, LaMonte McLemore, and Ronald Townson—had won six Grammys, including two for Record of the Year. The 5th Dimension won basically every prestige Grammy—and no Grammys in the R&B or "Black" categories. In 1976, Marilyn McCoo, with her husband, Billy Davis, Jr., released "You Don't Have to Be a Star." It was a number-one R&B hit, a number-one pop hit, and won a Grammy. Songs with Marilyn McCoo on lead have sold millions and millions of albums over her multidecade career. And yet McCoo is often forgotten by music fans.

It's occasionally reported that McCoo was Miss Bronze California, 1962. The Miss Bronze pageant was established in 1961 by Oakland journalist Belva Davis in response to an officially canceled but still operative rule that all Miss America Pageant contestants be "in good health and of the white race." In her 2011 memoir, *Never in My Wildest Dreams: A Black Woman's Life in Journalism,* Davis says the contest "gave our young contestants the confidence and self-pride they needed to pursue the dreams they held of breaking through the crust of doubts about their own self-worth." The Miss Bronze—a pageant deeply problematic for its prioritization of light-skinned girls—was a phenomenon in California's 1960s Black communities. When she was seventeen, my aunt Victoria was Miss Bronze Bay Area, 1965.

Thinking about her pageant days, McCoo chuckles. "I was never a Miss Bronze," she told me via phone in 2014. "I was *in* the pageant, and I won the Grand Talent award. . . . I may have sung 'Our Love Is Here to Stay.' I used to sing a lot of pop songs." She also won—"I was shocked," she says—Miss Congeniality. With her grand talents, McCoo was on her way to UCLA, which had hosted Black students, including Jackie Robinson, since the 1930s. "For the most part I was pretty outgoing. I had an element of shyness, [but] I knew I wanted to sing . . . and I wanted to act."

McCoo was paying attention to Lena Horne and Dorothy Dandridge, and she watched others as well. "I looked at . . . Judy Garland and . . . it never occurred to me that I *couldn't* because I was Black. . . . My mother always taught us that in order to accomplish anything, we were going to always have to work harder and be better."

The Miss Bronze pageant figures largely in McCoo's destiny. In the mid-1960s, she was a part of the Hi-Fis. Soon calling themselves the Vocals, they backed Ray Charles on the road. When that group dissolved, McCoo and fellow Hi-Fi Lamonte McLemore (who had been a photographer for the Miss Bronze pageant) regrouped with singer-violinist-actor Florence LaRue, who won the Miss Bronze Grand Talent award a year after McCoo. Ron Towson, who had dreams of being an opera singer, was called in. Billy Davis, Jr., brought gospel bona fides. McLemore, Towson, and Davis are all from St. Louis, Missouri.

The new group christened themselves the Versatiles and were promptly rejected by Motown Los Angeles. "Some bands have pop voices," LaRue said in 2016, "so they become a pop band. Some have gospel voices, so they do gospel. We happened to have such versatility that . . . we could do everything from *Pagliacci* to pop." The Versatiles became the 5th Dimension, signed with a smaller label, failed with their first single—and then things clicked. Their first big moment was a 1967 cover of the Mamas and the Papas' "Go Where You Wanna Go."

"It wasn't the direction we saw our music going in," McCoo told me. "We had a mixed feeling of not being true to our music—but yet wanting a hit. Johnny Rivers, who was head of [Soul City Records], believed it could hit for us." The song was top twenty on *Billboard*'s pop chart—and it helped that the 5th Dimension's style was bold. One day they looked like crew from the original *Starship Enterprise,* and the next they're in the middle of a Golden Gate Park drum circle. It's the rocking color blocks of the costumes. The earnest, theatrical acting-out of their songs. I knew this language, of believing hard in make-believe.

The title song of their 1967 debut album, *Up, Up and Away,* was a grand slam. "We *loved* that song," says McCoo. She recalls the day the single was recorded: "[Hall of Fame songwriter-arranger] Jimmy Webb was sitting at the piano. We were working on some harmonies . . . and

Jimmy said, 'I'm working on this song. Let me play it for you.' He played [it] and we just all fell in love. . . . We said, 'We want to record that song!' And we were saying among ourselves, 'We know it won't be a hit, but it's just such a wonderful song.' It didn't sound like anything else out there. It was a song that you wanted to sing." When it came out, though, "people didn't know," says McCoo, "we were Black."

The quintet fairly leap from *Ebony*'s October 1967 cover, and the accompanying line is "The Fifth Dimension: White Sound in a Black Group." An adjacent cover line is "How to Stop Riots." In the photo, the group is mid–dance move on a suburban street. Like so much Black music imagery of the era, the image claims mobility and joy when the United States is at a tipping point. The rise of the 5th Dimension runs parallel with over 150 uprisings that occurred in the summer of 1967. Their rise runs parallel to the civil unrest that unfurled in the aftermath of the assassination of Martin Luther King, Jr. Against a backdrop of Black people choking on poverty, discrimination, disenfranchisement, and police brutality, the 5th Dimension, called "homogenized," was both too much and not enough.

"They had problems categorizing us," Billy Davis said in 2020. "Here's this Black group singing these pop songs. The Black radio stations had problems playing our music because it was too 'white' for them, and the pop stations had problems because we were Black, and they thought we should have been singing R&B." Yet their sales and radio play skyrocketed.

In 1969, the same year McCoo and Davis married, the 5th Dimension released *The Age of Aquarius*. The title song, "Medley: Aquarius/Let the Sunshine In (The Flesh Failures)" set the culture on fire. When the group falls into the "Sunshine" part, it's like we all wake up in a Baptist talent show. The deftness of the code-switch is both familiar and astonishing. Is the mash-up of two *Hair* songs a stunt? Is it knowing, high-concept art? Is it the tactical recording of songs from a culturally disruptive Broadway rock opera in which 30 percent of the cast is Black?

It's all three, plus magic. Yet even after the success of the song, McCoo told me, the group felt isolated from other Black artists in the struggle for equity in pop. The challenges with labels, producers, publicists, booking agents, the media—according to McCoo, it was hard to talk about. She cited Dionne Warwick as being "like we were," but said of the biggest Black artists of the time, "We didn't run into one another that much on the road. Everybody was working. You did talk about [the challenges] from time to time, but . . . you laugh about it and you move on. Because you knew that that was the way it was."

"Aquarius/Let the Sunshine In" is symbolic of the entire 1970s. It spent six straight weeks as the number-one song in America and won the prestigious Record of the Year Grammy over mainstream beloveds Peggy Lee, Johnny Cash, Henry Mancini, and Blood, Sweat & Tears. The 5th Dimension toured internationally with Frank Sinatra, and did the demeaning, dazzling work of headlining in Vegas as it inched away from its Mississippi-of-the-West era. The group ended up releasing twenty Top 40 singles. But it's the image of the 5th Dimension playing Richard Nixon's White House that stands out, fluorescent.

"There was a fifty-governor conference on drugs," McCoo said in 2012. "One of the songs that the 5th Dimension did was a musical interpretation of the Declaration of Independence. If you read the Declaration, it is very patriotic, but it was really talking about revolution. So here we are in the midst of the Vietnam War, singing about revolution at the White House. When we finished the song, no one applauded. Utter silence. When Nixon started applauding, everyone applauded. A very awkward, interesting moment."

In the ensuing years the 5th Dimension played a state dinner for Philippine president Ferdinand Marcos and his wife Imelda at the Reagan White House. McCoo and Davis attended the first President Bush's Christmas tree–lighting ceremony. McCoo and Davis played George W. Bush's 2001 inauguration. There are a lot of interpretations of that Nixon performance. The blog Voices of East Anglia notes that there may have been a standing ovation, and that "this performance alienated the band from their Black fan base. Things would never be quite the same for them again."

In August of 1969, on the third day of Woodstock, rising British singer Joe Cocker closed his legendary set with a cover of the Beatles' "With a Little Help from My Friends." It has become the definitive version, and it lifted Cocker to superstardom. The song was heralded as a call-and-response soul and gospel anthem.

On the record, Cocker's responders are all women. There is Madeline Bell of New Jersey, who sang behind Donna Summer and Dusty Springfield and had her own group, Blue Mink. Patrice Holloway was signed as a solo artist to Capitol but is best remembered for voicing the groundbreaking Valerie in Hanna-Barbera's original animated series *Josie and the Pussycats*. Rosetta Hightower, previously lead singer of girl group the Orlons, had a top-ten hit with 1962's "The Wah-Watusi" and sang background on Dee Dee Sharp's "Mashed Potato Time." Heather "Sunny" Wheatman is a British session singer who sang with her sister as a part of Sue and Sunny. It's an iconic performance simulated at Woodsotck by male bassist Alan Spenner and male guitarist Henry McCullough, singing in falsetto. The crowd of 400,000 went wild.

And then, after Cocker's set, it began to rain. And in that stormy break between sets, near one half million people spontaneously broke out singing the 5th Dimension's brilliant medley. The group wasn't on the Woodstock bill at all, but a near all-white crowd the size of Minneapolis or Tulsa reached en masse for the 5th Dimension's buoyant "Aquarius/Let the Sunshine In" energy.

Yet with all of the sales, and Grammys, and influence on culture, the 5th Dimension has not been nominated for the Rock & Roll Hall of Fame. And I haven't seen a Soul Train Music Awards tribute either. "We think about those groups who were similar to us—and they're in [the Rock Hall] and we aren't," McCoo has said. "We've decided that there's no way to ever explain it, or understand it."

The network variety shows that were a requirement for me in the mid and late seventies were *The Marilyn McCoo and Billy Davis, Jr., Show, The Carol Burnett Show, Donny and Marie, The Sonny and Cher Show,* and *Tony Orlando and Dawn.* When Freddie Prinze, my *Chico and the Man* hero, appeared on *Tony Orlando,* I sat there wishing I could touch his hair. On January 28, 1977, in front of his manager, Prinze shot himself in the head. He died the next day, at the age of twenty-two. I was twelve, and I read a long June 1977 *Playboy* article about Prinze's life and the events leading to his death.

On Hi Point, Alvin kept the magazines in his bathroom, atop the toilet. I stared at the photos, and when TV-show hosts mentioned Playboy Bunny bios, I got the jokes. Aside from a *Highlights* story about a boy learning why ordinary days count as much as special ones, the *Playboy* piece, by Peter S. Greenberg, is the magazine story I recall most from childhood. The title: "Good Night, Sweet Prinze."

I reveled in the play on words, and in the way everything *looked*. I didn't have the vocabulary back then, but aside from album covers, where else was I going to see fonts and page design and heds and deks and art all together, telling a story about people relevant to me? The Alan Magee illustration, with glass cracking through Prinze's temples, haunts me still.

I liked *Ebony* and *Jet. Essence,* too. It was where I could see and read about Marilyn McCoo and Chaka Khan. I could see Donna Summer on a cover with her baby daughter. I thought *People* and *TV Guide* were fine. But all five magazines looked plain to me. I wished for a magazine that was designed like *Playboy* and *Rolling Stone,* but that had people of all colors throughout. I loved Cynthia Horner's *Right On!* magazine. *People* and *Playboy* and *Rolling Stone* sprinkled us in like cayenne.

On Hi Point, I hear the front door opening. Replace the magazines exactly. I ease out the back door, hop on my Huffy. Time to get out of Dodge, as my mother would say, before sundown.

I watched the variety shows only occasionally on Hi Point Street. More often I watched television when visiting family, or babysitting. It was on other people's lawns and in other people's living rooms that I had my own life. Afternoons spun out like whole seasons when my friend Sean and I talked. He skated while I watched. Or I skated and he laughed. I hated the man playing father in my life. Sean believed his father to be Sonny Bono. We sat on curbs in cutoffs. Sean's bangs flopped on his forehead like he was Freddie Prinze.

My other friend, Stephen, had moved to Los Angeles from New York in the middle of a school year. His skin and hair were the same cider brown. We talked in his moss-covered courtyard about his father in New York. He may have been a session player. He may have tried for custody of Stephen. All Stephen wanted was to get back to New York, his friends, and his dad, who I pictured as Louis Armstrong, but younger.

Stephen and I memorized intricate plans for stealing money from our parental figures. Wondered how we might get identification beyond laminated junior high school cards. Brainstormed places that might hire thirteen-year-olds. There were cousins of Stephen's I could crash with in New York. We fondled these dreams. We knew exactly what we'd wear on the day of our clean getaway.

Raised in Prince George's County, Maryland, Linda Greene was an artistic teenager. It was the mid-1960s, and the county's middle-class and wealthy white residents had fled as middle-class and wealthy Blacks steadily moved in. Greene recalled Prince George's as "magical."

Her father was a construction worker, and her mother worked as an accountant for the federal government. "To have access to a city like [Washington,] D.C.," Greene said wistfully, "cousins and family were there, and just this amazing collection of art and music [from] every nation." At that time, Prince George's County's Wilmer's Park concert facility was a beacon on the chitlin circuit. And in 1968, twenty-five miles from Prince George's, Black Baltimore—locked by discrimination into poverty cycles, reeling from the assassination of Dr. King—went up in flames.

Greene studied classical piano from the age of six, under a teacher who taught at Howard University. Inspired by Josephine Baker, Lena Horne, and Diana Ross, and prodded by her own talents, Greene was restless. At seventeen, she moved three hours south to Virginia Beach. In the 1960s and '70s, Virginia Beach's Atlantic Avenue was a music hub, and Greene was singing in a Top 40 cover band. "It was an all-white band, and I'll tell you why I did that," Greene told me in a 2015 interview (echoing Sweet Inspiration's Myrna Smith on working with Elvis Presley). "They seemed to have the best equipment, the best cars, and the best situation to just relax in."

The Rhondels were local heroes and played at shabby-chic venues like the Top Hat and the Peppermint Beach Club. Crowds trotted up from the shore to sip stingers, and to see touring artists like the Shirelles, Roy Orbison, and Fats Domino. Greene's parents weren't loving her situation. They wanted her to be a concert pianist. "But they let me make the choice," she said. "They . . . raised my sister and I to understand that when you get to be eighteen, you're out of here. It was an exact number. But it doesn't mean they're cutting all ties with you."

Greene also got in with the Rhondels because she wanted to appeal to all audiences. "From the get-go, it was two white guys that liked black music, which in 1959 was hard to find," drummer and band cofounder Ammon Tharp told *Virginia Living* in 2011. "We were white guys playing soul, that's what changed us up from the other bands. . . . They said we were a beach music band because we played on the beach."

Beach music. Shag music. Beach pop. All apparently more of a geographical designation than a race-based genre. The tags tarnished any claim to rock seriousness. The categorization also camouflaged theft from the large majority of Black artists who, due to collusion by white venue owners and bookers, could not get booked beyond chitlin hotspots like Wilmer's Park.

"It's an aura or sound, a cultural kind of thing," Ripete Records founder Marion Carter told folklorists Brendan Greaves and M. C. Taylor in *South Writ Large*. "Based on 'sweet soul'—a style of music [typified by] groups like The Temptations, The Radiants, The Four Tops. It's a style of singing where you would never get anything like a scream or a howl like Wilson Pickett would pull off. It's all controlled, nuanced singing—this is the root of Carolina Beach Music." More than covering songs, the Rhondels were covering Blackness. And, just by the fact of their whiteness, their sound was considered safer even than the crooners' from charm-schooled Motown.

Linda Greene had no gospel training that might escape as a howl. She also simply liked singing the way that she did. Greene grew up on pop radio—Lulu's "To Sir with Love," the Supremes' "Reflections," "Alfie" from Dionne Warwick. "We had a great beach club on the main street of Virginia Beach," she said in 2015. "There [weren't] very many people of color, and I found myself . . . among the only two or . . . three Black people someplace. . . . I learned how to turn that into a positive."

She had experience. Prince George's County, having avoided merging its segregated systems for twenty years after *Brown v. Board of Education,* was forced in 1974 to bus students. The vast majority of whites were opposed to desegregation. Only 32 percent of Blacks wanted it. But Greene was a part of it.

"In high school, I had to be among the first to go to a school regionally, as opposed to it being mandatory to go to a school closer to you," Greene told me. "When I had to be among the first two or three Blacks in certain circles, I got accustomed to just knowing how to present myself, and being considered welcomed, and interesting. Doors opened to me because of that—that were not always open to everyone."

Virginia Beach in the seventies was a mess of hatred sitting on the undying simmer of Jim Crow. Blacks weren't even allowed to walk on Virginia Beach until the 1960s. Black shore neighborhoods didn't have electricity, or a sewer system. Yet "everything that was pop at the time, [the Rhondels] did that," said Greene. "They were interested in all of Motown."

Everybody was. In 1972, Motown had been dominant for a decade, and remained (along with the Beatles, Elvis Presley, and the Beach Boys) where radio lived.

Singing "sweet soul" Motown songs, the Rhondels opened for Sly and the Family Stone, and for the Average White Band. Greene honed her craft with them on the beach, living her dream. As of this writing, Linda Greene isn't mentioned on the Rhondels' Wikipedia page, but at rateyourmusic.com, she's listed, without the last "e" in her last name, as "vocals, 1971–74."

All through the morning rain I gaze / The sun doesn't shine /
Rainbows and waterfalls run through my mind.
—"STRAWBERRY LETTER 23," FROM THE BROTHERS JOHNSON, 1977

We ride our bikes around La Brea Tar Pits. My sister and I see signs for King Tut. I know the Steve Martin song about it. My sister and I are well known to the security guards at the adjacent Los Angeles County Museum of Art, where there is not yet a fee to enter. The guards are bemused. The guards are concerned. We sit on wide benches near Roth-ko's red *White Center*. I want to know what the rules are for getting your stuff hung in the museum.

We eat plums stolen from the farmer's market on Third and Fairfax. I have white-bread sandwiches of liverwurst and bright mustard. Sugar-and-butter sandwiches for Quel. The burly museum guards do us no harm.

I believe we can be like the siblings in E. L. Konigsburg's *From the Mixed-Up Files of Mrs. Basil E. Frankweiler*. In it, Claudia plans to run away from home and live in an art museum—and she and her brother, Jamie, actually do it. They blend in with students on tours. Bathe in a fountain.

We bike the long way home via a visit with our friends Lisa and Dawn on Hayworth Street. Lisa's mom, Emily, always has on the radio. Each time I hear "Reunited" on it, I know I will one day be reunited with a boy who was a fool to ever leave my side. I am twelve. Or thir-teen. I was twelve or thirteen for ten minutes. I am invited to see *Star Wars* at Grauman's Chinese Theatre (so, then, I was almost twelve). Like my skateboarding friend Sean's mother, Emily is an actress. I think she had connections. We see *Star Wars* on the day it opens.

> Gary James: When you co-hosted *Solid Gold* with Andy Gibb, you said you found yourself constantly having to prove yourself. . . . What did you mean by that?
>
> Marilyn McCoo: Well, notice the word that you used, "co-hosted" *Solid Gold*. I co-hosted *Solid Gold* for two years and I hosted *Solid Gold* for three years . . . hosted it longer than I co-hosted it. But your memory is of me co-hosting. . . . The fact that I had to point that out to you is one of the ways that will answer your question.

Marilyn McCoo keeps strict limits on the time she has allotted for our conversation. Speaking from her home in Los Angeles, she has no time for the foolishness of biographical questions that someone like me should already know. "I came out here from the South," says McCoo. She was

born in Jersey City, New Jersey, but was in Columbus, Georgia, before
arriving in L.A. at the age of seven. "Los Angeles was different in many
ways," McCoo says, "and yet not that different in other ways."

The Black population of L.A. grew from sixty-four thousand in 1940
to over a quarter million by 1970. And while McCoo lived in an
integrated—Black, white, Japanese—neighborhood on Tenth Avenue
between Adams Boulevard and Twenty-Fifth Street, the area was a rare
melting pot. As the *Los Angeles Times* states about the situation in general:

> City council districts were drawn to divide black political power,
> black students were segregated, and the LAPD declared that no
> white cop should take orders from a black person. . . . Police brutally
> established order. . . . Restaurants put up "No Negroes" signs. Blacks
> could not use public swimming pools, bowling alleys, boxing rings,
> ice rinks and ballrooms.

Not even close to an Age of Aquarius. McCoo grew up in what she
remembers as Walter Mosley's devil-in-a-blue-dress neighborhoods.
Back then it was cul-de-sacs and tunnel car washes. Unlicensed nightclubs in buff-colored buildings. Before McCoo's time, Hattie McDaniel
was sued by her neighbors for breaking a whites-only covenant there.
Butterfly McQueen had homes in the area. Johnny Otis, who produced
Big Mama Thornton's hit "Hound Dog" years before Elvis Presley covered it, and one of the more prominent white men in early R&B, lived in
the area. In 1984, Marvin Gaye was killed by his father nearby, in front
of his home.

There was sun shining over the Ferris wheel at the Santa Monica
Pier—if a Black girl could get on it. Until about 1960, as at Virginia
Beach, California's shores and riverbanks were segregated. There was
an "inkwell" at the end of Pico Boulevard, at Santa Monica—a two-
hundred-foot strip of sand and surf was where Blacks were allowed to
enjoy the glory of California's coastline. In 2021, Marilyn McCoo's old
neighborhood is known as West Adams. It is 38 percent Black and 56
percent Latino.

McCoo's parents, Mary and Waymon McCoo, were both doctors. Waymon, an ob-gyn and an Alabama native, pursued a singing career of his own for a short time in New York City. During the 1950s, they both practiced in Georgia before moving to Los Angeles with their young family. Mary McCoo's death in 1989 warranted a full-page obituary in *Jet,* where she and her husband had been covered since the midfifties. McCoo's older sister, Glenda Wina, was a television reporter and then longtime Los Angeles newscaster. Her younger sister, Mildred McCoo, was with the Foreign Service. According to Marilyn, the family went to church only occasionally. A Black jet set was forming in the City of Angels, and the McCoos were toward the front.

Marilyn's high school, named for Los Angeles, was, as she puts it, "integrated and segregated at the same time." She navigated her way through L.A. High's whites-only and "mixed" fine-arts clubs. After McCoo auditioned for a school production of Arthur Wing Pinero's romantic *The Enchanted Cottage,* she was called back and told she "wasn't selected, because it was a play with a small number of characters, and there were no Blacks in that play."

"When I was not selected to have . . . even one of the smaller roles in *Enchanted Cottage,*" says McCoo, her situation became real-life front-page news. The headline: "Little Rock, Arkansas, Comes to L.A. High." Journalist and civil rights activist Almena Lomax founded the *Los Angeles Tribune* in 1941. The paper, published in service to Southern California's Black community, was run by a multiracial staff, and according to Lomax's 2011 *New York Times* obituary, "had a reputation for fearless reporting, publishing articles about racism in the Los Angeles Police Department."

Having already led protests against Otto Preminger's *Porgy and Bess* and Douglas Sirk's *Imitation of Life* (both from 1959), Lomax wasn't having McCoo's predicament, and the *Tribune* article caused a stir. "She took them on," says McCoo. "They called me into the drama department, and they said, 'We just want you to know that it's not like that, and that we just didn't have a part for you.'" Marilyn McCoo pauses. "But they did respond."

McCoo, as she speaks, is seventy. Her voice is crisp, and she is not resigned. McCoo says her feelings remain hurt. "But I had," she says, quickly back to sounding as she did hosting *Solid Gold* for a good chunk of the 1980s, "a very strong support system at home." McCoo eventually transferred to Dorsey High, which she says was "quite integrated."

I hate the song with the lyrics *I ain't gonna bump no more / With no big fat woman*. It's clear he's talking about a Black woman. My brain: *Who would want to dance with you anyway, Joe Tex?* I hate the Commodores' "Brick House." At twelve I am a 36C, and men shout that and worse at me. They grab at my breasts on the RTD's Pico bus route. That's but one of the reasons I'd rather pedal.

I attend leadership camp with the junior high school leaders. Having lost my bid for student body president, I am instead vice president of Girls League, so still in "leadership." In a ferned and misty part of Southern California we stay in cabins. Most of the camp kids are white. Nancy, Rafe, Robert, Teddy. Some of them had been with me at Carthay Center. I'd seen some of them in the Westside Jewish Community Center's production of *West Side Story*.

At leadership camp the goal is to meet our fears and overcome them. We must walk under a waterfall on a ledge of stone slimy with algae. I know I will fall. The counselors coach us. We are yelling. Hanging back, darting out. It's hysteria. We cheer for one another. We are wet, and have come within inches of falling millions of miles to our deaths. We make it to the other side.

There is talk into the night about the state of the handball courts, the ninth-grade court, and who is known for kissing whom. I like Rafe, but everyone likes Rafe. He can skate, his mom lets him keep his hair to his shoulders. His dad is a producer of *Slap Shot,* the Paul Newman hockey film, and we'd half watched a cut of it at Rafe's house, on a projector, before it was released. After leadership camp I am invited to all the bar mitzvahs and to Nancy's bat. Robert's invitation is brown velvet embossed with gold letters. I am forbidden to go. Alvin says I will not be a Black token at a fancy Jewish birthday party. So they can look good, having a little negro in there. I am twelve.

Perhaps if I had attended even one of the celebrations? But since I don't go to any, it is felt, Nancy tells me at the door of Mrs. Faulkner's world civ class, that I'd faked liking them at leadership camp. Friendships faded. *I told you they weren't shit,* Alvin says. *Just because you didn't go to their little parties. They wanted you up there, yet let one of them li'l boys want to marry you. It'll be hell then. Fuck them. I told you.*

Since 1966 there have been a half a dozen Peaches. And one Herb. The first Peaches was Francine Barker, born Francine Hurd, and with the stage name Francine Day. "Peaches" was her childhood nickname. She and Herb Feemster, better known as Herb Fame, had several R&B hits and became known as the "Sweethearts of Soul." Marlene Mack was next. Then Linda Greene.

Since Linda Greene, there have been Patrice Hawthorne, Miriamm Wright, and Meritxell Negre. Hawthorne and Wright have never recorded with Fame—they sang the hits with him on the road. The same was true for Negre until, in 2009, this iteration of Peaches & Herb independently released *Colors of Love*. The duo, as of this writing, has no problem selling out good-sized rooms in Las Vegas, or Atlantic City. In 2009, *The Washington Post* called Herb Feemster a "working-class soul man," in part because he had not yet retired from his position as a deputized court security officer for the U.S. Marshals Service. Feemster has been married to his wife, Yvonne, since 1959.

The myth is that Linda Greene was a model, living in Fame's neighborhood, and he "discovered" her. In truth, says Greene, "I was doing a *bit* of modeling. . . . I'd gotten tired of living in Virginia Beach . . . but I wasn't going to leave . . . because they were so good to me there."

She already felt like a star. "I just kind of pulled myself together that I felt like one," she told me in 2015. "Doesn't mean I walked around acting like it. It meant I felt free as an artistic, creative person." Tommy Chong, who'd run through Virginia Beach on tour with his comedy partner Richard "Cheech" Marin, encouraged Greene's desire for more. "He was saying, 'You could really further your career. I can see that you have what it takes.' " He was going to "do that for [her]," but she wasn't ready. "I was leading up to it," she told me, "but at that moment . . . I could . . . be in my own world, performing in kimonos and raggedy jeans. . . . I was already enjoying the pop culture that hadn't been sort of like *announced*. It's what I liked."

Herb, whom she calls her brother, grew up singing in church. He worked in a record store where he met producer-songwriter-executive Van McCoy. McCoy's 1975 "The Hustle" would be a number-one pop hit and inspire a disco-dance craze a decade later, and he would produce for David Ruffin, Aretha Franklin, Gladys Knight & the Pips, the Stylistics, and more. McCoy signed Fame to a Columbia Records subdivision as part of a vocal trio. After that group came to nothing, Fame and the first Peaches, Francine, became a duo in 1966. A few singles worked, but not well enough. In 1970, Herb shut it all down and entered the Metropolitan Police Academy in Washington, D.C. In 1976, Fame reached out to McCoy again. The D.C.-area Black community being as small as it was, Linda Greene's father had done some construction on McCoy's D.C. home. McCoy suggested Greene to Fame.

Greene had other assistance as well. "Natalie Cole was there in Virginia Beach," she told me. "Our relationship had grown in the two summers that she'd come down. She . . . tried to convince [McCoy] to help me." On a late '70s family outing to see Cole perform in D.C., Greene pretended to be Natalie's sister in order to get backstage. It was crowded back there; Cole was sitting on the huge hits "This Will Be" and "Inseparable." She was being referred to as "the new Aretha Franklin."

"And so . . . Van's standing there," said Greene, "and my [real] sister starts talking about 'Remember my dad? He worked at your house? Well, remember Linda was in a talent show, and you saw her?' And he goes, 'Yes, I do remember her.' That's when I said hi to him. And then Natalie comes in the door, says hi . . . and gives me a big hug. Van goes, 'Let me introduce you to Linda,' to his creative partner Paul [Cohn]. And Paul goes, 'Herb is . . . looking for a new partner. Would you be interested in something like that?' And I'm thinking . . . this could be a launch for whatever else life has in store for me."

Greene had another thought about that turning point. "I was lucky with the fact that Van happened to be gay," she says slowly. "That was one of my reservations . . . about some of the doors that we women have to go through, the tests . . . you have to go through, to be a woman in this business. Unless you have family in this business, or your daddy has a shotgun with him . . . I can't imagine what a lot of people have really gone through."

The good times are in Mrs. Klimes's creative writing class. I have band with Mr. Cooper. I have leadership class with random faculty advisors. I have World Civilization with Mrs. Faulkner and her calligraphic chalk-board lessons. When I'm not learning for the fifty-eleventh time that the word "spartan" has roots in an ancient place called Sparta, my seatmate Anne Kobayashi helps me reimagine my penmanship. This is us "taking notes." We both still get high marks.

Mrs. Klimes is very about a billowing cowl-necked sweater. She is about enthusiasm. We scoot our desks in a circle and read one another our stories. With Klimes telling us to "Speak up! Read it like you wrote it."

She tells us to choose a television show and write our own episode. The best teleplay will be given a table read. I write an episode of CBS's new basketball-themed *The White Shadow*. There are Black people on the show who have the mannerisms of real Black people that I know. The weekly plots are often about the Black students. Thomas Carter is beautiful to look at.

But my favorite is Kevin Hooks as Morris Thorpe, the moody, be-spectacled smartass. The conflict in my script: Thorpe must choose between art and athletics. He chooses art, but manages to get to the gym for the last moments of his game. Carver High wins! I get the table read.

This is me happy.

Ride nine miles west on Pico Boulevard from the Hi Point duplex. Take the sidewalks all the way to the actual and true Pacific Ocean. Walk the grimy Santa Monica Pier, play air hockey until it nips into your soda money. My sister and I don't talk much until we get to the water. We pedal. Hair in face, hot as hell, no helmets. We may have four dollars between us.

This is us happy. Even riding the nine miles back.

My grandmother's friend Louise tells me to add cream of tartar to milk before adding milk to mac and cheese. Aunt Louise tells me, during her barbecues, that I can "go in the back" and read. Her husband, Benny, hunts, and there is pheasant sometimes, frog legs, and venison. Uncle Benny has what they whisper is a "steel plate" in his head from his time in "the service." That plate doesn't seem to go well with whiskey after whiskey. So Aunt Louise gives us bowls of mac 'n' cheese and mustard greens and sends us to cool air, *Jet, People,* and a radio. She sees our tentativeness and smooth skin and Louise knows she is saving us.

When I heard from my mother that Louise was unwell, I was in my thirties. Benny had been dead. I went to a lemon-scented convalescent home to thank Louise but couldn't quite say for what. On her radio was Ruth Brown, and Louise thought I was hardworking and glamorous because I lived alone in New York City. This was me, for a moment, happy. Then Louise told me I didn't have time to sit inside with her on such a sunny day. She made me take a bottle of Rive Gauche cologne from the top of her bureau.

Carver High wins! I go with my sister to see *Grease*. Sit through it three times. We are Rizzo over Sandy. We are "Hand Jive" over "Hopelessly Devoted to You." We escape to Westwood with my mother to see *Bugsy Malone*. Escape Alvin again to see *The Goodbye Girl*. I can't shake the theme song. The lyrics soothe, picking at my every scab. My mother tells me that the writer of the film, Neil Simon, is married to the lead actress, Marsha Mason, and that Simon wrote the movie "for her." I think this fascinates both of us. This is me happy.

I met Herb's wife, Yvonne, and without having me sing or anything else, we just kind of talked. She said to me, "I think you're the one."

—LINDA GREENE, 2016

Greene got the call from Herb the day after the Natalie Cole show. To get to know each other, they went bowling. "Herb just wants to sing," said Greene. "He doesn't want to get in your business. He's not a needy person. He [knew] if he got in the right circumstance again, he was not going to be walking that block [as a police officer]."

The newly christened Linda "Peaches" Greene and Herb made 1977's *Peaches & Herb* (MCA), with Van McCoy producing. The album's "We're Still Together" was a lightweight hit, but the project fizzled. The duo soon signed with MVP/Polydor. They met with songwriter and film composer Dino Fekaris, who, among other things, co-wrote Rare Earth's 1971 "I Just Want to Celebrate," and co-wrote Gloria Gaynor's undying "I Will Survive."

Songwriter and producer Freddie Perren, Fekaris, Fame, Paul Cohn, and Greene went to Southern California to record album two. Toward the end of the process, when there was room for just one more song, the group of men suggested Linda choose. This was in no small part because Greene had loved the demo for "Survive" and was melancholy about it having gone to Gaynor. The team listened to a bunch of new demos. "All of a sudden," Greene told me, "they play 'Reunited.'" As plain-spoken as a Carpenters jam, "Reunited" became the song to request and to *dedicate* at your local station, be that station marketed to whites or to Blacks.

"Because we were singing romantic! There was a certain amount of acting, and playing up to the words and the meaning of the song," says Greene. "And Yvonne would be right there. She was okay with it because she trusted me—and she could."

Greene had gone from Virginia Beach cover band to number-one pop act. "From then on," she said, "I could *see* Sonny and Cher . . . Sonny was there, but it was always Cher."

Kids in my neighborhood are excited about the movie *Car Wash* way before it's released in 1976. There are rumors that it's going to be filmed at a tunnel car wash near the Hi Point duplex. There are rumors that there are auditions being held for Black boys who can skate. There's a boy named Hen from our neighborhood who can really go. Hen has clear Caddy wheels on his skateboard. Hen has eyelashes longer than mine. Hen is a magnet for ambitious, sad girls like me, and for guys with sketchy plans for getting money. Guys like his older brother Owen, who is always just out of County. When we glimpse Owen, his hair is long and chemically relaxed. He has muscles, is in his early twenties, and has girlfriends as old as my mother. Owen holds keys like he's been driving since he was twelve. He looks through us like we have it easy.

Car Wash was filmed at a facility on Rampart and Sixth Street, far from us, near downtown. Now, every time I see the movie, and the Black boy who regularly skates across the car-wash parking lot, I think of Hen and Owen. How little was available to them. How little I knew them. How being from a middle-class family didn't save them. When Hen skated, he was so free. Gone! That quick on his board. Just kind, and methodical, but still reckless.

Ray Vitte, the actor who portrayed DJ Bobby Speed in *Thank God It's Friday,* had two years previously played Geronimo in *Car Wash.* He'd appeared in stuff like *9 to 5* with Dolly Parton. He appeared in episodes of *Charlie's Angels, Quincy, M.E.,* and *What's Happening!!* By the early 1980s, Ray Vitte was costarring in a doomed ABC show called *The Quest,* and on February 20, 1983, he was dead in the back seat of a Los Angeles Police Department cruiser. It was reported he'd been "chanting and shouting," and that he'd "placed a curse" on the police officers. Vitte was sprayed with tear gas. He was carried screaming to their car, and in there, "ceased breathing."

I was a senior in high school by this time. Alvin was gone, so I had no access to *Playboy.* I could not find a deeply reported, deeply designed Freddie Prinze–type story with a haunting illustration and fancy fonts. I needed something detailed, worthy of Vitte's life and the days leading up to his death. The absence of Ray Vitte's story ate at me. Who were the ones at these places where they made the magazines that decided Bobby Speed was undeserving? Who were the ones who decided *I* was?

The Beverly Hills-Hollywood chapter of the NAACP held a news conference at Donna Summer's recording studio. Vitte's pregnant wife was there.

Summer, per a newswire report, "bitterly":

A man who's basically minding his own business in his own home, who happens to be creating a disturbance somehow, is now dead because his neighbors called the police. . . . We're less one person because his neighbors complained about some noise. That doesn't make sense to me. . . . It's more important to have the man, and if the man is noisy, OK, that's one thing. But I think our priorities are very drastically off. . . . I'm devastated, because he's also my brother in Christ and I love him.

Between the dreaded "Ebony and Ivory" and my beloved "Forget Me Nots," Vitte's death was a hot topic on Black radio for weeks. Ray Vitte wasn't beaten. That was noted. There was no evidence of a chokehold. That was said. There were no needle marks. That was noted. There were calls to halt the brutalization of Black people. I couldn't relax in the back seat of the Monte Carlo. Grandmaster Flash and the Furious Five's "The Message" was a bat signal from the rest of my life. DJ Bobby Speed was gone.

STEPHANIE + THE WIZ

I n March 1983, there is a freak tornado in Los Angeles. Trees torn up by their roots. Mudslides. Sirens. That same spring, with whirling dancers and wide ribbon, we make our own tornado at St. Mary's Academy. It does not get me to Oz, but the beats of rehearsal and memorization are comforting. Along with my job at the public swimming pool, the play gives purpose to my nonschool hours.

I bring my *Music Man* and *Fiddler on the Roof* experience to *The Wiz*, and as quirky Addaperle, the Good Witch of the North, I have a whole scene. "You better cool it," I say, going for LaWanda Page as *Sanford and Son*'s Aunt Esther, "or I'll turn you into something."

It's senior year. I don't understand why Michael Jackson is singing about Billie Jean King. I don't understand why white people are on the radio singing about the rains in Africa. My grades are good, though. I'm in love with a girl at my school. I'm in love with a boy lifeguard at the pool. In my grandmother's fourplex, I live with my mother and my sister in a two-bedroom apartment. My sister has varsity tennis and wild friends. My mother has work and what else we don't know. Outside of bedtime, we are rarely all home together. We are not a family that takes a lot of photos. Framed portraits are a vanity. We are not a family that stands long before mirrors.

As a teenager, I don't drink (except for that one Halloween) or smoke. I have no desire to chemically remove myself from reality—I'm about physically moving myself from the apartment. My nonschool life is half dream, half scheme. I have friends at school, but by the time *The Wiz* closes, after five sold-out nights and a school-bus tour of other California parochial schools, I am mostly done with them. First Carthay, then John Burroughs, now SMA: another school, another jagged ending.

Sweet thing, let me tell you 'bout the world and the way things are. It's my song. Addaperle is a chatty crossing guard at the curb of the Yellow Brick Road. The "sweet thing" is Dorothy, played in our production by senior Sheryl P. with the flamboyant smile. Our original Dorothy, a sophomore named Grace, had to leave the play right before we opened. Illness is mentioned. Bereavement is whispered. And the inconvenience of strict Christian parents. I wonder if meek Grace with the glorious voice has an Alvin who snatched her from *The Wiz* for shining. Sheryl the understudy moves like the athlete she is. We are mesmerized by her glowing skin. Sheryl has to be six feet tall.

I can't reach my high notes, but that's the charm of Addaperle. As in *The Music Man,* I appear in a matronly dress and a wide hat. My fear of being unable to appear on opening night is in my head. Alvin is not there to intimidate. When he is by the two-bedroom apartment, he is low-energy and thin, with beige teeth. My skin is rashy. I ask my mother often about my biological father.

> *'Til this day, I think* The Wiz *is the biggest thing that has happened in my career. Even though my albums have been successful, my goal— one of my goals—is still to make one of my albums that big.*
> —STEPHANIE MILLS TO ANGELA STRIBLING OF BET, 1989

During the late 1960s, a Black, Juilliard-educated piano prodigy named Charlie Smalls worked on the road with artists like Queen Esther Marrow and Sammy Davis, Jr. At the same time, a white ad producer and comics writer named William F. Brown was easing into the life of a playwright. There was also a sometime actor (*Another World*) and radio executive named Ken Harper. He'd been nursing a big idea. Harper went to Smalls and Brown with a suggestion that they adapt *The Wonderful Wizard of Oz* for an all-Black cast, incorporating Black slang.

They took a cherished all-white story about overcoming fears and turned it into one about the Black American dream of the home we never had. They did this to the tune of seven Tony Awards on eight nominations. *The Wiz,* a proof-of-Black-humanity precursor to *The Cosby Show* six years later, was a mass pop product, and was envisioned as such from early on. "*The Wiz,*" wrote an executive at Twentieth Century Fox, which had backed the show for first option on a film version, "is as black as *Fiddler on the Roof* is Jewish."

When *The Wiz* initially struggled, Twentieth Century Fox funded *Wiz* television commercials, featuring Stephanie Mills and whites in the audience. It was the second-ever national campaign (after *Pippin*) for a Broadway show. And as would happen with the pilgrimages to New Orleans's Essence Festival decades later, Black people planned vacations around seeing *The Wiz* in New York City. And when the show toured the States, grassroots support was organized and successful.

"There was a big push by producer Ken Harper to bring in the African American communities," Dee Dee Bridgewater—who won a Tony for her role as Addaperle's sister, Glinda, the Good Witch of the South— said in 2015 on NPR's *Here & Now*. "Busloads of people," from church groups and African American organizations. Night shows in New York City were fifty-fifty, Black-white, with many in the seats reporting *The Wiz* as their first Broadway show. In 1984, *The Wiz* toured Japan.

The magnetism of Stephanie Dorothea Mills is central to it all. Stephanie Mills is one of the most beloved, and one of the most underrated, Black female recording artists in history. Mills put in years embodying the role of Dorothy, and, while laying the groundwork for big Black-centered shows like *Dreamgirls, Rent,* and *The Lion King,* introduced a generation to Broadway.

Mills had been releasing albums since 1974 (*Movin' in the Right Direction, For the First Time*), but it wasn't until her 1979 *What Cha Gonna Do with My Lovin'* that she made more impact as Stephanie than as Dorothy. The 1980 follow-up, *Sweet Sensation,* included "Never Knew Love Like This Before," which was a top-ten pop hit and won the Grammy for Best Female R&B Vocal Performance. By the time of "I Have Learned to Respect the Power of Love" (written by Angela Winbush and René Moore), Mills was deep in a zone of zealously intimate R&B.

The future star was born in 1957 to beautician Christine Mills and city employee Joseph Mills. Her family lived in Brooklyn's Bedford-Stuyvesant neighborhood when nearly half a million residents lived on its 653 blocks. Bed-Stuy, the gentrifying setting of Spike Lee's 1989 *Do the Right Thing,* was by 1960 the second-largest Black community in the country, after the South Side of Chicago. Trash was barely collected. The Harlem uprising of 1964 had sent fiery tendrils into Bed-Stuy. People were calling it Brooklyn's Birmingham.

> The area's high schools had a 70 percent drop-out rate. Infant mortality, delinquency, and unemployment rates were twice the city average. Underemployment was at 28 percent . . . when the city's unemployment rate was just 3.7 percent.

Stephanie Mills sang at Bed-Stuy's Cornerstone Baptist Church from the age of three. Before her *The Wiz* debut, she appeared on PBS's *The Electric Company* and worked with New York City's Negro Ensemble Company. She spent time on Brooklyn's talent show circuit, and in 1968, Mills made her Broadway debut in *Maggie Flynn* as Pansy, an orphaned child of runaway slaves.

At eleven, singing the Jackson 5's "Who's Lovin' You" and Stevie Wonder's "For Once in My Life," Mills held down the Apollo Theater's Amateur Night with first place wins for six weeks in a row. "I'd been singing in church, so I didn't have any fear," Mills said in 2010. "If I'd been older . . . I probably wouldn't have done it, because I would've known what rejection was."

There used to be a giant billboard for L.T.D.'s 1978 *Togetherness* album on Los Angeles's Crenshaw Boulevard. I feel like it was there for a decade. L.T.D. lead singer Jeffrey Osborne went solo and became a pop star in 1982 with "On the Wings of Love." But in December of 1979, after my mother's first cousin Thurman was murdered, Jeffrey and his brother Billy Osborne (also of L.T.D.) sang "Everything Must Change" at his funeral. Thurman was home in his bed with a girlfriend when they were both shot in the head by a hired killer, who was eventually convicted of the capital crimes. Thurman was thirty-four.

He left behind my younger cousins Leafy and Ammy—two daughters not old enough to understand. He left behind an older sister, Gail, who seemed to me an international super spy. Thurman left behind an ex-wife so softly lisping and chic I stared. At the age of five, I'd been a flower girl in Thurman and Pam's wedding, and assumed they'd be moving to a castle in the sky.

Truly, my whole adult family was desolate and angry. They had seen it coming. Because of Thurman's work "in the streets," he'd been forbidden for years from family functions. I heard the elders talking: being around Thurman was "dangerous." But whether he was nearby or not, he had the glow of a golden boy. Thurman was tall and smelled of Earl Grey. When he was allowed (or when he dipped in minus consent), Thurman moved through beach picnics and holiday dinners like a movie star. He drove fast new cars. He bought me a Sly Stone album when I was, like, seven. Best of all, T.D., as family members called him, seemed a rebel, and brought upon me a fever of feeling seen.

I wasn't allowed to attend Thurman's funeral, but I saved the program, and I still listen to the many versions of "Everything Must Change," my favorite from Quincy Jones's 1974 *Body Heat*, trying to picture the grief. Jazz singer Veronica "Randy" Crawford's 1976 version of "Everything" towers above even Nina Simone's and Sarah Vaughan's efforts. I heard in the aftermath of his murder that T.D. was on a list of "beautiful people" thanked on Prince's self-titled second album, the one with the Pegasus. I looked at Thurman's name for so long. It made Prince human to me.

Thurman died in my fourteenth year—the year Alvin slapped me down on the playground in front of my friend Taylor and ten or twelve other kids. Also in my fourteenth year, I saw a poster at my junior high

for the Fountain Valley School in Colorado Springs. I called for a brochure. I wanted to start over, and from where I sat, Colorado looked like
a big square of peace. Girls in the Fountain Valley brochure were on
horses, in a green pasture. I set up an appointment for my mother to
speak with a school representative. There were scholarships available.

My mother said it made no sense for someone else to raise her child.
She didn't know those people, she said, for them to have such an influence. I was stunned by her response. But at the same time, I was starting
to truly get it: I have to keep doing for me. I felt like a giant blister. But
I kept walking.

When I met my cousin Marjorie for the first time, she had on a
St. Mary's Academy uniform: navy skirt, white blouse, gold tie. Some of
my family had learned of her existence at Thurman's funeral, and she
was by my grandmother's fourplex to meet more of us. Marjorie is Thurman's oldest daughter, looks exactly like Thurman's mother, and really
like our whole Louisiana side of the family. I was intrigued by her situation and her poise, but I didn't have time for a lot of chitchat. I asked
Marjorie about the St. Mary's process. There was a test to get in. I wanted
to take it.

My grandmother said that there was likely a discount for actual
Catholics, and that her mother had my baptismal certificate. I called
Gram in Oakland. She had my certificate. And for a while, Gram helped
my mother with tuition. Because I did pass the test. And my great-
grandparents were into me being at a Catholic school.

About my high school: (1) Each class wears a tie, one of four colors,
that marks their time at SMA. I'm a red tie (the best tie!) of 1983. (2) *Deus
illuminatio mea* is the St. Mary's motto. (3) St. Mary's girls are the daughters of dentists and lawyers. (4) St. Mary's girls are all pretty. (5) St. Mary's
girls are called "hoes." Guess the four truths about us, and the lie.

By the time auditions for *The Wiz* came around, the teen mezzo-soprano
Mills was a battle-scarred veteran with tiny butterflies and flowers
painted on her fingernails. "I had gone to so many auditions I didn't

get," she told Margaret Carroll of the *Chicago Tribune* in 1976. "It always seemed that it was twice as hard for me to get work [that went to] some of the other kids I knew. I told my mother I thought people didn't like me for some reason."

Mills didn't audition for Dorothy until the second call. "It was in [director] Geoffrey Holder's home," she said. "They told me how they wanted Dorothy to be, and I read from a script. The second time I auditioned, I sang. The third time I auditioned, I got the role." Her overall ambition was in line with that of composer Charlie Smalls. *Jet*'s September 23, 1976, issue ran an item reporting: "Pretty pixie Stephanie Mills becoming a student at New York's Juilliard School of Music this fall. The 17-year-old delight will be a co-ed by day and will continue to 'ease on down the road' with *The Wiz* cast on Broadway at night."

Surrounded by big, white-centered musicals like *Annie, Beatlemania,* and *A Chorus Line,* and in defiance of headlines like *The New York Times*'s January 1975 "'The Wiz' Misses," *The Wiz* lit up Broadway for four years. As Stacy Wolf says in *Changed for Good: A Feminist History of the Broadway Musical,* Black theatergoers' resistance to mainstream messaging "negated the presumption that a white perspective is objective or universal." Exactly. Out of necessity, and with habits refined during the Jim Crow and Civil Rights times, Black people were their own media. Way before overindexing on social-media platforms like Twitter, we had the ability to make ideas and language and cultural moments go viral.

St. Mary's Academy is the oldest continuously operating all-female Catholic high school in the Archdiocese of Los Angeles. It's on Grace Avenue, flanked by the now-defunct Daniel Freeman Memorial Hospital on one side, and Inglewood Park Cemetery on the other. My swimming pool workmate Marcus-the-lifeguard died at Daniel Murphy. Ella Fitzgerald is buried at Inglewood Park, as well as Etta James, Willie Mae "Big Mama" Thornton, and singer-songwriter Syreeta Wright. The Los Angeles Lakers played at the fabulous Forum, about three blocks down Florence Avenue. My senior year at St. Mary's coincided with Magic Johnson's third season in the NBA.

We often saw Magic zipping down Florence in a pale-gold Mercedes-Benz. He knew our school. The Laker Girls practiced in the huge room that served as our gym and auditorium. It's where we had *Wiz* rehearsals and performances. It's where we had dances in which nuns monitored how close we slow-danced with boys to Heatwave's "Always and Forever" and Stephanie Mills's "Feel the Fire," a duet with Teddy Pendergrass.

The oldest nun on our small campus I recall as Sister Eunice. She was a librarian at St. Mary's, and one of the few to still wear her habit daily. Sister would push bound issues of magazines toward me over her counter, disapproving of my fascination with the Beatles and the "Summer of Love" as covered by *Life*. Sister Eunice suggested I read Herman Wouk's *Marjorie Morningstar,* about a young Jewish woman who wants an artistic life, has a devastating affair with a selfish artist, and then ends up with a plain man and an ordinary, suburban life. I was a fifteen-year-old Black girl fascinated by the idea of a life of few rules. But I would have slit my wrists for ordinary.

In my senior year at St. Mary's, I wrote a paper about the Beatles' effect on the youth of America. I wish I still had it. I loved the screaming girls, the girls who fainted, the ones who tried to block the Beatles' limousines from rolling. They threw their weight around. They wanted more. I knew their desire to touch their heroes.

I screamed at the Jackson 5 concert my mother took Quel and me to for my seventh birthday. And in September of 1981, I was in the rafters at the Forum for the Jacksons' Triumph tour. My friend Kim's college-aged sister stood on line for tickets, and we three were there for one of four sold-out nights. Michael and his brothers were the size of fireflies, but jumbotrons were new and hypnotizing. I screamed until my ears rang and my throat hurt. Kim, her sister, and I were dancing, and singing every word, down to the ad-libs. It would have been easy to dive to my death. I had had enough. That's how wild was the rapture.

But the girl Beatles fans were rarely respected by rock writers. Even as recently as 2014, in a *Time* retrospective:

One of the reasons the band stopped touring so early in its career, and retreated to the studio for the last four years of its remarkably short life, is that the sound erupting from their frantic fans made concerts an exercise in futility: enveloped in a non-stop collective [primal scream] the lads literally could not hear themselves play.

These white male writers not only clutched pearls, they were hostile, and they shamed the young women. In 2010, Boomtown Rat, Band Aid cofounder, and Nobel Peace Prize nominee Bob Geldof told *Q* magazine:

I remember looking down at the cinema floor and seeing these rivulets of piss in the aisles. The girls were literally pissing themselves with excitement. So what I associate most with the Beatles is the smell of girls' urine.

One, get over yourself. And two: it's a claim disputed by the girls themselves.

As a sixteen-year-old just starting to read music journalism and criticism (it wasn't easy to find, and I didn't know to ask for it by name), I felt that men writers were jealous of the girls' wild and sweaty emotional response—group response—to other men. They were angry at the girls' assertiveness. None of the bylines seemed to be female. And since seeing my cousin Thurman's name on Prince's album, I'd started reading album liner notes, fascinated by the credits and the thank-yous. I didn't see that many women's names there. It didn't sit right with me.

To scream at a show, to get drunk on bass vibrations, to sing memorized lyrics loudly in unison with people you don't even know? It's the burningest, most crackling current, and to stay in it for a full show? You're linked with the world again, golden and new. I wanted to write about that. I didn't want to stand away from it, gazing at it like a painting, or with envy. I wanted to be where culture was happening. And to know more about it, from within. I played flute, in my junior high school band. I could read music. I sang in choruses. In *The Wiz,* I sang alone. What I wanted to be when I grew up had to do with music. And writing. And photography. And conveying what was not being conveyed.

At the apartment in my grandmother's turquoise fourplex, my world runs on Angela Bofill, Rick James, and the Police. It runs on Oki-Dog pastrami-and-cabbage burritos. At St. Mary's, I am intense, and often in the guidance office. I'm shooting black-and-white for the yearbook. I have a poster of Prince—he's seminude in a shower—taped in my locker. I fill out college applications. I'm accepted to USC. My mother is surprised at my letter, as she doesn't know I applied. I don't respond to USC.

On a date with a boy from the Jesuit school, I see the Go-Go's live at the Hollywood Bowl. At the Greek Theatre, I see Liza Minnelli and Joel Grey with my mother. With Thurman's sister Gail, I see the Whispers and Richard "Dimples" Fields at the Greek. I'm happy at all these shows. I am at home. I feel like people are trying to help. Because my grandmother's neat fourplex is in a neighborhood claimed by the School Yard Crips. It's mostly peaceful, but I see shit happening around the chipped motor hotels on La Brea. I see fools acting out in the parking lot at the World on Wheels rink. The boys on our blocks don't really bang. They sell dope so they can buy Blaupunkt speakers and kitted Volkswagen Sciroccos. They cruise girls too young for them. "Why," my grandmother would say, "would you ever go out with a boy who is old enough to drink at the bar, who would go out with someone who is not old enough to drink at the bar?" This makes sense to me. I cut off Barry and his pristine Datsun 260Z.

I rate a Brown University alum-to-student interview. It takes place on an outdoor staircase overlooking a UCLA lawn. Like I had when Quel was in counseling there, I ride the back of the Wilshire bus to UCLA. I'm in my navy-and-white uniform with my red tie. I am ashamed of my winding answers.

I want to be at Brown because it's far from California, because you can take whatever classes you want. Because kids are lying on a lawn in the brochure. *What are things that I wouldn't know about you from your application?* I have polished my saddle shoes. Nothing I say sounds chronological, or complete. Nothing I say sounds true.

I take the Wilshire bus to La Brea. La Brea bus to Pickford Street. Walk up wooden stairs to the flat roof of the carport. There are clotheslines for the fourplex tenants. Cars ride by. I hear Zapp's "Dance Floor" from Barry's speakers. I hear the S.O.S. Band's "High Hopes"—Tony's Blaupunkts. Jeans and fitted sheets hang damp and heavy. I need to hear Stephanie Mills sing her part of "Be a Lion," but for that I have to go in the apartment, to the stereo. We have Marlena Shaw singing "California Soul." We have the soundtrack to the Broadway production of *The Wiz*.

I didn't know back then that the original cast recording was produced by Jerry Wexler for Atlantic Records. Wexler produced records for LaVern Baker, Ruth Brown, Roberta Flack, and, most famously, with Aretha Franklin.

And with no fear inside / No need to run / No need to hide.

Stephanie Mills sang it out, just for me.

And the touring cast of *The Wiz* was inspired by Mills's evocations. Renee Harris was in the role of Dorothy Gale when I saw the show at Los Angeles's Dorothy Chandler Pavilion. Harris wore the ruffled ivory sundress. She had her very own Toto—a West Highland white terrier. It must have been my twelfth birthday. I was with my mother, my sister, and one of the Crispy Critters I loved best. Todd Bridges, then known for *Fish, The Love Boat,* and *Little House on the Prairie* (particularly for a scene about being a "nigger"), was seated with his family, a few rows ahead of us.

> *If on courage*
> *You must call*
> *Then just keep on tryin'*
> *And tryin'*

With empathy and encouragement, Harris sang to the Lion. A fever simmered under my skin. I looked around the audience. The Lion was us. More than a few grown people, with eyes wet as mine, looked back at me.

Michael Jackson saw *The Wiz* at least three times. There were rumors of a romance between him and Mills. "Yes, it's true," Mills says in a 2004 radio interview, when asked if she and Michael Jackson ever dated. "I was his only little chocolate drop," Mills says. A particular date took place in 1977 at New York City's Regine's. "Andy Warhol took us out to dinner. [He] did an interview." The radio jocks hoot and holler as she speaks. "In fact, it's in Andy Warhol's book," she says. "I was dating Michael back then. I thought I was going to marry Michael, but you [know] I'm a little too . . . I'm too dark."

The hosts don't follow up on Mills's statement. She's a Black woman calmly speaking about colorism, and to them, her pain is mundane. That pain comes through her work as depth and compassion, and what the hosts could have pivoted to is that if this were a world in which Black vocals were judged with the same grace as white vocals, Mills and Teddy Ross's "Be a Lion" and Mills's "Home" would stand next to Judy Garland's performance of "Somewhere over the Rainbow" in the pantheon of American music. Mills is asked if she and Michael ever had sex.

"No."

And then the Grammy winner is asked, "Did you ever see *it*?"

"Michael was very much a man. He was very loving . . . but we've never had sex. Only saw him with his underwear on, and he looked very cute." Without judgment she says, "He was brown-skinned at that time."

The photos of them together are intimate, awkward, happy. Michael had not yet recorded 1979's *Off the Wall*. Mills and Jackson had both been working and contributing to the bottom line of their families' lifestyles since their grade school years. Mills and Jackson both wanted to leave behind the work of their childhoods. They were both ready to get away—literally and figuratively—from their family compounds. Both Stephanie Mills and Michael Jackson wanted to be pop stars. They learned from each other, and each was influenced by the other. They may have used each other. They probably liked each other a great deal.

So there had to be disappointment when Michael's friend Diana Ross was cast over Mills to portray Dorothy in the film version of *The Wiz*. Ken Harper bought the show back from Twentieth Century Fox and got in business with Motown and Universal Pictures. Michael, nineteen, was set to be the Scarecrow. The 1978 film flopped. And some believe it haunted the Black film landscape for the forty years until Ryan Coogler's *Black Panther*. "The failure of *The Wiz* seemed to prove that multimillion-dollar productions starring Blacks couldn't make money," Roger Ebert said in 1981. "And Hollywood didn't need more than one movie to prove that to itself."

There's no doubt that director Sidney Lumet, producers Rob Cohen and Suzanne de Passe—as well as Ross herself—underestimated the degree to which audiences treasured Mills in the lead role. Also in play was iffy distribution: theater chains in many white neighborhoods refused to run *The Wiz*. "White films were for white audiences," author Steve Knopper writes in *MJ: The Genius of Michael Jackson*. "Just as black music, despite brief exceptions such as Motown and disco, had been for black radio stations and white music for white radio stations."

In 1980, after a three-month courtship, Stephanie was married by the Reverend James Cleveland to Shalamar's Jeffrey Daniel. She was twenty-three. Jeffrey Daniel is credited with teaching Jackson the moonwalk, the dance he debuted in March 1983 during NBC's *Motown 25: Yesterday, Today, Forever*. The show kick-started Michael's elevation to global phenomenon. Though she credits him for helping her get past her insecurities, Mills filed for divorce from Daniel in 1981. "I know society has a thing about beauty," she said to *Ebony* in 1982. "People are into that tall-pretty-girl-with-long-hair thing. . . . I used to feel intimidated when I was around those gorgeous ladies, but I don't feel that way anymore."

The crochet of connections is tight. Michael had been with Motown since forever. Ross is credited with "discovering" the Jackson 5. On the set of *The Wiz,* Jackson and musical director Quincy Jones solidified a relationship that led to *Off the Wall, Thriller,* and *Bad.* Mills visited the set of *The Wiz.* "I'm a big fan of Diana Ross," she told BET *Video Soul* host Angela Stribling in 1989. "And at the time, I was signed to Motown. But things just didn't work out with me doing the film. Was I disappointed? I don't think so. . . . I don't think it would have affected me like . . . if I was older, and that was my big, big break . . . or this was my one thing in a lifetime. It's proven to not have dampered or tapered my career."

Mills famously passed on an opportunity to appear in what would have been her own 2012 episode of TV One's important *Unsung* series. Featuring stars like Betty Wright, Phyllis Hyman, Billy Paul, and Roxanne Shanté, the show documents the careers of Black musical artists from the 1960s through the 1990s. Artists that don't tend to shine brightly in white imaginations. But Mills's position is that she is not unsung. "I've had a wonderful career," she said in 2017. "I've done wonderful things, and met so many wonderful different people. So I don't feel like I'm unsung at all." What stings me is the fact that *The Wiz* won seven Tony Awards. Mills was not nominated for any Tony, at all.

My mother and grandmother came to the first and last performances of *The Wiz* at St. Mary's. In addition to my full scene in Act 1, Addaperle returns in Act 2 and sashays through the audience, tapping people and flicking them with her natty feathered boa. On closing night, one of the people I tapped was Magic Johnson. He was having a great time. He waved to the packed house. The Lakers were having a great season. No one didn't love Earvin.

We were set for our tour of four other schools. Over the next week, before we packed school buses with sleeping bags and got on the road, Kim, the friend I'd screamed with at the Jacksons concert, handed me a folded sheet of ruled paper. On the outside was written the word "controversy." In quote marks. Everyone knew I loved Prince. The poster from his *Controversy* album was taped inside my locker.

When I unfolded the paper, the sentences were about the two girls I'd been exchanging love notes with. Two girls who listened to me. Held me. It's not like I'd been wholly secretive. Besides, we were a small, all-girl school. We all knew who was pregnant and having the baby. We knew who had been pregnant and terminated, without the nuns finding out. We knew which senior believed she was in a loving relationship with which male lay teacher. We knew which junior had our women's volleyball coach strung out and waiting by her car every day after school. We knew which nun our director of *The Wiz* wished she could marry.

So the thing that pissed me off was the fact that the note told me that certain girls were afraid to sleep next to me on *The Wiz* tour. Apparently, there was "controversy" about my sexuality. I needed to ask myself, said the note (quoting Prince), *am I straight, or gay?* Kim told me she could no longer hang with me, because she could take no chances that the people at college would learn she hung out with a gay girl at school. The note listed several other girls who were deciding if they could still be friends with me.

I was in a Black prequel of *Veronica Mars*. And if fools wanted to cut me off, then we could make it mutual. By the age of seventeen I was skilled at what the next generation would call ghosting. I could compartmentalize so concretely that when one compartment somehow leaked into another, it was like a shiv. I could vomit from the nausea. I burst with rashes on my inner arms, inner thighs, lower back—the softest skin. But crossover between silos was rare. Besides, I'd been accepted to UC Berkeley. I was graduating from St. Mary's on June 6, was headed to Cal's Summer Bridge program on June 11. My dreams and schemes were coming to fruition.

The night Magic Johnson was in the audience, Sheryl P. sang her "Home" finale like she had listened to Stephanie Mills sing it a thousand times. She went for Mills's intonations. She engaged with Mills's spirit. I was in the chorus singing background, and we all were weeping. As Dorothy, Sheryl was the personification of rejoicement. This was my farewell.

There was a standing ovation. Magic Johnson was asked to the stage as we took our bows. I can't recall what he said, just that his smile was wide. Magic reminded me of the lifeguard, Marcus—good-looking, and with an aura of possibility. Johnson was tall, but so was Sheryl. She reached up, like to hug him, and kissed him hard on the mouth. They tongued each other down long enough for the cast and most of the crowd to gasp and cheer. Some of the nuns seethed. Some of them smiled.

I love my high school. I am a red tie—the best tie—of 1983. There is a class reunion every five years. I'm on the email lists and in the Facebook groups, and I love my red-tie sisters. I always think hard about going to the reunions. I feel a pull. But I've never attended.

JODY + DENIECE

ody Watley was a magnet, to my tense teen mind, for loving-attention. I imagined the "real" Jody had sprung from a life of frocks from The Limited, picnic dates with sincere boys, and pure peace. What problems Jody ever had I knew could be solved with her unflappable gaze.

I worked to perfect mine: calm yet unpredictable. I loved Louise Jefferson, and Florence Johnston, and Helen Willis. But in the late 1970s, outside of Berlinda Tolbert as Jenny Willis on *The Jeffersons* and Bern Nadette Stanis as Thelma Evans on *Good Times,* we didn't have young Black women regularly being sexy and cool on television. Janet Jackson didn't arrive on *Diff'rent Strokes* until 1980, just as the dynamic Stanis, with the cancellation of *Good Times,* faded from regular public view.

Watley, dancing on *Soul Train* and flourishing in Shalamar, was very cool. The first music video I ever saw was for Shalamar's 1978 "Night to Remember." I yelled to my sister, "Come see! There's a little movie to the song!" Watley was central in a new television medium. On the strength of that, and down to her boyish name, she was in defiance of existing cultural conditions. I was in love.

But there were a lot of cool Black chicks making big pop in the eighties. They were very often written off as corny. They were willfully unacknowledged by mainstream cultural gatekeepers. A short list of those insufficiently covered in relation to their artistry, sales, and impact: Deniece Williams, Sade Adu, Anita Baker, Chaka Khan, Patrice Rushen, Cheryl Lynn, Angela Bofill, Cherrelle, Stephanie Mills, Patti LaBelle,

J O D Y W A T L E Y · G R E A T E S T H I T S

Caron Wheeler of Soul II Soul, Patti Austin, Phyllis Hyman, Barbara Weathers of Atlantic Starr, Sheila E.—and Jody Watley.

Watley's self-titled 1987 debut was a number-one pop album. Written and produced by Jody and former Prince affiliate André Cymone (with an assist from Chic's Bernard Edwards), it sent forth five hits: "Looking for a New Love," "Still a Thrill," "Don't You Want Me," "Some Kind of Lover," and "Most of All." By her own account, few expected Watley's immediate and explosive impact. Probably no one expected her "hasta la vista, baby," from "New Love," to zip into the zeitgeist with such authority that Arnold Schwarzenegger uttered it four years later in 1991's *Terminator 2: Judgment Day.*

Jody Watley sold four million copies worldwide and set up her 1989 *Larger than Life,* which featured the huge hit "Real Love," and sold another four million. Watley still records for a passionate—if smaller—audience, maintains a lustrous social media presence, and tours successfully. But it is her 1987–90 solo run, when she was neck and neck with Madonna and Janet Jackson, that shines bright like a diamond.

There are similarities between Watley and Jackson. That they're both Black girls who came of age in Los Angeles just five years apart is only a piece of it. They also broke away from highly popular musical units, took the reins of their careers, and walked solo toward stardom. Watley and Jackson also both created huge albums with former members of Prince's musical crew. Jackson worked with Jimmy Jam and Terry Lewis, original members of the Time ("Jungle Love," "Get It Up"), a group featuring Morris Day that toured with the Purple One. As Jam and Lewis were beginning their careers as producers of sixteen number-one pop songs over three decades, they were helped along by then–SOLAR Records' in-house writer-producer, Leon Sylvers III, who figures big in Jody's life.

For her solo debut, Watley worked with writer-producer-bassist André Cymone, who was central in Prince's teenage Grand Central era, and she worked with André through 1981. Jody and Cymone married in 1991 and have a son, born in 1992. Shalamar was signed to SOLAR Records, so Sylvers produced all of Shalamar's 1978 *Big Fun* and 1979's

Three for Love. He also produced half of Janet Jackson's self-titled 1982 debut. Sylvers and Jody Watley have a daughter, born in 1980. As Jody writes at her website, "Leon and I were engaged to be married—actually, he ended up being engaged to me and another girl, she [was] a member of the group Dynasty. I'm wearing my engagement ring on [Shalamar's] *Friends* album—a diamond cluster. 'I'm in love with you both,' [he said]. What a revelation."

During Jody Watley's late-seventies Shalamar era, my sister and I lived in my grandmother's unit in her turquoise fourplex. Gramma was a bookkeeper in a velvet-jammed fabric warehouse. Gramma made her own clothes, and we stayed in her sewing room—with the knitting machine and yards of gabardine, cellophane-wrapped needles, and sacks of hooks and eyes. Gramma was often gone in her ice-blue Lincoln Continental. I was in love with a boy named Lee. My sister yearned for Guess overalls. The living arrangement had "temporary" written all over it.

Our mother was still living on Hi Point with a fading and unemployed Alvin. He was selling off antiques. Barely driving, because he had no gas money. Our mother, who was well employed, came by the fourplex often. But Quel and I navigated alone my grandmother's zone of thirsty roses and bungalows. We had bus passes. We knew dead-eyed boys with hand-me-down Chevy El Caminos who lingered at intersections. Kenwoods blasting Cheryl Lynn's "Got to Be Real" like the perfect song that it is.

The multioctave Lynn was lead writer on 1978's "Real" and also sang her own background vocals. Among others, the song's team included David Paich of Toto (co-writer, production, and keyboards), and David Foster (co-writer), who went on to produce dozens of songs by Black women, including Whitney Houston's 1992 "I Will Always Love You." "Got to Be Real" felt solidly post-disco, but Shalamar was a distillation of a high-kicking *Soul Train* energy. Shalamar was a new style. And Jody Watley, with all respect to Howard Hewett and Jeffrey Daniel, was the shining star of Shalamar.

While Gramma taught me to whip eggnog and whisk gravy, I listened for Jody on the radio. Things I knew without being taught: Gramma didn't actually cook or eat much. Gramma, like my sister, was thin and knew the value in it. Gramma got away on cruises and to jazz festivals. Gramma stayed at the Hyatt Regency, with its piano bar and great glass elevator. This was in my 1979–80 season. In my grandmother's 1951 season, the one that shattered her, she was twenty-seven and widowed with two daughters. Little Lottie married four more times.

At her fourplex, Gramma played long jags of Billy Eckstine. When she wasn't home, I played Nancy Wilson's "Guess Who I Saw Today" on repeat, waiting for the last line to be a different last line. Wilson sings so conversationally about stopping to have "a bite" of food at a "most attractive French café and bar," she might have been friends with Little Lottie. Black women with jangling bracelets and just-waxed cars who just keep going. Women with long days and specific cocktails. The kind of brokenhearted women who throw the best parties.

The eldest daughter of an iron foundry worker and a housekeeper, Wilson had a wary sophistication that seems precursor to Watley's wrought-iron cool. *The Nancy Wilson Show* (1967–68) won an Emmy, and she was for a while as much a household name as her inspiration, Nat "King" Cole. "I didn't know I was a 'black artist,'" Wilson told *Essence* in 1992, "until I was nominated for a Grammy in a black category." Just a few years older than Dionne Warwick, she and Warwick share bearing. There's a deliberate grace in how they both take up narrow cylinders of onstage space.

I experienced Nancy Wilson at Lincoln Center's Allen Room during the 2010–11 season. The three-time Grammy winner was seventy-three then and had clearly spent her life nibbling the same slivers of dinner as my grandmother. Wilson spun in gowns that whispered couture and resembled the dresses my grandmother made herself and wore with earned vanity. Nancy Wilson had to sit for part of her set at the Allen, where a wall of glass overlooking the Manhattan sky and Central Park was her backdrop. We all leapt to ovation.

Gramma, at least with us, was rarely one for chitchat. Tucked into her (off-limits) fluffy bed, she watched a lot of *Quincy, M.E.*—post-*Odd Couple* Jack Klugman starring in an early autopsy procedural. Each week, motives behind misdeeds were outlined. White criminals got their comeuppance. My sister and I could hear the show's brassy theme from the sewing room. In there, sleep—after years atremble—arrived dreamless and hard.

Jody Watley began dancing on *Soul Train* at fourteen. A sophisticate in satin blouses and silver slippers, she flicked folding fans as she worked the *Soul Train* line. "I've been dancing all my life," Watley said in an interview for *The Lincoln Center*. "But I'm not a trained dancer. My vibe has always been more freestyle. I'm a person who just wants to be inside the music, to get lost in it, and I don't think there's a right or wrong way to do that, no matter what kind of music it is. It's just total freedom."

Jeffrey Daniel, also without formal training, is the dancer-choreographer who taught Michael Jackson to moonwalk. Watley and Daniel's unselfconscious dance-floor partnership was a building block of the Black cool *Soul Train,* created and hosted by Don Cornelius, and was elevating.

Like *Soul Train* itself, Jody was born in Chicago and blew up in Los Angeles. Middle- and upper-class Blacks were moving to L.A. suburbs like Altadena and Pomona in the late 1960s and '70s. Led by lawyers, doctors, and newly flush entertainment industry professionals, Blacks also moved into city enclaves like Baldwin Hills, Windsor Hills, and Ladera Heights.

None of this was quite Jody's situation.

Like Marilyn McCoo, Watley graduated from public Dorsey High, which was by then a mostly Black school in L.A., famous for its sports teams, school spirit, and "gang activity." Jody lived in a hilly area of the Crenshaw District called the Jungle. In the 1970s you could—like you can in 2020—hear Los Angeles Police Department helicopters hovering low. You can see the searchlights turning midnight into noon.

Jody Watley had been on the move for a while. Watley's mother, singer-pianist Rose Watley, grew up in Harlem. She wanted to be a model. But, as Rose says in an interview with Jody for Jody's website, "Little did I know, marriage was in my horizon." Jody's father, John Watley, Jr., was a Chicago gospel radio host and a Pentecostal preacher. He also golfed. In fact, John Watley was the first Black player to win the

1952 Chicago Herald–American Junior Open championship. The win meant he qualified for the Hearst National Junior Open in New Jersey. It isn't known whether John had the means to participate in the Hearst Junior Open, or if he would have been welcome if he had.

What is known is there was no going pro for Blacks until 1961, after the Professional Golf Association finally dropped its Caucasian-only clause. Instead John Watley found a profession in which Black men could lead. "But he definitely wasn't," said Jody when I interviewed her in 2016, "a buttoned-up Pentecostal minister." John also put together secular events featuring his show-business friends.

When her dad was losing his church, the family—Rose, Jody, brother John III, and sisters, Vanessa and Michele—traveled with him by car as he searched for church work throughout the Midwest and the South. It was a grind, but Jody's mother and father kind of glittered. "[They] were both fashionable," Watley said to me. "Music was always in our home despite the sacrilegious aspect of it. My parents were jazz lovers, so I grew up surrounded by that."

Young Jody was influenced by her mom's aspirations and her dad's rebel ways. "I was the child who was always imaginative . . . not just a dreamer, but a girl trying to do and be something." It didn't hurt that, while on the road, they met up with artists like Sam Cooke and Bobby Womack. The Black church circuit often crossed the secular chitlin circuit. Nancy Wilson was a friend of the family. Jackie Wilson was in fact Jody's godfather. "We called him Uncle Jackie," she told me.

The first time she was ever on a big stage was with Jackie Wilson. "He brought me out in North Carolina. . . . The women," she told me, "were going crazy for him. I was shy, [but] I just went . . . off. Danced like I'd danced in front of thousands of people before." She was seven, maybe eight years old. "I wasn't scared . . . and that made a big impression on me. I loved all of that energy." On her own, she pretended she was in the Beatles or the Supremes. Watley never sang in church. "It never appealed to me . . . and that's very unusual," she said. "For a preacher's kid."

When Jody was attending a Kansas City junior high, she saw this new thing called *Soul Train*. "I kept saying, 'I'm going to be on that show.' I planned to be on *Soul Train* not knowing that my father would eventually drive us [to California] in our broke-down station wagon, looking for opportunities." The family was shifting. Jody's brother, John III, joined the army. Michele became "Midori"—model, exotic dancer, adult film star, mother. "By this point," says Jody, "my mom and dad had divorced." In the Jungle, they lived in apartments and motels.

Black Los Angeles can be a small town. Watley had her mom stop their car one day because she saw Tyrone Proctor, who had toured with the original Soul Train Gang, on the street. "He kinda wished me luck," she said. But soon thereafter, fate again tilted in her direction. "A dancer by the name of Bobby Washington came up to me after [church]—and I'll never forget, I had on a black vintage dress with a black beret; I was very stylish." Watley was fourteen at the time, younger than you were supposed to be to dance on *Soul Train*. But Washington stepped to the teenager.

"He said, 'I don't want to be rude, but I dance on this show, *Soul Train,*'" Jody told me. "And my heart dropped. He said, 'My dance partner is out of town, . . . You have a nice look, and I wanted to know if you would be interested in coming to the taping with me this weekend.' Needless to say, I was like, 'Yes!' It was meant to be."

Rose Watley was open to it.

"I didn't have to convince [her], . . . She was at church with me that night, . . . He was just a nice guy, . . . He took me to *Soul Train* the first time." But she didn't need Washington the next time. "Once I knew where it taped? The next month I went up there by myself. Took the bus."

It's pretty much a straight shot from the Jungle to Hollywood Boulevard and Gower Street. If Watley took the La Brea line to the studio, along the way she saw a shipshape, working-class Los Angeles as well as rich Hancock Park. Back then, *Soul Train* was taped in a shabby industrial area of lower Hollywood, where young Black people with garment bags stood on line in the sun. I had friends whose older sisters waited on that line. They'd prepped clothes for weeks. And if my mother had errands over that way, we'd see the hopefuls smoking cigarettes and taking up all the space on the sidewalk.

The kids seemed wild, and far ahead of us—just for gathering publicly in loud clothes. This was 1975 or '76. Just ten years since the Watts uprisings. And *Jet* had to publish a guide each week just so we could find Black people on television. Bern Nadette Stanis as Thelma Evans was one. *Good Times* was in prime time 1974–79.

Brooklyn-born and trained at the Juilliard School, Bernadette Stanislaus was raised in the housing projects of Brownsville. Her father was a store manager, a saxophonist, and a community activist. The money her parents could have used to move out of Brownsville they used to send their five kids to Catholic school. Stanis's Thelma had a Black girl's many hairstyles—and the triumphs and problems of any working-class teenager. With her long legs and lush body, Thelma was stylish, earnest, and unintimidated by her brothers. Her smile was everything. It was as if Stanis knew she was all we had.

Good Times was a five-year pop hit, loved not only by African Americans, but by Americans. And like *Soul Train,* it continued the glacial process of bringing Black culture to the masses. "The Thelma character," Stanis says, "was a positive character. . . . She could still be educated, a good girl . . . trying to be the best she can be." Thelma dances so freely and unselfconsciously, so often, on *Good Times*. In one such scene, J.J. shouts, "*Soul Train,* watch out!" *Good Times* is set in the projects of Chicago, where *Soul Train* was launched in 1971. American Blackness was self-referencing on network television. And Thelma looked like she was born to the *Soul Train* of Jody Watley's hungry dreams.

Jody and Thelma learned from and moved beyond Motown's influential charm offensive. They expressed urbanity, and 'hood idiosyncrasies. *You grew up ridin' the subways / Running with people / Up in Harlem / Down on Broadway.* That's what Thelma dances to in a 1978 *Good Times* episode: Odyssey's 1977 "Native New Yorker," with Lillian Lopez on lead vocals. *Talkin' that street talk.* Who Thelma embodied were the Black pearls Yolanda "Yo-Yo" Whitaker rhymed about fourteen years later. The young, gifted, and Black women Nina Simone (1969) and Aretha (1972) sang about. To paraphrase Yo-Yo: We'd been in the background far too long.

———

Don Cornelius didn't so much choose Jody Watley for *Soul Train* as recognize Jody Watley. "The backstory," Watley told me, "which I didn't
know until years later, was that Don knew my father. They'd been on
the radio together in Chicago. . . . I don't think they liked each other. But
it all was destiny. . . . He'd never heard me sing, but he knew I could sing
because he knew my mother could sing."

"Shalamar" is a group concept created by Don Cornelius and the
notorious music executive Dick Griffey. It jumped off with an album
featuring session singers only. The second album featured Jody Watley,
Jeffrey Daniel, and Gerald Brown. It wasn't until Ohioan tenor Howard
Hewett joined the group in 1979 that the big hits—"Second Time
Around," "Make That Move," "This Is for the Lover in You," and (co-
written by Jody Watley) "Full of Fire"—popped off. "Being an integral
part of the sound and visuals of Shalamar, being our . . . co-choreographer
with Jeffrey—a lot of the time he was chasing girls and whatnot, so I did
a lot of the work."

One afternoon, my girlfriends at St. Mary's Academy brought me a
grocery-store cake to sewing class. The words "make that move" were
piped in red on top of white icing. It was a nudge for me to have sex for
the first time. Lee and I had been together for over a year. Virginity
games were watched hungrily at SMA. Stakes were high, a soundtrack
was required, and Jody on lead vocals seemed to cosign whatever came
after girlhood.

But the soap opera of Shalamar was not paying off. "I think Dick
Griffey—not 'I think,' I *know*—he definitely had a preferential thing
going on with Howard Hewett," said Watley. "[Griffey] was banking on
him to be more the focus of the group, and also to launch him for a solo
career. That happens."

It was 1983, and Michael Jackson's *Thriller* had just happened. The
boundaries around Black pop seemed to evaporate. And in May, when
Jackson debuted the moonwalk on *Motown 25: Yesterday, Today, Forever,*
the dance and the show were a sensation. Everything seemed possible.

Watley—who, when her family was living in a Los Angeles motel, "scraped up" money to buy *Right On!* magazine because that was where the Jacksons were covered, who begged ushers to let her and her mom into the Forum when the Jacksons were performing—decided to quit Shalamar.

"'This is going to be the biggest mistake of your life,'" said Watley. "That's what everyone in the group was telling me . . . and Dick Griffey." People thought she'd lost her mind. "We were so unique," she said. "Everybody brought something special to it. Ultimately, Griffey was the manager, the agent, the concert promoter, the record company, and giving preferential treatment and monies that we weren't getting to Howard. That erode[d] the fiber of the group. . . . The business side [of Shalamar] kind of folded under its own lack of foundation."

Watley hopped a plane to London. "I didn't know what was going to happen. But I knew I was going to be successful in whatever I did, even if it was just . . . being successful at being happy." Jody was living with former Shalamar dancer and backup singer Jermaine Stewart when she was invited to be a part of Robert Geldof's Band Aid project. The song was "Do They Know It's Christmas?"

"London," she says, "it gave me . . . freedom—being away from America. I didn't want to deal with the pressure to get back in the group. . . . I wanted a fresh start." By the end of the Sunday Band Aid session, Jody had worked out a future duet with George Michael, who was riding high on his recent hit "Careless Whisper." Watley's flatmate, Stewart (who died of AIDS-related liver cancer in 1997), was working up to his own U.S. top-five pop single with 1986's "We Don't Have to Take Our Clothes Off." It seemed everyone around Jody was moving toward something bigger. "I soaked in all of that creativity," says Watley. "Like, *Yeah I still want to sing, so well how am I going to do it?*"

Back home was a crowded field. Janet Jackson was still recording for A&M Records. Madonna was writhing in a wedding gown at the first MTV Music Video Awards. Tina Turner hit number one on the pop charts with *Private Dancer*'s "What's Love Got to Do with It." And June

Deniece Chandler, recording as Deniece Williams, and nine years Jody's senior, hit number one with her "Let's Hear It for the Boy."

Gary, Indiana, was founded by U.S. Steel. And in a clump of circumstances that included local politics, ingrained segregation, a massive, job-shedding mill, and resentment about Black mobility, Gary, during Deniece Williams's adolescence, could not hold on to white people. They wanted out. Tolleston, the neighborhood of Williams's high school, was all white until the 1950s, when legal segregation came to a halt. By the mid-1980s, Tolleston was almost entirely Black, but June Deniece had thrived during its fleeting era of actual integration. "We were the only area and only school in our town, out of four other schools, that had a melting pot of people. I've been very grateful—that prepared me for the world."

Born in 1950, June is the eldest of four children born to a security guard and a nurse. She sang in church along with her parents and as a teen, worked at a record store where she listened to the current hits, but also to her old-school favorites—Nancy Wilson (for her "class and elegance"), Carmen McRae (for diction), Lena Horne, and Doris Day. Williams made the rounds of the local talent show circuit along with Gary natives the Jackson 5 and the trio—Wanda, Sheila, and Jeanette Hutchinson—that would become the Emotions (known for 1977's "Best of My Love").

The owner of the record store asked Williams's mother if he could introduce her to some "record people," and young June Deniece was soon signed to nearby Chicago's Toddlin' Town Records, and then to Lock Records. Chandler's cousin John Harris was a childhood friend of Stevie Wonder's. Harris gave Wonder some of Williams's work, and soon she auditioned, with twenty-six others, for Wonderlove, as Stevie's background singers were known.

At the tryout, Deniece Williams sang "Teach Me Tonight," the first song on Nancy Wilson's 1960 album *Something Wonderful*. Williams, who had been studying at Purdue University and working part time as a phone operator, got the job with Wonder.

She was engaged at the time of her audition to Ken Williams, whom she'd known since she was eleven. They married and had two sons together, fourteen months apart. So, as Wonder was touring with the Rolling Stones, Williams was "was going back and forth between the group and her young family."

Managing motherhood and marriage and making a name for herself was hard. Of the man who became her ex-husband, Williams has said, "He is one of my dearest friends. But we were children, and we had no idea what we wanted out of life, or where we would go. We . . . went in two different directions."

Williams sings on Wonder's most classic and awarded albums: 1972's *Talking Book,* 1973's *Innervisions,* 1974's *Fulfillingness' First Finale,* and 1976's *Songs in the Key of Life.* She contributed background vocals on projects for, among others, Roberta Flack, Minnie Riperton, Tom Jones, James Taylor, the Weather Girls, and Earth, Wind & Fire. She sings on the Emotions' 1976 *Flowers,* and their elite 1977 *Rejoice.* There was a very short second marriage. In the way one will when one must, Williams kept it moving. She had thirteen Grammys to be nominated for, and four to win.

The coloratura soprano left Stevie Wonder's crew in 1975 to go solo. Earth, Wind & Fire's Maurice White produced Williams's debut, *This Is Niecy,* in 1976. They hit with "Free," a song Williams co-wrote with some of her Wonderlove colleagues.

The song begins with a mesmeric thirty-seven seconds of vibes and chimes, and then another forty of balladry, before softly bursting into a midtempo that implies lovers in motion. *I gotta be free / I've gotta be free / Daring to try / To do it or die.* The bluesy assertiveness has appeal for all, but for Black Americans the call for freedom can ring on the most subconscious levels. It can seem a field holler—Keep going!—from the not-so-distant past. "Free" was a global pop hit and must have influenced Donna Summer's 1978 "Last Dance." In the mid-1970s, Johnny Mathis, the Black pop sensation from the 1950s and '60s, was looking for a change. So he got in business with Deniece Williams.

Mathis ("Chances Are," "It's Not for Me to Say"), who sold upward of 360 million albums worldwide over thirty years, was influenced by one of the first Black women to suffer the triumph of being a huge musical star. Johnny's father, Clem Mathis, a San Francisco pianist doing domestic work, would drive him to the swanky Fairmont Hotel to see Lena Horne sing. Dad sat in his truck smoking while his son snuck into the Venetian Room. "There was something electric and magnificent about her," Mathis told me in 2011. "She would mesmerize me. And that was the thing that motivated me the most. . . . She was the shining light. I wanted to be that good."

Horne's husband, Lenny Hayton, even eased Mathis into the foyer near Horne's dressing room so he could speak to her after she was made up and gowned. Mathis recalled Horne as standoffish, but he took it with a grain of salt. "She was a Black woman in a white world," he said, "doing all these . . . things, making roads for people like myself. . . . She was the person, even more than Nat 'King' Cole . . . who I thought was the epitome of what it would be like to be a singing star."

Shimmering chunks of music history are stacked in Williams and Mathis's 1978 "Too Much, Too Little, Too Late." Parts of Lena Horne, Maurice White, Stevie Wonder, King Cole, and Nancy Wilson live in the song alongside encouraging fathers, quick marriages, ambition, and divorce. Plus, Mathis was playing for his legion of fans the role of a straight man. He came out to his father as a teen, and after years of hedging, came out to all in 2017 on *CBS Sunday Morning*—at the age of eighty-two. How Black pop from the 1980s can be experienced as cheesy is beyond me. "Too Much" is three minutes of triumphant melancholia. A true blues, it makes beautiful the banality of a mutual goodbye. As I hear it:

> *Pity all our bridges*
> *Tumbled down*
> *Were there a chance*
> *We'd try*
> *Let's face it*
> *Why deny*
> *It's over*

Mathis and Deniece Williams, the veteran and the upstart, went to number one.

I saw him perform at Carnegie Hall in 1993. I reviewed the show for *The New York Times,* and the headline was "Still Smooth, with a Tinge of Sadness." In 2011, I interviewed him for *Billboard,* and I asked a layup question as we headed toward the buzzer. "Do you have a lot of regrets?" Mathis, who was pleasantly surprised to be speaking with a Black reporter, reminded me that he was blessed with a beautiful life. He did wish, though, that he'd asked reporters to refer to him as John instead of Johnny. "I think of myself," he said, "as John."

Cheesy—inauthentic, tacky, not cool or fresh—remains the lowest hovering descriptor for the 1980s. The tone-deafness of Bobby McFerrin's 1988 "Don't Worry, Be Happy" notwithstanding, from Whitney Houston's "Greatest Love of All" to Tina Turner's "Private Dancer" to Lionel Richie to Tracy Chapman to Janet Jackson and her brother Michael, this was the era that many music critics—most of them white—dismissed large swaths of popular Black music as bland, and not genuine. It's interesting, because it was during the 1980s that Black pop made massive steps toward dominating the cultural landscape.

It was when I began at St. Mary's Academy in 1980 as a tenth grader that I started paying closer attention to old magazines. Inside at lunchtime, away from hundred-degree noons, I read vintage issues of *Rolling Stone, Ebony, People,* and *Life* at the library. I had mixed feelings about the rest of the library's offerings. *The Scarlet Letter* and *Their Eyes Were Watching God* left me quite angry, and high. *The Catcher in the Rye* and *Zen and the Art of Motorcycle Maintenance* remain wholly uninspiring. Overall, I was weary of reading about white males working through their disenchantment by swimming in other people's pools.

I searched for stories about Stacy Lattisaw. Her 1980 "Let Me Be Your Angel," recorded when she was thirteen, was modern Black-girl yearning performed at levels I'd never before seen. She opened for the Jacksons on their 1981 Triumph tour. Yet, outside of Cynthia Horner's

Right On!, with rare exception, I couldn't find astute stories about Lattisaw anyplace. She was well aware of her situation:

> I'm not . . . boasting, but I was one of the first child stars who reached a level of success, and I opened doors for other artists who came after me. I was before Alicia Keys, before Whitney Houston . . . and quite honestly, my record label and management company weren't promoting me. Neither was the industry. I was never acknowledged by the Grammys or the American Music Awards. I began to feel as though my talent was being overlooked. There was a time when I would watch the AMAs and the Grammys and I would cry, because I was never acknowledged.

Nine years later, after the bodacious "Where Do We Go from Here," a number-one R&B hit duet with Johnny Gill, Lattisaw left the music business. "God had more for me than the R&B music industry," she said. "The industry was asking for more than I could give."

I've been on countless conference calls, in editorial meetings, and in deep conversations at bars in which it seemed people were riffing from a long memo that had been sent out to mainstream editors across the nation: Resist acknowledgment of 1980s Black aspiration. Resist documentation of the new swag of post-1970s Black creatives beginning to feel empowered in the business of music creation (and pro sports, but that's a different book). The memo goes on: Please abstain from noting the authentic creative glee and achievement and money and feeling of fairness and validation that comes from finally making it with regularity on the *real,* the *main,* the historically white *pop* charts. Also resist earnestly liking a song like Deniece Williams's gorgeous, teen-dreamy "Silly" or "Let's Hear It for the Boy," as there is little pathology there to gaze upon from the relative safety of awe. The songs' bright blues provide little fuel for white teen rebellion—or cribable trauma.

What if you were, like me, Black and twenty in 1985? Or, like Latifah, fifteen. Yo-Yo, fourteen. What if the music of your childhood and tween years was pop careening so high it had to break into the million pieces that hip hop snatched up and stitched into music that inspired folks disillusioned by respectability politics, 'hoods left to rot, and the pathology of Republican policies? This bold and weary generation— Gen X, I guess, we spit our unwelcome blues. *All you supersonic people try to bite our rhymes. Fuck the police. Fight the power. Can't you feel the music pushing hard? Ladies first.* We spit them to sounds we built around the boss pop we vibrated to as tweens and teens, as well as in the womb.

It's 2016, and Jody Watley is pragmatic. "I have a Shalamar medley in my show," she says. "It kicks butt, and people love it. I feel fortunate to be associated with a group that was successful, and to come out of it being even more successful as a solo artist. That's unique. Generally, the most successful person out of the group is the quote-unquote lead singer. And although I sang lead, I wasn't considered the lead singer of Shalamar."

At the 1988 Grammy Awards, Little Richard waves an envelope that holds the name of the Recording Academy's Best New Artist. Before announcing the winner, he delivers an oration. Macon, Georgia's own Richard Wayne Penniman reminds the mostly white music-industry audience that he is the architect of rock 'n' roll, and that he has never received a Grammy. That the audience shown on television did not seem uncomfortable is amazing. Because behind the pancake makeup, Penniman is furious. When he opens the envelope, Jody Vanessa Watley is the winner.

In an azure frock, oversized motorcycle jacket, dozens of bracelets, and her trademark choker-sized hoop earrings, Watley thanks by name everyone from her manager to her video director to her lawyer and publicist and more. Her hair is glossy and massive, and Little Richard looks upon her with pride. "I wanna thank everybody for believing in me, and supporting me," Jody says. Her hand is over her heart, and she's fighting tears. "When a lot of people . . . didn't."

PART III

WHITNEY + ARETHA
Grammy Parties, Hotel Lobbies, and Other Halls of Fame

For a time in the year 2000, if on a Thursday evening you walked into the lobby restaurant of the Rihga Royal Hotel in Midtown Manhattan, you'd run into the most famous and most hardworking people in the business of music. There was a particular summer night when you might have run into me, Grammy-winning singer-songwriter Gerald Levert, and his father, Eddie Levert, of the O'Jays. We were having dinner. It was the second time I'd had dinner with both Eddie and Gerald. And on both occasions, we'd interacted with Whitney Houston and Bobby Brown.

The first time, back in 1996, was at Clive Davis's annual pre-Grammy gala. Eddie, Gerald, and I were seated at an outlying table for eight. I was thirty years old and the music editor of *Vibe,* and, along with Gerald's manager Leonard Brooks, father and son kept me laughing through courses of dainty and unseasoned food. I asked Eddie questions about "Use ta Be My Girl," the flawless Gamble and Huff production that brought so much joy to my thirteenth year.

Clearly I hadn't been the only one to love the song's unpredictable arrangement and mix of pride and regret, because it was a number-one R&B hit and a number-four pop hit. Like Peaches & Herb's "Shake Your Groove Thing," Chaka Khan's "I'm Every Woman," and A Taste of

Honey's "Boogie Oogie Oogie"—all from 1978—"Use ta Be My Girl" unfurled on the world with a snap.

It was a treat to meet Gerald in 1996. I talked with him at the gala about how he came to write Barry White's huge 1994 hit, "Practice What You Preach." It's a song so in line with White's then-grandfatherly persona, it's as if Gerald had been hearing an authoritative gospel-rich baritone his entire life and knew precisely how to write for a man double his age and rarely acting like it. On that night at Clive's gala in 1996, though, Gerald waved me off and changed the subject. Rumor going around the ballroom was that Whitney Houston was at the pre-Grammy gala. The lightweight scandal buzzing: "But she's not gonna sing."

Houston was at a pinnacle. In 1993, the soundtrack for *The Bodyguard* stayed at number one on *Billboard*'s pop album charts for twenty weeks and sold eighteen million copies, more than 1977's Bee Gees–heavy *Saturday Night Fever* soundtrack or Prince's 1984 *Purple Rain*. *The Bodyguard* remains, in 2021, the number-one bestselling soundtrack of all time.

The album broke the single-week sales record held by Guns 'n' Roses' 1991 *Use Your Illusion II* and became the first album in history to sell one million copies—in one week. The soundtrack has twelve songs. Six of them are Whitney's. One of those, "I Will Always Love You," was America's number-one song for fourteen weeks in a row. A number-one hit in almost every country that keeps track. Whitney told me that *The Bodyguard* changed her life and wrecked her marriage.

As my former *Village Voice* editor Joe Levy wrote in a 2012 issue of *The Hollywood Reporter,* "Whitney copped [Linda] Ronstadt's arrangement. . . . Parton's original is actually much closer to a classic soul ballad. . . . But [Houston's] vocal takes Parton's high-lonesome pain as a jumping-off point and goes wild from there, rounding through operatic technique, blue yodels and gospel before climaxing in pure Elvis-in-Vegas glory. It's almost like a historical tour of American singing—or America itself."

Joe was also executive editor of *Rolling Stone* during the 2000s, and we held the same position—editor of *Billboard*—one behind the other. Joe edited me on everything from Madonna to Jodeci at the *Voice,* back when white editors weren't lining up to assign white art to Black critics. I remember seeing Levy outside of Houston's New Jersey funeral, both of us wrecked but working.

Houston's pinnacle also included November 1995's "Exhale (Shoop Shoop)" from the soundtrack to *Waiting to Exhale*. I'd read Terry McMillan's 1992 bestseller when it was new, and the law was clear: if a novel was published by McMillan (or Bebe Moore Campbell), it was to be purchased, inhaled, discussed, and lent without expectation of return. Whitney costarred in the film, which remains historic for its four Black female leads, its surprising (to mainstream white people) success at the box office, and Angela Bassett's fearless and transformative scenes. Bassett, in black lingerie, strutting from a car full of her cheating spouse's expensive and burning clothes—which she set afire—is a meme for all time.

And McMillan wanted Houston to play Savannah Jackson from the jump. "Whitney represents something wholesome and down-home," the author told me via phone in 1995. "Little-town girl makes it big. There's an innocence to Whitney, a vulnerability. Sometimes people think it's false, but it isn't. She takes a lot of criticism with grace and finesse. I've watched her."

And the soundtrack album, featuring an all-Black, all-woman lineup, was on its way to seven million in sales. All of the songs were written and produced by Kenneth "Babyface" Edmonds, but Houston had her input: "Whitney was down for the female artist thing," Edmonds told *Billboard*'s Trevor Anderson in 2015. "But she said, 'I get the last say-so of who will actually be a part of it.'"

A part of it, in addition to Houston's own number-one pop song, "Exhale (Shoop Shoop)," was Brandy's platinum number-two pop hit "Sittin' Up in My Room," Mary J. Blige's platinum number-two pop hit "Not Gon' Cry," top-ten pop hit "Count on Me" from Whitney Houston and CeCe Winans, and the platinum number-one pop single from Toni Braxton, "Let It Flow." "Exhale" was nominated for Song of the Year at the thirty-ninth annual Grammys. Whitney is central to two of the most successful soundtracks in the history of American music.

The whole *Exhale* project was a phenomenon, and Whitney Houston was leading the surge of Black women owning white mainstream pop airwaves that, in the moment, were quivering with Coolio, Bon Jovi, Montell Jordan, Celine Dion, Metallica, and Tupac. But after ten number-one pop songs, it is "Exhale (Shoop Shoop)," her eleventh, that is the last number-one single of Whitney Houston's career.

It is only the third song in *Billboard* history to debut in that top spot. She was standing on the shoulders of Dionne, of Aretha, of Marian Anderson, of Donna Summer, of Diana Ross, and of Tina Turner. A leaning tower of American culture. She could not talk about or sing about being, or having been, in love with a woman. She was married to Bobby Brown. Whitney was thirty-two.

Four years later, in 2000 at the Rihga Royal, I note boxing promoter Don King holding court across the room. Eddie Levert squints toward me as I'm seated beside him. He has memory of me but acts the part of dear acquaintance. Eddie does this with the charm that has seen him through sixty years in what O'Jays lead Walter Williams called "this very mean business." Williams said this from the podium in 2005, without smiling, as the O'Jays were finally inducted, in their sixth year of eligibility, into the Rock & Roll Hall of Fame.

At the Rihga, Gerald, sitting next to me, quietly says, "I told you folks was out."

He says this because he knows I hadn't felt like coming into the city from Brooklyn. But I am glad I pulled together my wannabe Sade ponytail and slid into my red-and-white-jersey Diane von Fürstenberg dress. Because the Rihga's energy is a-crackle, and I am familiar with the kinds of music industry nights when it feels like something is about to happen.

For example: Watching the dance floor from a mezzanine at Digital Underground's San Francisco record release party for *Sex Packets* in the few minutes before Too Short and his crew burst in and started flipping shit over. This was 1990.

For example: At the Radio City Music Hall celebration concert for the tenth anniversary of Jay-Z's *Reasonable Doubt.* Jay, in collaboration with Questlove and the Roots, decided to perform the whole album, but in reverse order of the fourteen-song track list. So we were all anticipating Mary J. Blige stepping onstage to belt the hook of "Can't Knock the Hustle." *I'm taking out this time / To give you a piece of my mind.* But instead of Blige, out walks Beyoncé—in white, and as if on water. It was 2006, and Beyoncé and Jay-Z were still secretive about their relationship. We all felt we'd been invited to see who they really were and how they truly felt about the other.

For example: Seated at the Grammys in 2009, when phones went trembling with word that Rihanna and Chris Brown had been in a car accident, and that she would not perform the show as scheduled. Details emerged on slow burn. I remember thinking—this has to be a lie, because why wouldn't they be in a limousine or Town Car, with a professional driver? I had put Brown on the October cover of *Vibe* in 2007, the year he and Rihanna were being referred to as "the prince and princess of R&B." Brown was eighteen then but seemed a smiling and ambitious twenty-five. He did actual backflips in the wide hallways of New York's Milk Studios. All night at the 2009 Grammys I was thinking, *Not one thing that Rihanna does right now can be the right thing, because she's shining brighter than he is.*

That night in San Francisco with Digital, the buzz was that Too Short's squad was carrying steel pipes. My sister and I—aware as always the mood of a room—were with the band and at the ready when the dozen or so of us were ushered by security through a door that let out into an alley. We piled into a revving limousine. Laughing. Half scared, half relieved. And ever more familiar with the insanely exciting work and lifestyle we'd no intention of leaving.

There's something wild and tight about these kinds of nights. If you stand up too fast, or whisper too loud, or look at somebody the wrong way, you're going to ruin the good, or hasten the bad. So you have to be in the flow.

But it's gonna do what it do, anyway.

The air is horseradish and butter. In the lobby restaurant of the Rihga Royal, knives ping on china and Edward Willis Levert of the O'Jays enjoys his dinner. Eddie was born in 1942 near Birmingham, Alabama, and came of age in the kind of Ohio no-water-for-niggers tension that culminated in the five-day 1966 Hough uprisings. Cleveland's neighborhoods remain not just segregated but hypersegregated, with many Black families living in social and economic isolation. In 2000, both Gerald and Eddie still live in Ohio. Eddie smiles at people who acknowledge him at the Rihga. Eddie asks me about Brooklyn. Eddie prods Gerald about work. Eddie watches the room like he knows fancy don't mean fine.

I hadn't seen Gerald in a while when we met for dinner that night at the Rihga, but was friends enough with him to know that, as loved as he was by his fans, and though he got to number five with 1987's "Casanova," he always worked toward a number-one pop hit. To score big on the R&B charts—which were the "race" charts when his father started recording—was an achievement, but he wanted to be top of the pops. The kinds of questions he asked me often: "Why can't me or my groups get mainstream press and television bookings? Like the white groups do, who sell less records and make less impact on radio?"

He knew the answers. But I reminded him that segregation in music is as segregation is in life: whites systemize spatial separation and unequal playing fields. The systems at that time—radio and retail—enforced white-made music as the main and enforced all other recorded music as subordinate and other. In 2017, author and American studies professor Eric Weisbard (2014's *Top 40 Democracy: The Rival Mainstreams of American Music*) told the writer Kelsey McKinney that iHeartRadio's *American Top 40* skews away from empirical numbers toward a program that is "softer, whiter [and] older." America's Top 40 is not America's Top 40, if it ever has been.

It tore Gerald up to get close to the all-around achievement of a number-one hit. He wanted the status that came with it. He wanted the financial reward. Gerald wanted to be—as Ja'Net DuBois co-wrote and sings at the top of every episode of *The Jeffersons*—"up in the big leagues." I love Brooklyn's own DuBois for her knowing lyrics and towering performance, and for the allusion to the cruel differences between Negro and Major League baseball. *Gettin' our turn at bat,* indeed.

Gerald Edward Levert's journey was a knotted one, and it stopped in 2006 due to an accidental mix of prescription and over-the-counter drugs. Gerald's brother, Sean, who was also a part of the group LeVert, died two years later at the age of thirty-nine. On the sixth day of a jail term, having pled guilty to the nonsupport of three children, Sean died as a result of withdrawal from prescribed Xanax. Angela Lowe, Sean Levert's widow, charged that jail policies contributed to her husband's death and, in 2010, was awarded $4 million.

Few in the music business are ever truly shocked when a pop star dies before old age. It can seem payment to a savage piper. Dope is accessible. Planes fall from the sky. And for Black artists—caught up in the circular pattern of white artists being rewarded for mimicking Blackness and Black artists being maligned or short-sold for trying to sound like white artists, who are trying to sound like them—it's easy to succumb to existential gloom. If there is banality and cynicism to be heard in pop music from whites and Blacks, this dehumanizing spin cycle is where it's born.

It's young Black women dancing the Charleston with the glee of the newly free, and white women stealing their moves to become the beloved, free-spirited, and culture-shifting "flappers" of the 1920s. It's Elvis Presley slicking his hair in a pompadour like Little Richard or Chuck Berry, who had straightened their hair to look like the silken white-boy thatch held up by Americans as superior to glossy coils. It's *Sex and the City*'s Carrie Bradshaw talking about "wearing ghetto gold for fun." It's the Kardashian empire. It's the fact that Blackness has more value coming from white artists. This is so normal that if you are a Black artist and think of it too much, you go numb.

And if you are a Black woman artist? In addition to being robbed, you must appear strong. You must bow to the tyranny of the swaying navel and maintain the twenty-six-inch waist. Historically, you must put off bearing children or hand off rearing them. Come last in pay, and in credit given. Be called a whore, or "loose." Manage being a low-value target of physical and mental abuse and rape. And the cherry on top: all of this is known and documented, yet little changes. And then, because she loves her craft and it is her livelihood, the Black woman artist, on alternate nights, must *sing the body electric* and *sing the blues because she's got them bad*.

———

At the Rihga Royal in 2000, on this night when folks is definitely out and laughter peals and the energy is taut, Whitney Houston strides into the lobby restaurant with her husband, Bobby Brown. Whitney is too effusive. The rollicking room levels down to a hum. It is Whitney, after all. She is not at her nineties pinnacle, but she is still Whitney. Wiry as a hanger, twisting and untwisting, she gives Don King a showy, rocking hug.

Whitney and Bobby both look higher than they ought to, but Bobby seems more high. Like his is a manic high. Brown doesn't like the hug; we can see that from where we are, and we are four or five tables away from where they are. I'm in the Grey Goose gimlets of my thirties. Gerald with his Hennessy.

King's cousinly hold on Houston is long. Bobby says something. Points. King's got Whitney like *Are you okay?* Holds her like we wish we could. King has known Cissy Houston, Dionne Warwick, and Whitney since forever. "Music is the ribbon that ties humanity together," King will proclaim on the occasion of Whitney's death. "And God had given Whitney the voice of life."

In the Rihga, most of us are seeing Houston that high for the first time. A bunch of us had been wanting to believe it was not as bad as it seemed, or as deep as we'd heard. We're frozen. How must we look? In our good clothes, nursing sweet drinks, with our mouths open?

Knives no longer ping, and Eddie Levert no longer eats his food. Eddie sees the flare before the fire. Still pointing, Bobby talks at King. Pointing, stabbing air, getting close. I can't hear exactly what's being said. Gerald senses my impulse to be closer to the action. Gerald with a calm hand on my knee all of a sudden, like *Sit tight, sis. Sit tight.*

Because who the hell is yelling at Don King in a crowded restaurant? In 1954, Don King shot a man in the back and did no jail time. After serving four years for stomping another man to death, King was pardoned. Eddie Levert and Gerald Levert are from Cleveland. Don King is from Cleveland. King ran the numbers racket in Cleveland. In addition to being the most famous boxing promoter of all time, King is also a touring entrepreneur who promoted, along with Katherine Jackson, the Jacksons' 1984 Victory tour. King promoted the O'Jays on the road in the 1980s. Don King promoted the depressing duel in which Mike Tyson bit off a chunk of Evander Holyfield's ear. King was inducted into the Gaming Hall of Fame in 2008 and has been investigated for ties to organized crime. King, who in the lobby restaurant of the hotel Rihga Royal still has Whitney in a hug, is not known for suffering fools. Bobby Brown, before us all, is suffering, and foolish.

Eddie watches. I don't know if Whitney can feel Bobby's energy, but she's not pushing away from King. Bobby doesn't quite yell, but he's a disturbance in the buttered air. King's security team on standby like the Fruit of Islam. Focused on Brown, focused sharply past Brown, and around the room—like they would, on King's nod, extinguish life.

King himself, at sixty-nine, looks like he could push a body through the Rihga's plate-glass windows. Brown, who—aside from being a founding member of the eternal New Edition—was responsible in 1988 and 1989 for two number-one pop songs, nine top-ten pop hits, and a number-one pop album provocatively titled *Don't Be Cruel*. Brown is a shadow of his former tenderoni self. At the Rihga, Brown is unironed and uncombed, and he is still hollering at the wrong Negro. Eddie Levert gets up from our table. Gerald makes a move to stand as well, but his father puts up a low hand: *Let's not make it too big a deal, or it will be too big a deal*. One would have to be high to run up on Don King.

Moving smooth, Eddie makes a path through the jammed tables and wraps Bobby up in his arms. Nods fast at King: *I got this, he's tripping, I got this*. Bobby squirms, then submits to Eddie's stocky embrace. Whitney finally hollers at Eddie to let Bobby go. Eddie communicates physically with Bobby, verbally with Whitney, visually with King. Eddie unsuccessfully aims for unobtrusive, quelling, even charming. King nods: *Nice you're here*.

Security guards: plain-faced, alert. Whitney urges Eddie to let Bobby go. There's little self-awareness on her part, or her husband's part. The most torturous thing is that the couple moves like this ado is happening behind a closed door. It looks like King is deciding if the better look is for him to stay for dinner at the lobby restaurant of the Rihga Royal, or to leave. *This is real*, is my thought. *And it's not going to end well.*

It took a dozen years, but it ended with Whitney Houston dead in a fourth-floor suite of a big, jutting hotel painted the color of marshmallow. Houston was facedown in a marble tub of very hot water at the Beverly Hilton. Blood was coming from her nose, and according to her autopsy, nearby was a "small spoon with a white, crystal-like substance in it."

Houston was acutely intoxicated with cocaine. And while it apparently did not contribute to her death, Xanax was in her suite (for anxiety and panic attacks), and the muscle relaxer Flexeril. In all there were twelve different medications from five different doctors.

In the still life of her stilled life there were both a popped bottle of champagne and an open can of beer. At the age of forty-eight, Houston was already in dentures. Coroner's notes: the singer of "I Will Always Love You," of "I Wanna Dance with Somebody," of "The Greatest Love of All," may have drowned in a bubbling cauldron. Or may have already been dying as she fell into the steaming water. Whitney Houston slipped into the abyss on the night before the British singer-songwriter Adele Adkins, with her second album, *21,* was set to win as many Grammys in one night as Houston had won in her twenty-seven-year career.

Whitney's early girlfriend and longtime best friend, Robyn Crawford, told the writer Tom Junod at the time of Houston's death, "I'm trying not to think of the end . . . trying not to listen to all the reports. All these people talking about drugs—well, a lot of people take drugs, and they're still around. Whitney isn't, because you never know the way the wind blows. I just hope that she wasn't in pain, and that she hadn't lost hope. She gave so much to so many people. I hope that she felt loved in return. She *was* the action, for such a long time. She's out of the action now. I hope she can finally rest."

———

At the restaurant in the lobby of the Rihga Royal Hotel, Eddie Levert sits back down with his son Gerald and me, and to his food. He gives us a brisk recap, something about walking them out to their car. Maybe telling their driver to step on the gas. That part is vague, the part I didn't see. It's Whitney Houston with glazed eyes and no composure that I will remember forever.

Eddie Levert is agitated, though. So am I, and Gerald, too. Food is cold, and it is thunderous in the restaurant, every whisper a shout. I can't see Don King or his personal police anymore. Tablecloths are aflutter, as if in the wake of a storm. I smooth my ponytail and scribble stuff on napkins.

With another soft squeeze of the knee, Gerald says, "You should tell him again how you feel about 'Use ta Be My Girl.'"

"Yeah? I told him last time."

"Tell him," Gerald says. "Folks say they love it. No one ever tells him that the song is a perfect song."

This is trial-and-tribulation music.

—MAHALIA JACKSON, 1968

The Rock & Roll Hall of Fame Foundation was established in 1983 by Atlantic Records cofounder and president Ahmet Ertegün and a small team that included one Black executive. Her name was Noreen Woods. She was Ertegün's right hand, and a bona fide legend in her own time.

Upon his 2006 death at the age of eighty-three, it was said by PBS that Ertegün's "personal and professional life comprised the history of popular music in America over the past seventy years." An Istanbul native, Ertegün called the United States "the land of cowboys, Indians, Chicago gangsters, beautiful brown-skinned women and jazz." Noreen Woods was his support for decades. A 1978 *New Yorker* profile of Ertegün describes Woods as "Ahmet's assistant and a vice-president of Atlantic, who is a woman of deep intelligence, deep patience, and (probably) deep cynicism." Woods is described elsewhere as Ahmet and Jerry Wexler's "joint secretary," as "formidable," and as "steely."

When Noreen Woods died in 1998, "there were more record industry people at her memorial service than almost anyone you could remember," Grammy-winning record producer Bob Porter said in 2014. "[Noreen] was eulogized as the women [sic] who kept the secrets." In the PBS eulogy, when the formation of the Rock Hall Foundation is laid out, Woods, who was a senior vice president, is not mentioned at all.

The Hall is meant to be a shrine not to perfection, but to talent, unquestionable musical excellence, and impact on what has been known as "rock & roll"—with the ampersand as opposed to the vernacular "rock 'n' roll." By the 1970s, the music was mostly referred to as the hard, white, "rock." Its origin stories, especially the one starring Cotton Plant, Arkansas's Rosetta Nubin, did not "fall into the shadows of history," as noted in 2018 by NPR's Bruce Warren, but were hacked off by white music fans and historians, like Kunta Kinte's foot.

Nubin, who—as Sister Rosetta Tharpe (1915–73)—was inducted into the Rock Hall in 2018. She had been eligible for thirty-two years. Chuck Berry, who himself is robbed of his full "rock" legacy, once said his entire career was "one long Sister Rosetta Tharpe impersonation." The Beach Boys and the Beatles in turn impersonated Berry's mirror of Tharpe, to the degree that he sued them for plagiarism and won. "Sister Rosetta Tharpe is the first guitar heroine of rock and roll," says the nominee video at the Rock Hall.

Yet Tharpe is most often referred to as the "godmother" of rock. This is no small distinction or tic of language. "Mom" gives birth. "Godmom" is friend or relative of parents who raises a child up in the faith of its parents if the parents die. A godparent shows up to family functions with tokens of love. Tharpe's relegation to this role is linguistically and strategically aggressive on the part of the white and Black music makers and historians. It rarely fails in the music industry that Black women originators are hashtagged during educational history months while the thieves in the temple are raised up like saints.

In the year 1983, when the Rock Hall Foundation was formed, Donna Summer was literally working hard for the money. She had been snubbed, in the year of her death from lung cancer, by the Rock Hall. "Our voting group," said a Hall of Fame representative of the faceless cohort, "has failed." Finally inducted in 2013, she had been passed over in the year of her death in a class that included the Faces and the Beastie Boys.

In the year 1983, when the Rock Hall Foundation was formed, there was also a project called *Thriller* from Michael Jackson (inducted into the Rock Hall as member of the Jackson 5 and as a soloist) and future hall-of-famer Quincy Jones that changed the course of music history.

In this wonderful year of music, the one in which I graduated from high school, there was Irene Cara and "Flashdance . . . What a Feeling." Patti Austin and James Ingram's impeccable "Baby, Come to Me." There was also the song that moved Peabo Bryson into the mainstream so seamlessly that he became the go-to guy for Disney films like *Aladdin*: his and Roberta Flack's "Tonight, I Celebrate My Love." The music industry was also buzzing with what looked to be the return of future Rock & Roll Hall of Famer Tina Turner.

Worshipped by legends and lovers of guitar- and blues-based rock, the former Anna Mae Bullock, at forty-three, was struggling post-Ike to get her label to support her. In a triumphant effort to get a big mood going, Turner and her manager, Roger Davies, staged three legendary shows in January of 1983 at the Ritz, a rock club in New York City. Those sweaty, star-studded nights led to the recording of 1984's "What's Love Got to Do with It" and *Private Dancer,* Turner's raging, romantic midlife renaissance.

Some critics were disappointed by this new, smooth Turner. Her rebrand, as it took the globe by storm, was pooh-poohed by mainstream white critics as sentimental. *Play small* was so much of the energy coming back at Tina. *Keep it within "Nutbush City Limits."* Stay comfortable being our gritty and soulful Black inspiration for white rock. Remain vulnerable to our cultural and emotional looting. Leave the big stages, babygirl, to us.

In 1997, Turner confirmed to Larry King that she in fact didn't really love "What's Love Got to Do with It," because "it's not really a singing song. It's a . . . cute little song. . . . I wasn't accustomed to singing those kind of songs."

King then says to her, "You're in the Rock & Roll Hall of Fame. You consider yourself rock 'n' roll?"

Tina, with bronze hair and dark brown roots, in a boardroom-ready black blouse, says, "Yes."

"That's your idiom," he says.

"That's my style," says Turner. "I take great songs and turn them into rock 'n' roll songs."

Six years after her divorce from Ike Turner, Tina's *Dancer* won four Grammys, sold over twenty million copies, launched an incomparable 180-date world tour, and brought Tina back to us, and to the universe. "I don't want anything bad to happen to her," Ike Turner said to *Spin* in 1985. "I made mistakes. I dealt with Tina physically instead of mentally. It's very hard to deal with black women mentally. It's like you have to put some fear in them to communicate."

The woman in the beaded minidresses who performed "Proud Mary" with Ike and the Ikettes so hard that as a child I thought Tina's name *was* Mary had in fact been on a brutal run-up to her destiny. *Spin*'s story is headlined, "Why Ike Beat Tina." Ike beat Tina because, as weak as Ike was, he was talented, and he was not dumb: he knew before anyone that, with regard to singularity and ambition, his wife was the clear winner.

All of this was simmering as the Rock Hall Foundation took form in 1983. In addition to Noreen Woods and Ahmet Ertegün, on the committee were the attorney Suzan Evans (also unmentioned in the PBS eulogy), *Rolling Stone* magazine founder and publisher Jann Wenner, the attorney Allen Grubman, and record executives Seymour Stein and Bob Krasnow. The first group of inductees, celebrated at New York City's Waldorf Astoria, included Buddy Holly, Chuck Berry, Elvis Presley, Fats Domino, James Brown, Jerry Lee Lewis, Little Richard, Ray Charles, Sam Cooke, and the Everly Brothers. No Rosetta Tharpe. No Bessie Smith. No Ethel Waters. No Aretha Franklin—who released her first album, *The Gospel Soul of Aretha Franklin* (Checker) in 1956.

Aretha Franklin signed with Atlantic in 1967 after a series of false starts at Columbia. Noreen Woods started at Atlantic in 1957, ten years after its founding. Woods was at Atlantic when LaVern Baker was rebounding from the white singer Georgia Gibbs's note-for-note copying her "Tweedle Dee," which Baker took to number four on the (Black)

R&B chart and number fourteen on the (white) pop chart. Gibbs's version went number-two pop, and Baker, a woman who came of age in an era when billing oneself Little Miss Sharecropper was sound business sense and a protective cloak against those who might think her too uppity, unsuccessfully petitioned Congress to make it illegal to copy an arrangement without permission. Baker is the first known entertainer to have written a petition of this kind. As with Dionne Warwick and Dusty Springfield, this kind of identity and artistic theft was often played in the mainstream press as nothing more serious than the Black girl having a bee in her bonnet.

Woods is the lone Black in photos celebrating Foreigner's iconic debut. Wilson Pickett credits Woods with coining the album title and eternal nickname *Wicked Pickett*. Woods's circle of influence was deep: her sister, Joan Brooks, was Doug Morris's assistant. Morris succeeded Ertegün as Atlantic Records president in 1980.

Woods was at Ertegün's right for the era that defined Aretha Franklin: "I Never Loved a Man (The Way I Love You)," "Do Right Woman, Do Right Man," "Respect," "Dr. Feelgood," "(You Make Me Feel Like) A Natural Woman," "Chain of Fools," "Ain't No Way," "Think," and the blithe glory that is "I Say a Little Prayer." In 1978, when Aretha Franklin married her second husband, Glynn Turman, Woods was among the bridal attendants. By 1978, Woods was senior vice president and assistant to the chairman of the board. Woods's appointment in 1974 (which was noted in *Jet*) to executive assistant to the chairman of Atlantic Records made her the highest-ranking woman at a major record company at that time.

But Woods, outside of Black networks, is largely unmentioned, a hidden figure. Her path was not uncommon. Starting as a secretary and ending up running the show was the path for another powerful woman who remains at the forefront of an ever-changing industry: Sylvia Rhone, with an economics degree from the University of Pennsylvania's Wharton School, began as a secretary at Buddah Records in 1974.

At a banking job, as Rhone told *Ebony* in 1988, "I wore pants to work, and all eyebrows turned up. No one actually said anything, but they made it clear that what I'd done was unacceptable." Inspired by her play-big-sister Suzanne de Passe (their moms were friends), Rhone left banking, took a pay cut at Buddah, and twenty years later became chairwoman and CEO of Elektra Records, the first woman and first Black person to be named chairman of a label owned by a Fortune 500 company.

In 2004 Rhone was named president of Motown and executive vice president of its parent company, Universal Records. Sylvia, like me, was inspired by the Jackson 5. Suzanne took her to see the group in concert when she was managing them. It's wild how these things are all intertwined. Sylvia Rhone was named chairperson of Epic Records in 2019. She and Suzanne are close to this day. And Sylvia Rhone and I have been like sisters for over twenty years.

As she told *The Atlanta Journal-Constitution* culture writer Sonia Murray, Aretha Franklin developed her fear of flying in 1983. At forty-one, Franklin was signed to Clive Davis's Arista Records and coming off her hit 1982 album, *Jump to It*. As she was on her way home to Detroit from Atlanta in violent weather after a performance at the Fox Theatre, the prop plane she was flying in shuddered like a soul leaving a body. Aretha said the plane went upside down for a moment, and did a couple of "dipsy doodles." How could she have not felt a cold clasp on her soul from Otis Redding, Patsy Cline, or Buddy Holly—contemporaries who had soared high in small planes, and then been slapped back to earth? Had she flown too close to the sun?

Apparently, it was this aviophobia that left Franklin unable to attend her 1987 induction into the Rock & Roll Hall of Fame. It took place at New York's Waldorf-Astoria. And in a 2015 history of the Hall on Cleveland.com, the artist with eighteen wins on forty-four Grammy nominations is tossed off as "a no-show." In fairness, Franklin's fear of flying in this case seems suspect, as Franklin knew the date weeks if not months in advance of her induction.

The Rolling Stones' Keith Richards says the following by way of Franklin's induction:

The dictionary's been used up. There's no superlatives left. Ummm . . . there's nothing to read, and anyway [laughter] you understand me, right? What can I say about Aretha? You're in, baby! [Laughter] My turn next, maybe!

Then Clive Davis reads a speech on Franklin's behalf:

It was late last night. The telephone rang. It was Aretha. It was snowing out there, and her pink Cadillac got stalled on the freeway of love. And she gave me these words that I wanted to read to you. And these are her own words. [Places shaded eyeglasses on face] *She said, "It is with my sincerest regrets I am unable to be with you tonight as planned. I'm highly honored to be held in such high esteem. Along with my peers and my old friends. To be the first woman inductee into the Rock & Roll Hall of Fame is a historical moment, and indeed a milestone in my career. It is a moment I hoped to share with you and the illustrious members of this esteemed committee. I would like to share this award with John Hammond, with Ahmet Ertegün, with Jerry Wexler, with Clive Davis, who have guided my career from its very inception to date. It is with many thanks and appreciation that I proudly accept and take my place in the Rock & Roll Hall of Fame.*

Then Davis speaks for himself:

A brief word to say that working with Aretha is like being a part of history. It's like no other experience I've ever had. She is the Queen of Soul. She is the Queen of Music. Here is her brother, the Reverend Cecil Franklin.

Here Cecil comes, bringing both mics together at the podium so everyone can hear everything.

Ladies and gentlemen, may I say first of all that it is indeed a privilege, a pleasure, and an extreme honor to be here to accept this award on behalf of my little sister—thankyouvurryymuch. My great sister, Aretha, uh, and, and, uh, before I go any further let me first acknowledge my, the president of my record company, Mr. Clive Davis. The president of our springboard, Mr. Ahmet Ertegün, and last but not least, certainly, Mr. Jerry Wexler. Can we give Mr. Jerry Wexler a hand?

This is not to say that creative and dogged music executives don't contribute deeply to success of pop artists, because they do. This is not to say every note must be a solemn one, because it doesn't have to be. But. All of them onstage. Laughing, backslapping. It's a good time, Aretha's induction. Cecil:

Thank you. Now, many accolades have been paid, many tributes have been given, many awards have been received, and certainly we are appreciative of them all. However, we feel that tonight is the greatest night of Miss Aretha Franklin's—the Queen of Soul, Soul Sister Number One, Lady Soul, whatever you'd like to call her—we feel that this is the greatest night of them all, because tonight, Aretha has been written into history. You, the board of directors, Ahmet, his colleagues, and the rest of the committee have written Aretha into history! [Takes mic in hand] Ladies! Can I hear from the ladies!! The first female and the only female to have been inducted into the Hall of Fame. The Queen of Soul—hello! Miss Aretha Franklin!

All the men. *I. My. Our. We. Whatever*.

For the prodigy, Aretha Louise Franklin. For a complex, anxious musical genius whose gashes include the lack of a childhood, whose scars show up as deeply harmonic sensibilities, and as otherworldly confidence in her vocal instrument. For the woman who sings in rare and dying emotional languages yet is understood by everyone. This uncanny empathy is what sets Franklin apart even more than her sublime notes and riffs: she hurts in the exact way that you do. Aretha is wrenchingly in love in precisely the way you are in love, every single time.

Imagine if, at Aretha Franklin's Rock & Roll Hall of Fame induction, someone had said something with the wholeheartedness that the

Reverend James Cleveland embodied that January 1972 day at the New Temple Missionary Baptist Church in Los Angeles, when director-producer Sydney Pollack and his motley crew were doing a half-assed job of taping a documentary that should have accompanied the release of Franklin's live album *Amazing Grace*. Pollack produced or directed the haunting *This Property Is Condemned,* the heartbreaking *The Way We Were,* the tear-jerking *Tootsie,* and the near perfection that is Gwyneth Paltrow and John Hannah in *Sliding Doors*. But show up at New Temple—to record Aretha singing—and the sound goes to shit. The sound.

But here comes Reverend Cleveland, so burly and gravelly it's difficult to imagine him as the young man hired by C. L. Franklin to be minister of music at his New Bethel Baptist Church. James Cleveland, who died of AIDS in 1991, is known both for benefiting from the problematic energy of a highly closeted era and for walking scores of gay Black gospel professionals into the music industry.

"Now," Cleveland says, "the young lady that we've all been waiting to hear. She's known by many names, and deservedly so. She's earned every title. It's my pleasure tonight to just say, 'My sister, Miss Aretha Franklin.'" When Cleveland met her and began working with her, Aretha was nine years old.

Cleveland, whose name is rarely lifted up alongside Clive Davis's or Jerry Wexler's in the discussion of Aretha, was born and raised on the South Side of Chicago and was inspired to the performance and business of gospel by Mahalia Jackson. He wrote or arranged over four hundred gospel songs. He has sixteen gold albums. Three Grammys. And was the first gospel artist to receive a star on Hollywood's Walk of Fame.

The relationship between James and Aretha, at least in the documentary—which was released in 2019 after years languishing, at Aretha's request, in a back room someplace—is one of mutual respect, creative partnership, and ease. It's Aretha who places Cleveland squarely at her beginnings, calling him "my earliest musical influence and musical mentor."

The documentary (even with less-than-perfect sound) functions as a pristine snapshot in time. The editing is so awkward as to feel homemade, and there are no blaring chyrons beneath talking heads. As a camera pans down a mural of white Jesus, Cleveland introduces the song that "needs no introduction." And as his fingers curve-press over the piano keys as background and punctuation, you see in another scene Aretha's fingers curve-press over the piano keys. In Cleveland's relaxed ownership of the piano you see Aretha's attitude toward the massive and iconic instrument, an orchestra on its own. Their cousinship is clear and beautiful. The teaching is clear as day.

"The other day in rehearsal, Aretha began to sing it," says Cleveland in the film. "When she got to the part that says, 'Through many dangers,' and I looked over at her and I saw the tears rollin' outta her eyes. 'Cause never did we think . . . twenty years ago, that God would do great things for us. *Hm,*" he says.

And Aretha hits it high and long. *Hmmmmmmmmmmmmmm.*

From James Cleveland in the mood of a laid-back and thoughtful pastor: "Can I get a witness here tonight?" And Aretha goes from the last of her *mmmmmmm* into "A-mmmmmmazing . . . grace." Young Aretha and James, eleven years apart in age. What joy must these two have created, what closeness to God must they have cultivated. We will never know precisely what dangers they dodged, and which the two of them were unable to manage.

At the time of the filming and the recording of *Amazing Grace* the documentary, and *Amazing Grace* the double album, Franklin was twenty-nine and coming off of nine straight hit albums—in four years—with Atlantic Records. At New Temple, Franklin is a vision in frosted lipstick and dangling earrings. Perspiration on her face like tiny dimes of mercury. She is incandescent, and lost in the work of performance, and the church work of praise and worship. Aretha sings under Christ along with James Cleveland's Southern California Community Choir, and when Aretha one-handedly twists a sweaty towel behind her back as Cleveland holds the other side of it for her, the rag might as well be a tourniquet on her soul.

Why? Because Aretha's marriage to Ted White was decomposing. White, wearer of peace-sign medallions, is well known as a pimp. White is the one who apparently changed the "emotional dynamic" between Aretha and her father. White beat Aretha Franklin.

"You could compare the Aretha/Ted situation with Ike and Tina," Etta James told the author David Ritz for an unauthorized Aretha biography that Franklin called "very trashy." Etta went on to say, "Ike made Tina, no doubt about it. He developed her talent. He showed her what it meant to be a performer."

Etta James's 1960 version of "At Last" is in the Grammy Hall of Fame. The song went to number two on the R&B/Race charts but oddly only to number forty-seven on the pop/white charts. Like Deborah Cox's impeccable 1998 "Nobody's Supposed to Be Here," which sat at number-two pop for a record-setting eight weeks (it could not move Céline Dion and R. Kelly's "I'm Your Angel"), Etta's "At Last," nestled in the most mournful of strings, is a cry of exquisite relief. It is restrained and Sunday-best in the way, during the early 1960s, that white people liked their Blacks, and in the way Black respectability demanded. James keeps everything very veiled-hat-and-kid-gloves, until she slyly repeats "you smile, you smile," and by the end of the song you don't know if she's singing in an ivory gown from the altar or from a bench in the afterlife, where the lover she murdered has humbly arrived.

James's "At Last" chart standings are odd, because "At Last" remains such a standard, even in 2021, on oldies stations, on jazz stations, on adult contemporary stations; a staple of commercials, and likely the most popular wedding anthem of all time. How might that have happened unless the record was being played on white radio stations (for the ratings) and not being reported to chart professionals (for the cultural credit) at *Billboard*?

Etta James never had a real home. Her childhood has been called Dickensian, and while he and his widow denied it, Etta thought her father, whom she never met, might be Minnesota Fats, a celebrated pool hustler inducted into the Billiard Congress of America Hall of Fame without having ever won a tournament. Etta was a heroin addict and then a cocaine addict. By her own word she would cook up a "mess of gumbo" for friends and stay high for days. You can hear Etta's voice and see her swagger in Tina Turner, and in Gladys Knight. Etta's men were usually criminals. James did time herself on drug charges, and for floating checks. She had frank thoughts about Aretha Franklin and her husband Ted, and about women and men in the music business.

> When I ran into [Ted] and Aretha—this was the sixties—I saw that she wasn't as shy as she used to be. . . . She'd become a hipper chick. . . . I'm not so sure that was bad for her, since she wanted to make it in the big bad world of showbiz. Ted gave her an edge she needed. And if things went bad for Aretha later on, Welcome to the party. That was the story of how it went with most of us and our men. They came on to promote us when we wanted help in the worst way. . . . They dressed us and trotted us out to the stage. At the time—and this is the part no one gets—we didn't mind it. We fuckin' liked it! We were hoping these cats would choose us and sell us and show us how to get over. That was the good side. The bad side was when the devil popped outta them and they thought they could control us forever. That's when the violence started. Just like Billie [Holiday] and Sarah [Vaughn], I experienced that. Just like me, Aretha experienced that. In the meantime, we became stars. Could we have had one without the other—a career without the pimps selling us? Who the fuck knows.

Some men who hover around women creatives, making them hipper chicks and bigger stars, are spoken of derogatorily, but more often they are awarded titles like "mentor." In addition to the decent guys there are a gallery of dudes who, for example, become producers solely to be around the business of women making music. They become bodyguards of women singers and rappers. They seek women creatives to publicize, and for whom to write songs. They are limousine drivers. Personal trainers. Gold diggers. Sometimes they deliver plates of thinly sliced cantaloupe. On red carpets, just out of the shot, they hold for their date an Hermès pocketbook. An embossed silk cape.

But these men have access to spaces off-limits to Black women. And incidents of resentment, abuse, gaslighting, and hate masquerading as love rampant. The phenomenon of male hangers-on is real. There just aren't as many songs—Sly & The Family Stone's 1968 "Jane Is a Groupie," 2Pac's 1996 "All About U," Ludacris's 2001 "Area Codes"—about male "groupies." And in films, these guys are dressed to impress.

As a girl I fell in love with Billy Dee Williams because of his portrayal of Billie Holiday's only husband, Louis McKay. He is suave for the entirety of 1972's *Lady Sings the Blues,* but when he comes to visit Diana Ross's vacant-eyed Holiday in the padded cell and offers her the diamond ring, well, I thought it was the most romantic thing ever. I had never in my life seen—onscreen or off—a Black man in a suit proposing to a Black woman. I was seven when the film came out. And where, on television or in theaters, would I have seen this?

The real McKay, whom Holiday married in 1957, was abusive, lost much of her money in bad real estate deals, and was referred to by those who knew him as "Louis Decay" because of his corrosive influence. He was her third husband and her sole heir. As such, he was a technical advisor on the set of *Lady Sings the Blues*. McKay turned himself into a hero in a fedora hat.

Billy Dee Williams at the age of thirty-five gleamed onscreen like a proper superhero. He was aware of his beauty but used its powers—as Gale Sayers in *Brian's Song,* as a community activist in *Mahogany,* as *The Empire Strikes Back*'s Lando Calrissian—for good.

McKay, on the other hand, was a violent groupie, a grifter, and gold digger. A bloodsucker dominating women on the chitlin-strewn path of a patriarchal world. Tina Turner told Larry King that she wished the film *What's Love Got to Do with It* could have been more real, packed with even more horrific details of her life. Disney told her the story just would not be believable. Would that Billie Holiday had the opportunity to leave and heal and live.

But no. Billie Holiday's fate on this earth was to be a heroin addict and a prostitute. The brilliant Billie Holiday's destiny was to transform Abel Meeropol's "Strange Fruit" and perform it relentlessly, even as retaliatory narcotic squads were on her tail. *The bulging eyes and the twisted mouth / Scent of magnolia, sweet and fresh / And the sudden smell of burning flesh.*

Billie Holiday's destiny—with fifteen fifty-dollar bills strapped to her leg—was to lie dying and under arrest in a Harlem hospital, worried that she would burn in hell for her hard living. I really don't care if Holiday was a hophead, or if their relationship was tumultuous, or if Billie—in that way that girls defending themselves are often said to—gave as good as she got. If there is a hell, and I hope there is, Louis McKay is there in a Billy Dee Williams three-piece, smelling like shit in the sun.

"I might be just twenty-six," Aretha told *Time* magazine in 1968, "but I'm an old woman in disguise—twenty-six goin' on sixty-five. Trying to grow up is hurting, you know. You make mistakes. You try to learn from them, and when you don't, it hurts even more. And I've been hurt—hurt bad."

Ray Charles, no prude himself, called Aretha's father's traveling gospel caravan—of which teenage Aretha was a featured performer—a "sex circus." While Franklin's unofficial biographer David Ritz has named a school friend of Aretha's as the father of her oldest child, Franklin never publicly confirmed this. The boy was named Clarence after her father and was born when Aretha was twelve years old. She was a mother again by the age of fifteen.

Aretha's own mother is the late gospel singer and pianist Barbara Vernice Siggers Franklin, born in 1917 in Shelby, Mississippi. Barbara's mother, Clara, migrated her large family to Memphis, where Barbara, the youngest daughter of seven siblings, was a stand-out student at the all-Black Booker T. Washington High School. Memphis was a capital of the South in the 1920s and '30s, and Beale Street was called the Main Street of Negro America.

Aretha Franklin's grandmother Clara couldn't financially manage her large family in Memphis, and they moved back to their Shelby farm. By 1934, Barbara was pregnant by a man who was apparently uninterested in her baby boy, Vaughn.

Clarence Franklin, who had been preaching on the Black Baptist circuit since he was sixteen, often visited Shelby from neighboring Sunflower County. Clarence saw Barbara at church, playing piano and singing, and soon Aretha Franklin's future parents were in a serious relationship. Clarence's home county, named for the blooms that line the banks of its silty Sunflower River, was at that time the kind of county where a Black man and a Black woman would get hunted down by a mob and be made to watch their own fingers being chopped off and tossed to a crowd of six hundred cheering whites who were feasting on deviled eggs and whiskey.

As just about all of American pop music, regardless of genre, is based in the blues, it's no coincidence that the state of Mississippi boasts more Grammy winners and Grammy Hall of Fame inductees than any other state in the union (and is home to the only Grammy museum outside of Los Angeles). "Blues" come from actual blues. After fingers were chopped and other tortures completed, the couple would be thrown on a fire and "allowed to burn to death." This terrorism and the culture of fear that surrounded it, is in the heart of Mississippi's actual and musical blues.

To Clarence, Barbara had beauty, musicality, and Memphis sophistication. For Barbara, Clarence was an ambitious 'round-the-way country boy who preached sweet fire. Aretha Franklin's mother and father were married in a June wedding at the home of a deacon, and Clarence, himself adopted by his stepfather, adopted Vaughn. Once Aretha's oldest sister, Erma, was born, both Clarence and Barbara wanted out of the Delta, where white terrorism was always simmering.

Clarence, in alligator shoes, preached all over the South, and in a Memphis congregation there was a twelve-year-old who he was molesting. When Mildred Jennings had a daughter in 1940 at the age of thirteen, it was a scandal, but Barbara stayed in the marriage. She dealt with more of her husband's infidelities and knavery. She still sang at St. Salem, the Memphis church. Barbara and Clarence's son Cecil was also born in the same year as Mildred's Carl Ellan Kelley. And in 1942, in a small house in Memphis, Aretha Louise Franklin came into the world.

The Franklins stayed in Memphis until 1944. They moved to Buffalo, where he took over Friendship Baptist, and where Barbara was his pianist and choral director. Both Barbara and Aretha sang at Friendship. Aretha's aunt Ruby, who was married to her mother's brother Simuel, said on the occasion of Aretha's death that Barbara Franklin "had a beautiful voice," and was an unforgettable gospel talent. She recalled Aretha as a child, climbing up to study the piano keyboard, when the family lived on Buffalo's Glenwood Avenue.

Two years after that they moved to Detroit, where Clarence took over at New Bethel Baptist. Clarence was becoming quite famous. He was friends with stars and civil rights leaders. In 1948, when Aretha was six, her mother moved back to Buffalo with Vaughn. It is often written that Barbara "left" her other four children. What if Clarence, on the strength of his gender and power, was more able to "keep" them?

Aretha visited her mother often in Buffalo, where Barbara was working as a nurse (or a nurse's aide) and spent summers there. Barbara was living with her mother, Clara, and her stepfather. Often the kids stayed with close neighbors. Aretha is remembered in the neighborhood as a tomboy, one who would climb over a fence or up an apple tree. There were lollipops and ice cream, and long bike rides. One of her childhood friends, Charlotte Rushin, told Sean Kirst of *The Buffalo News* that "as kids we weren't thinking of her becoming famous. She was a fun person to be with, and she wasn't singing around us like that. I loved her in Buffalo because she was just Aretha Franklin." It's a beautiful portrait of young Aretha, one of the exceptions that prove the rule of one-dimensional reporting that predominated when Aretha died.

Over the course of her life, Aretha, with her siblings Erma, Cecil, and Carolyn, came to Buffalo often to visit their mother's grave. Barbara died in 1952. In 2016, Aretha was inducted into the Buffalo Music Hall of Fame. According to her autobiography, "Barbara would climb the porch steps, settle into a rocking chair, and . . . draw Aretha and Carolyn to her side. . . . Barbara Franklin would rock the children and speak to them 'of better things to come.'"

Clarence and Barbara had never divorced. It was after her death that he launched the C. L. Franklin Gospel Caravan. Aretha was on the road with the bacchanalian troupe and pregnant at the age of thirteen.

"I cannot describe the pain, nor will I try," Aretha wrote of her mother's death. She remembered sitting on the curb on Lyth Avenue "for a long time" after returning from the cemetery. Mahalia Jackson has said "After [Aretha's] mama died . . . the whole family wanted for love."

Most everyone said they had nothing in common, but that's not true.

Whitney Houston married a man who called out Elvis Presley with the title and best single from his second solo album. *Don't be cruel* goes the hook of Bobby Brown's top-ten pop hit, *'Cause I would never be that cruel to you.* In 1956, Presley went to number one on three charts— country, R&B, and pop—with his (completely different in every way but the title) "Don't Be Cruel," which currently sits in the Grammy Hall of Fame.

Bobby, a badass from the housing projects of Boston, was a pop star—from the awkward joy of "Girl Next Door" to the flawlessness of "Roni." He had a glorious three-album run—1986's *King of Stage,* 1988's *Don't Be Cruel* (a number-one pop album), and 1992's *Bobby.*

Over her almost thirty-year career, Houston is credited as songwriter on only three songs, and one of them is "Something in Common," from *Bobby.* The video for the song is set mostly in 1990s-McMansion video luxury. It's heartbreaking to see how beautiful they look, and how full-throated they sound, individually and together. Whitney's style alternates between glam in a black limo, bikini top in a sparkling pool, and suburban house frock. Bobby steers a speedboat. They dance together, they show off Houston's quarter-million-dollar wedding ring. *We have something in common. Yes, we do. Yes, we do. Yes, we do!*

And at the end there's a quick shot of the couple with their new daughter, Whitney feeding her from a bottle. "This one's dedicated to those who don't believe in real love," says Brown. "Especially our love."

He and Whitney had in common the work of succeeding at top levels. They had in common a daughter who would be found, like her mother, unconscious in a fancy bathtub. Whitney's water had been hot. Bobbi Kristina was facedown, in a tub full of cold. In the wake of this grisly scene, one man was under suspicion of aggressive codependency, and another was found civilly liable for her wrongful death. Bobbi Kris,

who I met when she was two, lay in a coma for six months before suc-
cumbing to pneumonia at the age of twenty-two.

Brown and Houston had in common the culturally performative as-
pects of talk shows and other kinds of white-framed media. They had in
common the stage itself, and the livid mockery of fans and critics when
one gets too famous, or when one is just not as hot as one once was. With
regard to cultural impact and genius-level talent, Whitney, even in
death, remains superior to her ex-husband.

Bobby was a pop and R&B star, but he and Whitney do not have in
common legendary accomplishment or status. He is not an icon. He will
not walk alone down any hall of fame. Deep inside, he knows this. It
can't have been easy to deal with—lust for and competition with and
love for and enviousness of one's partner—but people deal with it.
Women of all stations deal with it all the time.

The iconic poster for *The Bodyguard* features Houston—being carried like a bride over a threshold by Kevin Costner. Whitney, her face
hidden, is protected from those who wish her ill. Kevin is stoic and white
and strong. Whitney has said to me that the ubiquitousness and lasting
success of *The Bodyguard* and its soundtrack ruined her marriage.

The only image of Houston—with a man—that is more indelible
than Costner with Whitney in his arms is Whitney leaping onto Brown's
chest, long legs wrapped around his waist. This was in 2000, outside of
the North Broward County Jail, from which Brown was being released
after serving sixty-five days on a parole violation stemming from a 1996
DUI. He had his personal belongings in a plastic bag. Whitney was
barefoot. They couple pulled away from the jail in a white stretch limo.

It's the kind of thing that would make people say "So fuckin' rock &
roll!" or "That's some real punk rock shit right there!" No such rebel
yells for Whitney, or even Bobby. That kind of cultural uplift is reserved
for couples like Sid Vicious and Nancy Spungen, Liz Taylor and Richard Burton, and Stevie Nicks and Lindsey Buckingham.

Four years later, early in 2004, I was in Atlanta on an *XXL* assignment, trying unsuccessfully to get an interview with the newly ordained
Reverend Mason "Mase" Betha. Whitney Houston and Bobby Brown
were living off and on in what was then the Ritz-Carlton in Buckhead,

and, for a few days, in a single queen a half dozen floors down from them, so was I.

Hotel scuttlebutt had it that toxic mold had been found at the Alpharetta mansion where Bravo would eventually tape the eleven cruel episodes of *Being Bobby Brown*. This is the mansion to which police responded in 2003 to a domestic-violence call and found Houston with a "bruised cheek and a cut lip." Where "evil eyes" were spray-painted by Brown on the walls, and where Whitney Houston's face was cut from the family portraits.

In 2004, though, the shiny lobby bar of the Ritz-Carlton functions like a den for Brown. One afternoon he hunches there alone over a highball glass, in a pout. A tipsy older white man smiles from the bar and points bigly Bobby's way.

"You! I know you. I know you!"

You can see it going wrong from across the wide hall. At his table, Brown sits up and waits on it.

"You're Whitney Houston's husband!"

Brown stands, heads into a spittled fit. He's the one pointing now, lurching toward Mr. I-Know-You. Security is quick and quiet and escorts Brown toward an elevator bay.

It was a sore point for him. "Something happens to a man when a woman has that much fame," Houston told Oprah in 2009. "I tried to play it down all the time. I used to say, 'I'm Mrs. Brown, don't call me Houston.'"

In the mid-1990s, Whitney Houston Brown's Mendham Township, New Jersey, mansion featured a Lilliputian guardhouse stuffed with a jumbo guard. It was at the start of a winding driveway six blocks long. I interviewed her in that home years before seeing her, in 2000, in the lobby restaurant of the hotel Rihga Royal. But for lightning, the stormy night was pitch-black in Mendham, a rich town of about five thousand. And as the racial makeup of the area is more or less 0.45 percent Black, it's safe to say all of us were in one place.

In the wide rumpus room, I told Whitney about my divorce from my first husband. Interviews are like first dates in that authenticity tends to win. It creates a tension: each person's desire for a next intimate step in the face of the other's suspicion. A race to see who, to quote Aretha Franklin, is zoomin' who.

For me, functioning both as a music editor at *Vibe* and as a writer on a story, there was the added pressure of knowing to the penny just how desperately we needed a particular cover story to happen beautifully, and on time. We needed this Whitney thing to happen.

I have never felt like I was ahead for too long in any conversation with Janet Jackson. Or with Mariah Carey. Or with Beyoncé Knowles Carter. I made the mistake of thinking I was ahead of Whitney Houston that night in Mendham.

This was the night I met the toddler Bobbi Kristina. I watched Whitney and Robyn Crawford go for long Nerf football passes in a massive living room. This was the night I was supposed to get twenty minutes of conversation with the woman who had gone from singing background vocals for Chaka Khan and Jermaine Jackson to representing America at the Super Bowl during the Gulf War to pushing, with her preternatural voice and energy, the culture-dominating soundtrack of *The Bodyguard* to $44 million plus in sales.

I stayed out in Mendham for more than three hours. Over the course of the evening, I told Houston truthful stories about my relationship with my first husband, so that she might relax and feel intimate enough with me to talk about her relationship with Brown. My personal empathy for her situation was as real as my professional desire to get "my" story for *Vibe*'s readers. At a moment when *Waiting to Exhale* was about to hit theaters, I wanted to know and to relate to her state of mind. I had fought to get the story.

It had seemed to me that Houston was going to give interviews to white magazines only, and this did not sit well with me. *Vibe,* as glossy as it was, was on the chitlin circuit. And my mottos were: (1) "We claim everything," and (2) to quote Special Ed, "This is a mission, not a small-time thing." As far as I was concerned, we at *Vibe* had more right to the time of any musical celebrity than any other publication, Black music being, as it was and is, the core of American culture. I also felt I knew something about men who were at odds with the professional ambitions of their wives.

I'd moved to New York City from California in 1993 with a gregarious and gifted guy. *Billboard* moved us for my new job as R&B editor, and he was working as a freelance photographer. On the plane from San Francisco to New York, the conversation I had with myself was about doing what I had to do to make real money.

My significant national media network had been built by awkwardly but consistently cold pitching myself via snail mail with my alternative newsweekly clips. This was reinforced by good people like the legendary hip-hop renaissance man Bill Adler recommending me for opportunities like the *Billboard* job. NPR's Ann Powers pretty much walked me into her job at *SF Weekly* and has been saying nice things about me when I'm not in the room ever since. It might have helped that my résumé and photocopied clips were beautiful—I'd worked for two years at Copymat and can change toner like a champ to this day.

But I didn't want to work at Copymat. I didn't want to sell Hanro panties or Armani ties at Saks for time-and-a-half on Sundays. I wanted to write more. I wanted to move higher up on editorial mastheads so that I could, as I had at *SF Weekly* as music editor, decide the direction and mood of music coverage.

This was a new state of mind for me, thinking about the future. Marriage had helped with that. My husband projected confidence, and it was rubbing off. Previously I'd worked to pay rent and buy groceries and cute pairs of shoes. Check to check was awesome for me, because the checks were regular. On that flight, with East Oakland behind me and health insurance in front of me, I decided that the idea of security—of already having four figures in the bank when the next check was deposited—was worth going for. This was a huge accomplishment for a person who couldn't get to the grocery store without tensing for the car accidents I believed would kill me at every intersection.

In retrospect, it would have been wise to bring Lamont into the conversation. There were times I wanted to talk, and to plan things around work and money and other things that frightened us, but we were in our twenties, and moving to New York City on someone else's dime had the feeling of a lifetime achievement. We both had parental figures who were substance abusers, so Lamont and I respected each other for being visibly whole and fun-loving. Anything else, if we dared articulate it, was gravy.

Journalism made me plan, though: a week, a month, a deadline, a publication. But the idea of success? What that meant to me at first, and began to mean to me desperately, was to not need anyone for anything, ever. The fact that Lamont couldn't smell on me the intensity of my commitment to have my own proved he didn't know me anymore.

I didn't know how to communicate my ambition. I had a quote, attributed to Goethe, penned in many a journal and daily planner: "Whatever you think you can do or believe you can do, begin it. Action has magic, grace, and power in it." Action. I was so good at it. And to be honest, I didn't feel Lamont—or anyone, really—deserved the courtesy of my truth. Over the course of my young life, what little I had vocalized had been used against me.

I quickly became not quite the girl Lamont married in an Alameda County judge's chamber. The girl in an ivory cotton knee-length skirt and sheer white polka-dot tights. Who'd survived running with the dope boys and the rap stars and was happy to write music reviews quietly and cook often and hostess and photo assist. It had been beautiful, our thing. We occasionally worked the same shows. We saw each other through some painful and embarrassing shit. I really used to sit in the darkroom with him, happily fascinated and nosy. He painted a room deep red for me and helped set it up like an office so I could really feel warm, and official.

Because it was hard for me to feel that way. I was self-conscious about having dropped out of school. And when I went home to family in Los Angeles, which was not that often, it was as if it was my fault that I had no money. And my education was entirely my problem, to solve alone. I'd lied about dropping out of Berkeley, and I was shamed for it.

The smart girl had finally gone dumb. The girl who could control things and make things happen for herself was flailing. This was why I had to get out of California, too. If I was going to be on my own, I may as well have geographical as well as emotional distance.

Between Lamont and me, I had the steadier gig. In the Bay Area I'd attended three or four shows a month; in New York, I was at shows twice a week or more. Other nights I was at listening events, or dinners. Lamont and I crumbled quickly. There was sabotage: him of me, and me of myself. There were more than a few raw and slippery confrontations.

At Whitney Houston's home in Mendham, I was sitting on a divorce that was final but for the signatures. I couldn't look into my future without seeing the stained-glass plans you make when you're twenty-three. They change the color of everything, forever. And by the time I was sitting up in Houston's rumpus room, I was deep into mistaking hard work and depression for new wisdom. In any case, it felt like maturity, and it was what I had.

I was the music editor of *Vibe* when I went to see Houston in Mendham, having left *Billboard* after just five months because Lamont asked me to. He said we'd be happier if we were both freelance creatives, as we had been in Oakland. I was committed to my marriage. Our relationships with our families were so thin that the only people in that Alameda judge's chambers aside from Lamont and me had been his father, my sister, and my friend Karen. Lamont and I were on the other side of the country, all we had was each other, and I had no intention of going back.

I knew how to be a freelancer. So, as I was prepping a resignation letter for *Billboard,* I called my editors at *Rolling Stone* and *The New York Times* and set myself up with freelance work. I did it in the same earnest tone I'd used calling Pacific Bell asking that my phone not be turned off due to nonpayment. My best white-girl, due-to-unforeseen-circumstances voice. I was relieved and emboldened by how happy editors were to hear from me. A new magazine called *Vibe* had been launched by Quincy Jones, and since I no longer had a proper day job, I went on the road immediately, interviewing people like Wesley Snipes for six-thousand-word cover profiles. And when I did go home to Oakland, it was for the "Pumps and a Bump" video shoot—and to interview MC Hammer for an inside-the-book *Vibe* piece that was just as in-depth as Snipes's.

I could drink Snapple with Wesley and find meaning in the grand emptiness of his Venice, California, beach home. I honed my childhood ability to listen to people's faces. I asked celebrities the roots of their middle names. I fell back on lessons from high school creative writing classes. Fell back on my obsessive readings of *Right On!, Seventeen, Playboy, GQ,* and those 1960s and '70s issues of *Ebony* and *Rolling Stone.* Fell back on repeated readings of Hurston's *Their Eyes Were Watching God,* Didion's *Slouching Towards Bethlehem,* hooks's *Yearning: Race, Gender, and Cultural Politics,* Derrick Bell's *Faces at the Bottom of the Well,* Janet Malcolm's *The Silent Woman,* and Michele Wallace's *Black Macho and the Myth of the Superwoman.* Turned over in my head Julie Dash's *Daughters of the Dust* and Spike Lee's *Do the Right Thing.*

I would continue my self-education. I would string together classes and fellowships at the good schools, and make myself feel whole. My editors at the *San Francisco Bay Guardian* and the *East Bay Express* told me that my experience actually made me an expert, that I was a dynamic and thoughtful writer, and if I thought something was important, it was.

I was fired up. I had my missions. And I would not go back to California. I had no idea what a generational curse was back then, but one of our family's curses is the impulse to passively discourage those earnestly trying new things. Maybe it began as a protective measure, but it's painful and it's successful. In addition, beauty is untrustworthy. And—maybe this is in every culture—strength and independence are a threat. Billie Holiday co-wrote it and sang it and it gave me spine before I ever even heard Diana Ross sing it in *Lady Sings the Blues: Mama may have / And your papa may have / But God bless the child that's got his own.* Holiday has said that it was an argument with her mother over money that led to the song. We all of us have been doing this wearying stuff for a long time.

For that MC Hammer story, which aimed to humanize the pop star who danced confidently into fried chicken commercials, I was edited by a Black woman named Diane Cardwell. I've never told Diane to what extent she changed my life.

I wanted to be Diane. To use her breezy and sophisticated editing vocabulary. To be plainly beautiful without all my baubles and ill-fitting bras. Cardwell encouraged Black writers like me to create with intention, to be bold with contrary ideas, and to not feel second best because we were from second cities and hadn't gone to Rutgers or Brown. She assigned me that Hammer piece because, like Stanley Burrell, I am from Oakland, and also because I had thoughts about how hard it was at that time to see a Black man smile unapologetically and publicly when so many were suffering. About how ambition was being derided, and about how pop hip hop itself was and remains powered by a spirit of reparation. Low-key payback for slavery and high-key payback for the successful theft of rock and R&B from the musical generations immediately preceding the pioneers of rap.

In addition to writing profiles and album reviews for *Vibe,* I was going to late-night rap shows at the Palladium for the *Times,* tearfully arguing with copy editors, and trying to be like Jon Pareles. The learning curve was steep, but I had pop music editor Fletcher Roberts in my corner, at least for my Sunday *Times* stuff. Fletcher lifted me up, and he let me down, too, when he had to—like when I reviewed Harry Belafonte's show at what was then Avery Fisher Hall at Lincoln Center.

> Many elements of this show—including the gold lamé costumes, the black percussionist in tribal dress and the songs filled with images of island inhabitants happily harvesting sugar cane—played to a 1950's vision of exotic island living that now seems badly out of place. The dynamic between the older, mostly white audience and the younger, mostly black performers in ornate costume was familiar and disconcerting.

Fletcher told me that Belafonte called one of the Sulzbergers himself and, in a conversation that stays with me after all these years, apparently asked the man who I was and demanded that "he" be fired. That was my last piece for *The New York Times* for decades.

After the thing with the *Times,* I wanted to be in the more powerful position of editing again. I'd been music editor at *SF Weekly*—editing album and show reviews, editing a music cover a month, reporting out stories myself, writing a column about Bay Area music happenings. I so deeply believed this prepared me for any editing job anywhere that when Alan Light, my generous reviews editor at *Rolling Stone,* called to say he was being promoted to editor in chief of *Vibe* and did I want to talk about possibly becoming music editor, the only thing we disagreed on was my taking an editing test. I didn't do it. *SF Weekly* was my editing test. Alan and I worked things out.

Vibe was young and in trouble. I wanted to help Alan make it work. I told Lamont, "If you fuck with me on this job like you fucked with me at *Billboard,* I'll leave you." It was the strongest and the nicest way I could say it. I was off to Clarkson, Michigan, to meet Janet Jackson on the July 18, 1994, stop of her janet. World Tour.

I was where I was supposed to be. I wanted to be cursed no more for staying out late at shows. I didn't want to be resented for getting assignments, or for needing time and peace to work. I didn't want to be paged and paged, being asked where I was and when I was coming home. I didn't want to scream and snot-cry and fight and be exhausted and depressed and embarrassed by antics. I didn't want to feel guilty for not cooking. I cooked well, and as often as I could, but I had a job, and I was serious about it. I had asked Lamont not fuck with me on this *Vibe* job, and he did. I had to go up to the *Vibe* offices after midnight to finish writing that Janet Jackson story, because at home I was being baited. I could do nothing right because, once I left the apartment, I was the girl with what we called back then a "title." This was hated.

By the time I went to Philly with photographer Dana Lixenberg to chase down Robert Kelly, I'd made up my mind, with the advice of my sister and mother, to leave Lamont. I was going home to Los Angeles so much, my mother told me, I had already left him—just hadn't moved out. By winter I had a sublet. By spring I was living by myself for the first time in my life.

Top floor, one bedroom, in a proper Brooklyn brownstone on Greene Street between St. Felix and St. John. I half-painted my half-den forest green. And, typical of a high-functioning depressive, I was soon in an intense relationship with a charismatic man who was centered almost entirely on himself. His smile was beautiful. He told me, for five years off and on, that I received my "elite" jobs and opportunities because I was light-skinned. He told me also that I was missing out on the *real* elite jobs and opportunities due to my chubbiness.

New York is a big city, but he fucked women I knew—or who knew me. Fucked them in our apartment. I received notes about how my cocker spaniel had been friendly, and how neatly I folded my bedsheets and towels. I was complimented on my bulbous wine glasses. Out of respect for all I was doing at *Vibe,* they felt bad, and felt it was only right—"apologies for not signing this"—to let me know.

I've been in this thorny relationship for a year or so, and in September of 1995, Whitney walks onstage at Radio City Music Hall with her husband, Bobby, to present the MTV Music Video Award for Video of the Year. Dennis Miller is master of ceremonies. "Here to introduce the final award of the evening is a talented woman who is known as the embodiment of elegance, charm, and beauty. Come on," he says with a quick explanatory shrug. "She's nice. I don't have to be a smartass all the time. Here's Whitney Houston and Bobby Brown, ladies and gentlemen."

Their walk-on music is Houston's Grammy-nominated global pop hit "I'm Every Woman," the follow-up to "I Will Always Love You." Bobby steps to the podium, cigar in hand. "I almost had to have a fight with one of the announcers earlier for not saying my name," says Brown. "But, um, thank you, Dennis."

Houston is smiley, nursery rhyme-y. "He did say your name." She's keeping peace before maybe ten million people around the world. Then Bobby mock-aggressively turns toward the wings, as if he might be staring down the aforementioned announcer. Houston says, "Not another one; no more fights." All in good fun as Brown is uneasily watching his wife read the intros for clips from Weezer, Janet Jackson and Michael Jackson, Green Day, and TLC. At the point where she reads, "What does it take to attain this lofty position?" Brown condescends to shake his head, amused.

A few weeks later, Bobby is reportedly at a New York nightclub, telling acquaintances he has moved out of their New Jersey home. He is showing off his left hand, sans wedding band.

———

By autumn, *Vibe* got Whitney. Her first cover for the magazine. I had the approval and high hopes of Alan. I knew how important *Waiting to Exhale* was going to be. I knew that *The Bodyguard* was a white film, and that *Exhale* was a swing back to Black. I had the pressure of the business side of the magazine. I'd negotiated an interview and cover shoot.

And then, on the day before I was set to interview Houston, it was reported in the *New York Post*'s powerful Page Six column that Brown, intoxicated, had, in Times Square, thrown his wedding ring down on the street.

Whitney's white, mainstream publicist, Lois Smith, called to postpone. Smith, who died in 2012, was a famed publicist to Robert Redford, Meryl Streep, and more. She was "part of a generation that changed the nature of the business by striving to limit access to their clients." I was part of a generation and culture that didn't know who she was.

She seemed to be handling all media for Houston for *Exhale,* or maybe just generally, as Houston's life had crises in need of management. But her prominence signaled to me that decisions had been made that placed the Black press, including *Vibe,* as low priority. This was even more irritating than usual, as *Exhale* was a Black movie based on a book written by McMillan, a Black author, and directed by Forest Whitaker, a Black director. In our short time working on this project, I realized that Lois liked to set a lot of rules and regulations. When she brought up the possibility of a short postponement of the interview and photo shoot, I feigned understanding.

This gave Lois the opening to pitch a rescheduling not just of the interview but of Whitney Houston on the cover of *Vibe*. Like, change the issue. And there was nothing on paper. Contracts for covers was not how we did business. I gently reminded Lois of commitments made. She verbally shrugged. With notable exceptions, promises tended to be kept between Black publicists and Black media organizations. And because at that time *Vibe* was the gem of magazine publishing's chitlin circuit, publicists usually had to come back our way. Not so with Lois. Her other clients were white, and her power relationships were with places like *Vanity Fair, Jane, Rolling Stone, Premiere, People,* and *GQ.* Lois politely ended the call, then had someone else call me back to outright cancel. Whoa.

Whitney Houston was scheduled for our December–January double issue. Things were always a little panicky around a double, an issue that remained at newsstands for six-plus weeks. Whatever the sell-through percentage was, it counted twice toward the yearly average. I needed the Whitney Houston interview to happen as scheduled.

I called PMK, Lois's company, and asked for her. And I called again. Not like an ass, but on the five-minute mark, every hour (I did have other stuff to do as well!). I really used to function like, in this situation, there really is no other option except for us to win. *Vibe*'s readers will not be denied. Who else was covering Black pop singers back then—female or male—with any kind of consistency?

What did I say when she finally picked up, irritated? Who can re-member? If I know myself, it was some version of a hard pitch I made often.

I'm not calling you because we need this. I'm calling you and holding you to your commitments because she needs this. Her side of things needs to be out there. This is not going to be a hit piece. I know, because I'm writing it. Why would Vibe *do a hit piece on Whitney Houston?* Vibe *is about her telling her story. Yep. Yep. I get it. I understand this is a sensitive time. No need to hang out all the damn day. I'll be in and out in thirty minutes. Photo shoot, yep. That is negotiable. If that's what you feel good about, and that's what you all feel represents her more than a fully styled new shoot, then of course, I can find photos. But she's got to speak. I'll be in and out! I know she doesn't want* Vibe's *readers to be disappointed, or does she? Does she place them on the same level as* People's *audience?* Vanity Fair's? *This is her main fan base. Her core. These are the people who buy her albums no matter what. Do you really want to alienate those fans, her most loyal, the ones she needs when pop audiences get finicky? Yep, I'll go wherever she is. I'll be in and out in twenty minutes.*

I'd given the speech dozens of times, in moods serene and cool, in moods loud and pissed off. I meant it every time.

In the end, Lois agreed. Her team sent a Town Car that took me way out to Jersey that evening. It got dark and rainy along the way. I had my tape recorder. I'd never met Whitney Houston before. The man in the guardhouse got the okay to let me in, and Robyn Crawford opened the front door. Crawford was like, "Yeah hi cool." And reminded me immediately of my twenty-minute time limit.

Crawford, in an "as told to" for *Esquire* on the occasion of Houston's death, talked about how the two of them met. "She was 16," Crawford said. "It was at a summer job. I was working at a community center in East Orange, New Jersey, and she was working just like the rest of us. . . . She introduced herself as 'Whitney Elizabeth Houston,' and I knew right away she was special. Not a lot of people introduced themselves with their middle names back then. She had peachy colored skin and she didn't look like anyone I'd ever met in East Orange, New Jersey." There were persistent rumors about Crawford and Houston being in love, in a relationship. Crawford functioned for many years—until soon after Houston's marriage to Brown—as her assistant.

While I murmured some kind of agreement to Crawford, in my head I was like, *Whatever for a time limit.* Crawford was businesslike, in jeans and a turtleneck. Wary. "I have never spoken about her until now," Crawford also said in *Esquire.* "And she knew I wouldn't. She was a loyal friend, and she knew I was never going to be disloyal to her. I was never going to betray her." Crawford led me downstairs to a large room, with a TV and low couches, coffee tables. And it was baby-proofed. Seated on a sofa, I tested my recorder.

Crawford walked Whitney in. She was gaunt, jaunty. In stretchy, comfortable clothes. She sat across from me on another neutral-colored sofa. After two hours of conversation, Crawford came back down. As if to distract Crawford from whatever she was about to say, Houston asked for tea, and asked if I'd like some. Yes, I did, thank you.

We were having an intimate conversation. Talking about God, and about love and men. I could see cover lines in my head. I could see pull quotes. Writer as music editor, music editor as writer—I knew what I was getting. And it was good. "They had it already set up," Houston said, picking up Bobbi Kris and sitting her on the table. Her daughter was two. "Who they thought I should be with, I mean." "Who?" I wondered aloud. "Costner?" We were in the ripples still of the *Bodyguard* tidal wave.

"I'm not the one to be talking about Black and white issues," she said to me, "because I don't come with a lot of that. But, well, we all know who runs this whole thing. We all know who's in power, right? Well, when they saw me, they saw me as their little princess and [figured], *She's going to marry a white man,* or whatever."

She told me she tried to tell people who she was. "I come from New-ark, born and raised in New Hope Baptist Church. All-girl school, mostly white-girl, yeah, but this is what I am. This is what I'm used to. This is what I like." She was referring to Bobby Brown. "What you-all may think it is, it ain't. Whoever set this little story up before I got here, it's changed. It's different. I'm not Diana [Ross]. I'm not."

I remember not liking talking about my divorce but doing it anyway. I rarely spoke about my divorce at that time—it was fresh, barely final. I hadn't yet figured out how to tell the story of that marriage, but I felt that it was somehow in the same galaxy as Whitney and Bobby's, that he was struggling with her ambition. That she was over-loving him, trying to be traditionally girly. At one point Houston said to me something like "You ask me about me and my husband—ask Lena Horne. Ask her about Joe Louis." According to Clive Davis, Lena Horne and Dionne Warwick were Whitney Houston's favorite singers when she was a girl. Lena Horne told me once that if there was anyone portraying her in a biopic, it had to be Whitney Houston.

The very first time Clive Davis introduced Whitney to television au-diences, he said to Merv Griffin, "There was Lena Horne. There is Di-onne Warwick. But if the mantle is to pass to somebody . . . who's elegant, who's sensuous, who's innocent, who's got an incredible range of talent, but guts and soul at the same time, it will be Whitney Houston. It's her natural charm. You either got it or you don't have it. She's got it."

Miss Lena Horne, with her eight Grammys and two Tony Awards. An Emmy Award. Honored in 1984 at the Kennedy Center. On the Hollywood Walk of Fame separately for her recordings and for her films. Horne got us from 1943's *Stormy Weather* to 1978's "If You Be-lieve" in the film version of *The Wiz*. Miss Lena Horne on the road in the

1930s with her actor mother, Edna. Miss Horne at sixteen dancing on the line at Harlem's Cotton Club, hearing Ethel Waters sing "Stormy Weather."

Lena Horne who sang "It's Not Easy Bein' Green" on *Sesame Street* with Kermit, and it felt like a coded message to all the Black kids. Horne's *New York Times* obituary states the horrific fact: "She might have become a major movie star, but she was born 50 years too early: she languished at MGM for years because of her race."

We focus on Horne's smile. On her triumphant 1981 one-woman Broadway show, *Lena Horne: The Lady and Her Music*. We honor her contributions to the Civil Rights Movement, are inspired by her relationship with Malcolm X.

While she was in Hollywood, the special makeup color created for her, Light Egyptian, was used on Ava Gardner, and on Hedy Lamarr while, as *Playbill* notes, "she was assigned to cameo roles that could be edited out when the movies played down South." She was deeply unhappy. "I used to think, 'I'm black and I'm going to isolate myself because you don't understand me,'" Horne said in 1981. "All the things people said—sure, they hurt, and it made me retreat even further. The only thing between me and them was that jive protection. The audience would say, 'She looks great, but she's cold as an iceberg.' I was literally freezing to death. I could feel nothing except my lack of love toward anybody, or anything."

There is tragedy in the fact that what Horne wanted, what she was qualified to do and what she worked for, was denied to her by white creative professionals, and what she did accomplish was hated on by the men she loved the most. Horne exploded in 1950 when someone in a Beverly Hills restaurant called her "just another nigger." She "jumped up, and threw a table lamp, several glasses and an ashtray at the man and hit him." God bless her.

"The performance of 'Stormy Weather' in *Cabin in the Sky* is one of the most profound performances . . . that you'll ever see from a Black woman of that time," Houston said in 1999. "You're talking about a woman who had so much to deal with. Here she is, in Hollywood, surrounded by—the white factor." Houston places "white factor" in air quotes. "She's a sister who has to deal with civil rights issues. . . . But she stands there the most poised . . . most confident—and fuhgettabout the beauty, it's just . . . it's beyond. And she puts on show for that second, for that time. . . . She gives us performance to last us a lifetime, that every little girl, every actress, singer, woman should look at and see . . . Never mind . . . what's going on inside . . . what she portrays on the outside, you would never know."

Joe Louis, "the Brown Bomber," was a pop star himself. Neither he nor his Black manager, the real estate professional and numbers runner John Roxborough, were into pugilism for the discounted fees and ragged venues on the chitlin circuit of boxing. Team Louis created rules of respectability for Joe—that included him never being photographed with a white woman.

Louis, who supposedly "transcended the color barrier," and presented as "polite, well mannered, and [knowing] his place," went for and won massive purses—not just for a Black boxer but for a boxer, period. As the columnist and author Robert Lipsyte (*Free to Be Muhammad Ali*) has said, "Louis was psychologically disturbed, eventually institutionalized, perhaps because of the pressure of a double life. He was an abuser of alcohol, drugs and women of all colors."

Louis pursued Lena relentlessly. Many say Horne began dating him at the suggestion of—or due to pressure from—her father, Teddy Horne. Details about Teddy's manner of making a living are vague. Many say he was a pimp and a gambler, with connections to the gangster Dutch Schultz. Lena had already, at eighteen, been married to a college grad seven years her senior. He has been characterized as a politician and a gambler, and as being "jealous" of her success.

In 1978, Horne shrugged off the infamous story of Louis choking her. She felt it was sad that toward the end of his life, the boxer had to be asked about the incident. "I met Joe as a child," she told *The Washington Post*. "He knew my father. An affair? If one goes around with someone I suppose that's an affair. But let me say this: Joe Louis was nicer to me than any of the bosses I had."

———

In 1999, in a conference room on the east side of Manhattan, I told Miss Horne that when I'd asked Houston about her marriage to Bobby Brown, Whitney had suggested I ask her about Joe Louis. Horne, fragile, but alert as a hummingbird, was unsurprised, and unoffended by my Joe Louis question.

She said things about women who have light around them. Lena Horne said that certain men are attracted to that light. And that what those men really need to do, what's really in them, is the desire to put out that light. Her words are stenciled on my heart.

"If we know ourselves, we are always home, anywhere." That's what Horne's angelic Glinda the Good Witch sings to Diana Ross's Dorothy in the film version of *The Wiz*. But what if we don't know ourselves? Or can't? What if our time in history doesn't allow it?

On the rainy night I was at her home, Whitney Houston didn't seem overly, or even very, vulnerable. And she was just chill enough and aware enough to make me—an admirer of women who present unselfconscious strength—like her right away. Not unlike Eddie Levert of the O'Jays, Houston had been charming people in and around the music business since she was singing backup for her mother, Cissy, at nightclubs in New York.

Whitney asked if I was hungry. She walked me up to the massive kitchen. Crawford was there, not quite glaring but far from warm. I got it: she had to protect Whitney at all costs. But no, I wasn't hungry, thanks. I was too busy staring at Whitney, trying to see who she was and how she did what she did. Houston shrugged at me in a friendly, *Bitch, what?* kinda way, like, *Hello sis what? I'm right here what are you looking at.* Big smile. Lonely smile. I'm. Right. Here.

I wanted out. Had what I wanted and needed. I had the urge to be on my way before anything could be asked of me, before anything could be reneged on, before some nugget could be recalled. But Whitney brought me into her jumbo living room. Told me that she and Bobby played catch in it sometimes, and picked up a nearby Nerf-like football. In my imagination, she asked me to "go long," and I declined, in order that I remain professional. In truth I kicked off my shoes, jogged that giant room, and went for it like Jerry Rice. Houston had a good arm. I missed the pass, though, and she laughed in that way pro athletes do when they're playing with kids.

Houston agreed then, though, to do our *Vibe* cover shoot.

The last time I attended Clive Davis's pre-Grammy gala was February 7, 2009. Called that year the Salute to Industry Icons, it's the music-industry party often referred to in timelines of the night Chris Brown beat up Rihanna. It was a Saturday night, and it was where they'd made their last public appearance.

The couple had in fact been hugged up at the Clive Davis event. My husband and I could see them from our table. Rihanna's pale pink lips, hoop earrings, pixie cut, glowing décolletage, bare shoulders. She had already won a Grammy for her 2007 "Umbrella," from her third album, *Good Girl Gone Bad*. The video for "Umbrella" was also named 2007 MTV Music Video of the Year. She and Jay-Z won the Grammy for Best Rap/Sung Collaboration, and it was nominated both for Song of the Year and Record of the Year. The song went to number-one pop in nineteen countries and was at number one in America for seven weeks. Her second number-one pop single only topped as the best performing single of 2007 by Beyoncé's "Irreplaceable," which remained at number one for ten weeks.

What a year. What accomplishment. What an impact on culture. The song, from Jay-Z's audacious *We Roc-a-fella / We fly higher than weather,* is juiced with arrival and sunlight and the happy cool of two poor kids—one an immigrant from Barbados and the other from the project hallways of Brooklyn—in love with life and seeing things from heights they had the nerve to imagine.

Chris, nineteen, still baby-faced, was in all-black everything. Davis acknowledged Rihanna from his podium—as he did everyone, from Paul McCartney to Island Def Jam chairman Antonio "L. A." Reid. Taylor Swift was there, Jamie Foxx, Keyshia Cole in a flowy yellow gown. Joan Collins. Kenneth "Babyface" Edmonds. Faith Evans. Rod

Stewart. There were at least a thousand people: managers, publicists, directors, songwriters, producers, CEOs of touring outfits, radio programmers and personalities, all of it. Barry Manilow was on the patio smoking a cigarette, no security. The applause for Rihanna was thunderous. She'd sold almost ten million albums at that time.

As the response to Rihanna's name calmed a bit, Davis asked Brown, whom people had begun comparing to Michael Jackson, to stand also. The applause for him was loud, but a whisper less so than the applause for his girlfriend. I noticed it, and I tensed for her. The dots were fluorescent, easy to connect: Clive Davis, the man Whitney Houston had often referred to as her "father" in the business, stood up at the most popular party during Grammy week and sprinkled Rihanna with his pixie dust. It was an anointment, a show of respect for who she was and who she was going to be.

And Rihanna stood that evening with the posture and the grace of young Whitney. Rihanna and Whitney had different gifts and different training, but the carriage was there. The room was full of insiders, and insiders knew that Reid, then chairman of the label Rihanna was signed to, polished his star-making skills working near Clive Davis when Reid and Babyface's LaFace Records were distributed by Arista (1989–2001). *Ah,* the industry crowd seemed to murmur at the graceful nod of Rihanna's head. *This is her time, her turn.* All this, even as we waited for the rumored "surprise" of the evening—the return of Whitney Houston.

Houston did perform one ballad, and she was rusty. But the headlines were elsewhere, because the next night Chris Brown handed himself in to Los Angeles police.

The day of Grammys, for the show's women performing artists, can begin at dawn, with hair, makeup, and nails to attend to, in addition to production meetings, rehearsals, soundcheck, and red carpet. On that day, there had been an escalated argument between Brown and Fenty in Hancock Park. Rihanna was supposed to have performed with Justin Timberlake that night at Grammys. Brown, who debuted in 2005 with the triple-platinum, Grammy-nominated, number-two pop album *Chris Brown,* and who was sitting on *Exclusive,* his 2007 triple-platinum, number-four pop album, was supposed to have performed his number-two pop hit "Forever." Since Grammy weekend 2009, Chris Brown has had three number-one pop albums: *Fame, Fortune,* and *Indigo.*

Back in 1996, at the Clive Davis pre-Grammy gala, when I was sitting with Eddie and Gerald Levert and Gerald's manager, Leonard Brooks, Keith Clinkscales walked over to me. We had actually come in together, but Keith, who was my boss's boss and CEO of *Vibe,* is a legendary room-worker, and I had not seen much of him all night.

"Danyel," he said near my ear. "You should go say hello to Whitney."

Me: "Whitney is here?" The story had been published. I'd heard nothing from her team. I had not seen her since the cover shoot, and I'd only stayed there long enough to see that we had a cover shot.

"You should go say hello," Keith said.

"I'm good," I said. But then also, "Where is she?" He pointed. She was standing near another sparsely populated outlying table. Houston was in casual clothes, talking and laughing with some folks.

"Go," Keith said. I feel like he pulled back my chair. "At least speak. You put her on the cover. Go over there. Be who you are."

Now Gerald is looking at me like, *What's the hesitation?* My hesitation is fear and awkwardness. I have never been a legendary room-worker. I am a legendary room-watcher.

I go over. "Hello, Whitney? Hey!"

She squints. It seems to take her a second to remember who I am. I see that Bobby Brown is among those seated. She's standing behind him. Unlike most everyone else in the room, Houston is not in formal wear, and she looks to be on the verge of motion—like the scene is kinda wack, and she could exit at any second.

"Hey, lady," says Houston. "Hey! How are you?" She puts her arms around her husband's shoulders from behind and squeezes. The embrace is an exaggeration. Brown seems oblivious.

Me: "I'm fine. Really good."

"Oh?" Whitney Houston says, with a wicked grin. Her husband lolls in her arms. "Well, I got my man back. How 'bout you?"

PART III

JANET

Do I want Michael's kind of success? Oh hells yeah.
Are you kidding? I'd love to. And he knows that, too.
—JANET JACKSON TO DANYEL SMITH, CLARKSTON, MICHIGAN, JULY 1994

There is a legend of Janet Damita Jo Jackson.

In the 1980s wilderness of American pop culture, there is a young Black woman heavy with the name of her large family, and unsure of her artistic identity. By the rare light of a blue blood moon, she steals away from a groaning California castle dominated by her brother, Michael the Great, and her father, Joseph the Mean. Weary of recording middling songs from trifling troubadours, Janet wades icy waters on her journey to meet the mysterious twin wizards, who honed their conjuration on Prince Rogers Nelson and Leon Sylvers III.

Tendrils clinging to her face, this young Janet arrives at Castle Flyte Tyme. In this bright and frozen land of Minneapolis—Janet, before a dancing fire, tells Sir James Harris III and Sir Terry Steven Lewis the tale of her life. To her surprise, they actively listen. She is inspired.

With Jimmy and Terry, Janet retreats to a creative chamber both modern and vintage. Surrounded by magic drums and pianos, she soon emerges with a batch of incantations that will change her world, and the world beyond Flyte Tyme, forever.

Did what my father said / And let my mother mold me / But that was long ago.

With soft jet hair like a cascading crown, Janet stands, shoulders padded against pushback—cradling the emancipatory trophy that is 1986's *Control*.

The Janet legend is compelling. On her quest for selfhood and greatness, our superstar conquers obstacles galore.

But not enough is made of the courage it took for Janet to compete with her brother Michael. It was a gargantuan challenge. Michael rose from the plains a true giant, and even a dragon. And when she was ready, Janet picked up sword and shield.

Michael was a pop star from the age of eight. He recorded genius music as the leader of the Jackson 5, then the leader of the Jacksons, and then as a solo performer. It's near impossible to count the number of awards he had won. As a touring artist, Michael had set new bars for attendance records. His haunted and haunting moonwalk was likely being performed on the streets of other universes.

"My singing is just . . . Godly, really," Michael said in 1980. "No real personal experience or anything that makes it come across. Just feeling, and God." Michael was speaking with journalist John Pidgeon at the Jackson family's Encino compound. He'd requested, as he often did in that heady era between *Off the Wall* and *Thriller,* that Janet sit in on the interview. "If you could direct your questions to Janet," Michael's publicist said, "she'll put them to Michael." Janet was thirteen. "Our main goal in music," Michael said that day, "is to integrate every race to one through music, and we're doing that."

After 1982's *Thriller*—which until 2018 was considered the best-selling album of all time—everyone wanted to be next to Janet Jackson's brother. By 1986, he was working with George Lucas and Francis Ford Coppola on the Disney attraction *Captain EO,* and with Quincy Jones on *Bad,* the follow-up to *Thriller*. The tabloids and shows like *Entertainment Tonight* leaned into Michael as his hair straightened, his skin went pallid, his black sunglasses became the rule, and his nose shrunk to a point.

All this as he was hanging out with Emmanuel Lewis and young Macaulay and Kieran Culkin, and indulging in then exotic-sounding home oxygen therapy. Janet, with *Control,* walked into the perfect storm of Michael's voice, dance, knotted charisma, and ambition.

> *And since you wanted to be Penny on* Good Times *and get saved from an insane home life by nosy Ja'net "Willona" DuBois; and since you desperately wanted a boyfriend like* Diff'rent Strokes' *Willis, who could take you for a sundae in Mr. Drummond's limousine; and since you lived for Janet as Cleo in* Fame *because she got to share tension-filled moments with Leroy, the pouty dancer, who was, at the time, the sexiest boy alive; because of what you wanted and what your life was like, when you finally see Miss Janet and she stares directly into your eyes, you catch something there, along with the twinkle. You may not be Janet or anything much like her. But you realize that she is looking at you, and what you represent, with the same amazement with which you are looking at her.*

> —DANYEL SMITH, *VIBE,* OCTOBER 1994

In 1994, at the age of twenty-nine, I was at the Pine Knob Music Theatre in suburban Detroit, sitting in Janet Jackson's myrrh-scented dressing room, talking with her about *The Bridges of Madison County* and how the wife should have gone off with the photographer. It was the first time we'd talked. She told me she'd like to marry René Elizondo "someday." They had been secretly married for three years.

That time at Pine Knob, during the eighth month of the janet. tour, we talked about how Janet always wanted to work the drive-thru window at McDonald's. And about how she used to go, incognito, to work at a clothing store with a high school friend. Janet would "pull clothes and stuff." We both fell out laughing when she said she never went so far as to work the register. We talked about wanting it all.

Blink, and now suddenly it's Janet Jackson's forty-second year. While her dewy face says twenty-five, Janet's hands, like mine, look like truth: she's been doing creative and manual labor since she was six years old. At Manhattan's Blue Ribbon Sushi Bar & Grill, Janet picks at salad, and then at her toro. Sashimi, to me, is a lunch or dinner food, so I'm on tea. It's eleven o'clock in the morning and Janet gives a look. Like I'm unsophisticated. I shrug. She's on her own chronometer, time zones long ago robbed of significance by intercontinental schedules and private planes.

It's my forty-third year. I'm back at *Vibe* magazine, as editor in chief for the second time. It's a privilege to be of service to a huge readership. Wonderful to sit with Janet, for the third time in my career. I'm happily remarried. The author of two novels. An undiagnosed depressive, I'm high-functioning and excelling. And the nightmare—where I'm a passenger on a commercial jet attempting to land on the Manhattan Bridge—is recurring. Wings are tangled in suspension cables, and we have been asked to remain silent.

At Blue Ribbon, a cast-iron teapot sits warmly by.

Me: "Is it harder to be twenty now than it was when you were twenty? Was everything more fun when you were younger?"

"No," she says with a smile. "It's still fun."

Janet was nineteen when *Control* was released. Before *Control* there were television shows, two albums, a marriage, and an annulment. Music is the Jackson family business, but Janet chose not to begin there. Ostensibly based on the success of the Mae West impersonations she did on tour with her brothers, Janet was cast as Penny, the foster daughter of Ja'net DuBois's Willona in Season 5 of CBS's *Good Times*. Penny's birth mother, portrayed indelibly by Laverne "Chip" Fields, famously burned Penny with a clothes iron.

"Since I was a kid," Jackson says, "getting up at ten years old, doing *Good Times,* I never had my mother wake me up and say, 'Time to go to work.' I'd set my alarm clock for five, five-thirty. Our driver would be out there waiting to take me to the set. I'd get myself up every day. It never struck me . . . that's a lot of difficulty for a ten-year-old." She combed her own hair on these mornings. "Even though it was just in a little bun," she says, "I had to do it. My parents . . . I don't ever remember them literally extolling [work ethic]. I don't know if it's something in the genes, or from watching my brothers, seeing them working hard, traveling and rehearsing."

Janet and Michael were close as children. She moved with the family to the wide warmth of Los Angeles at age five and must have seemed to Michael untouched by the Gary, Indiana, household of his youth. "I just remember hearing my mother scream, 'Joe, you're gonna kill him, you're gonna kill him, stop it,'" Michael told Martin Bashir in 2003's *Living with Michael Jackson.* "I was so fast he couldn't catch me half the time, but when he would catch me, oh my God, it was bad."

Joe had been a Golden Gloves boxer, and as his family grew, he worked full-time at U.S. Steel as a crane operator. In between, he played guitar in a band with his brother. The Falcons never secured a record deal. Legend has it that Janet's brother Tito found the guitar and, though fearful of his father's likely response, began playing.

How might Joseph have worked out his disappointments on his family? From afar, his fatherhood reeks of commonplace artistic funk as well as the halitosis of swallowing one's own humanity. From within clouds of envy and sanctimony, he witnesses carefree young people who, by accident of birth year, would live lives of comparative freedom. "My kids was brought up in a way so they respect people," Joseph Jackson told Piers Morgan in 2013. "They were brought up professionally."

Perhaps on his mind were words Janet said to CNN's Morgan in 2011. "I think my father means well. . . . And wants nothing but the best for his kids. I just think the way he went about certain things wasn't the best way. But it got the job done." Morgan reminded her of a moment in the self-help book she co-wrote, *True You: A Journey to Finding and Loving Yourself,* when Janet recalls stepping out of a bathtub, and her father whacking her with a belt. She was not yet eight when it happened. "I can't remember what it was that I did," she says, her smile out of place, a tic. "I can't remember if I truly deserved it. My father's never touched me, aside from that time. He's never whipped me."

Cynthia Horner, editor in chief of the Black teen magazine *Right On!* during the 1980s, counted Michael Jackson as a friend and is a longtime supporter of Joe Jackson. "There aren't a lot of fathers like Joe who are going to put that much work into developing a family act," Horner told me in 2016. "Joe Jackson was working three jobs and still managing the Jacksons. He got criticized . . . because people felt he was very strict. If he had not been strict, there would not have been any Jackson 5, because you can't expect any children to be that disciplined."

I asked Cynthia if she recalled the first woman celebrity she sat down with. "Janet Jackson," she said. "But she wasn't really a celebrity at that point. She was Michael Jackson's little sister."

Janet was cast as Willis Jackson's (Todd Bridges) recurring girlfriend Charlene DuPrey in NBC's *Diff'rent Strokes*. There was also a stint as a daughter of Telma Hopkins's character in the short-lived *A New Kind of Family* (ABC). Janet and her real family may have known Hopkins from around, as she was a background singer at Motown and one third of Tony Orlando and Dawn. The trio scored three number-ones, including the Grammy-nominated "Tie a Yellow Ribbon Round the Ole Oak Tree."

By the time Janet portrayed dancer Cleo Hewitt on the television version of *Fame* (1984–85), she was an old hand on sets, but still soft-spoken. "When Janet first came on the set, she was kinda *introverted,*" the late Gene Anthony Ray told me in 1994. He portrayed Leroy Johnson in the *Fame* film and television series. "Very Michael. All that whispering. We brought her out of that real quick."

With her father's management, Janet released *Janet Jackson* in 1982 (with Angela Winbush, René Moore, and Leon Sylvers III at the creative helm) and *Dream Street* in 1984. Janet's first music video, the low-budget "Dream Street" (lackadaisically produced by Giorgio Moroder, who co-produced many Donna Summer hits) was shot in conjunction with *Fame,* and in it, Janet is unselfconscious, lightly styled, and natural-istically choreographed. She portrays a girl working service jobs while trying to make it in a world bigger than the one she left. I was familiar with that decision. I too had the baby-faced swag of abbreviated child-hood. I too was thick and had married young.

Dream Street sold . . . okay. But Stacy Lattisaw, with "Love on a Two-Way Street" and "Let Me Be Your Angel," was the young queen of the kind of achy teen stuff Janet was recording. Plus, since both Rebbie Jackson and La Toya Jackson released albums in 1984, it looked like Joseph Jackson was throwing stuff against a wall to see what would stick. Michael dropped some background vocals on *Dream,* but the idea of Janet excelling in Michael's arena was not yet a whisper on the wind.

The adolescent vibe of *Dream Street* also clanked against the fact that Janet had recently eloped with James DeBarge, youngest of his clan. Under the names Switch and DeBarge, iterations of the DeBarge siblings had created R&B and pop classics for Motown since 1978. Janet and James had known each other since childhood. *Jet* coverline: "Marriage Unites Famous Families." The James-Janet union was scandal and a fairy tale. A paparazzo's dream. In most every shot, the couple looked like awkward high schoolers on the way to the prom. But Janet was working every day on *Fame,* and James was in the recording studio with DeBarge. "We could never spend time together," she's said, "the way we wanted to." And James was rumored to have had a cocaine problem.

In the wake of the new marriage, Janet's father was interviewed by *Jet.* "I never got involved in Janet's situation," he said. "Soon as she was eighteen . . . she decided that was what she wanted to do. I did not want her to get married. . . . What I was trying to do with her career was such that matters could wait. . . . You can't just build an artist the way you would like to, and deal with the marriage situation at the same time." The marriage lasted less than a year. In 2014, at fifty, James DeBarge was arrested—as he has been many times over the decades—for drug possession.

A lesson Janet Jackson apparently takes from her nineteen-year-old self is to resist the announcement of marriage. It wasn't until he filed divorce papers in 2000 that Janet Jackson confirmed her 1991 marriage to "boyfriend" and creative collaborator René Elizondo. In February 2013, Janet Jackson revealed that she had been married since 2012 to Qatari retail billionaire Wissam Al Mana. Shortly after the 2017 birth of their son, Eissa, Wissam and Janet broke up. As of 2021, the search for anything proving the finalization of the couple's divorce is a rabbit hole within a wormhole within a classic Janet Jackson maze.

With Janet, when we did Control, *we weren't trying to cross anything over. There was nothing on pop radio that sounded like "What Have You Done for Me Lately" or "Nasty." There wasn't really a female who was using really aggressive beats like that. The beats*

we made were beats that would be more for a man, a male artist,
than a female artist. But we felt it fit her.

—JIMMY JAM

Janet Jackson began to sour on *Fame*. And while she often recalls her "sheltered" teen life, the early-eighties gossip had Jackson speeding down Sunset Boulevard in a convertible wearing sunglasses at night. People swore they saw her partying at what was then the grungy Santa Monica Pier arcade. At my St. Mary's Academy in Inglewood, the consensus was that Janet was enrolled at Santa Monica's chic Crossroads School, near the beach. Over the years, attendees have included Minnie Riperton's daughter, Maya Rudolph; Gwyneth Paltrow; and Baron Davis. Actually, Janet graduated from San Fernando Valley Professional High School, which counts as alumni Tiffani Thiessen and Alfonso Ribeiro.

In the run-up to Janet's escape to Minnesota, she went for advice to family friend and A&M Records executive John McClain. McClain had attended the Walton School in L.A.'s Panorama City neighborhood with several of the brothers Jackson. "When I was two," Janet said in 1987, "John used to change my diapers. He's like a son to my parents. . . . He's always been there for me." McClain was so close to Michael Jackson that he was named, at Michael's willed request, coexecutor of his estate.

McClain suggested Jimmy Jam and Terry Lewis to Janet. She'd seen them in concert as a part of the Time when she was sixteen. "They were great," she said, "and soooooo nasty."

As tabloids screamed that her family might disown her for marrying DeBarge, Janet headed out to meet Jam and Lewis. At the news of the annulment, a popular theory was that Janet had, under duress, caved to family. But McClain had not been into the marriage either. "I tried to convince her that she's a teen idol and people just wouldn't accept it," he told *People* in 1986. He said he "hounded" her for eight months and finally persuaded her to annul. "Hey," he said. "I'm trying to make her a star."

As Michael Jackson, Lionel Richie, and Quincy Jones wrote and produced "We Are the World," and Michael bought the Beatles' catalogue for $47.5 million, McClain, according to *People,* "put Janet on a diet, sent her to voice and dance coaches for three months and shipped her to Minneapolis to record under the tutelage of Prince protégés Jimmy Jam and Terry Lewis." *People* also quotes McClain as saying Joe Jackson okayed the whole Minnesota idea, and would have "backhanded him" had it not worked. The plan McClain pitched to Janet: "Let Patti [LaBelle] and them sing their lungs out," he told her. "You just concentrate on being a better Michael." The runaway child narrative played well to the masses. The superconnected, supercoached baby sister narrative played well to insiders. Janet, like most ambitious underdogs, simultaneously played and flipped the hand she was dealt.

"The albums before [*Control*] . . . she was making . . . because her dad wanted her to," Jimmy Jam told me in 2016. "She had a good voice, but she had no input. Nobody asked her, 'Did you have an idea?' Listen . . . we had five days. We went to the movies. We went to clubs. We drove around the lake."

Janet wanted to know when they would begin working—like in the studio. This kind of creativity was new to Janet. "Me and Terry were like, 'Oh, no, we *are* working.' Then we showed her . . . lyrics to 'Control' and she was like, 'Wait a minute. This is what we've been talking about.' She said, 'Wait a minute, whatever we talk about, that's what we're going to write about?' Yes. It was like a light bulb went on in her head: 'Oh, okay, great. Let's write about those guys in the club, those nasty guys in the club. Okay, great, let's write about that.'" Her stories were the stories.

It took a bit longer than five days to figure out what *Control* was going to be. And it took two months to record. As Janet began to talk about what her videos might be like, McClain suggested Laker Girl Paula Abdul, who the Jackson family had hired to choreograph a Michael-less Jacksons video for a song called "Torture."

It was starting to feel like a spit-and-glue production. As Jimmy Jam said in 1990, "When someone says, 'Well, she brought in Jimmy Jam and Terry Lewis,' you've got to remember that we weren't exactly the hottest producers around. We weren't Quincy Jones. . . . *Control* was our first . . . smash. The same with Paula. It wasn't like Janet was hiring Fred Astaire. . . . She took a chance on all of us."

Janet released her fourth album, 1989's *Rhythm Nation 1814,* eight months after her brother Michael returned from his Bad world tour. This was the tour with the epic "Man in the Mirror" performance, and the rabid pageantry of "Leave Me Alone." There were reports of fans being crushed toward the stage, of fans abjectly screaming for their Michael until they fainted. This was four years before the LAPD first investigated Michael due to allegations of child molestation.

When I saw the Jackson 5 at San Carlos's California Circle Star Theatre, I was eight, and I broke away from my mother and ran toward the stage with the older fans. I have little memory of the moment, other than darting into the aisle and running toward Michael's face and voice. I feel like they were on "The Love You Save," their third number-one hit. *S is for "Save it" / T is for "Take it slow" / O is for "Oh, no!" / P is for "Please, please, don't go!"*

I didn't know they were singing about a "fast" girl. I heard a Black boy's earnest, soul-filled voice—and that delivery, really from both Michael and Jermaine Jackson, has never stopped ringing off in my body. I saw Janet that night, too, in her Mae West drag. I thought she was the luckiest girl in the world to be onstage in front of people, and to be Michael Jackson's sister.

The Bad tour was on pace to become the second-highest-grossing tour of the 1980s, and team Janet was prepping for her first solo tour as well. They had brilliant material. The brawny and blissed out "Miss You Much"—co-arranged and co-produced by Janet with Jam and Lewis— was the first song recorded for *Rhythm Nation 1814.*

I was in a friend's car the first time I heard "Miss You," crossing the old Bay Bridge from Oakland to San Francisco. I was working three jobs—at a youth parole nonprofit, at Saks Fifth Avenue, and as an editorial intern (for no pay) at the *San Francisco Bay Guardian*. I wrote photo captions and covered conferences, but what I really wanted to write about was my hometown, the crack culture that ruled it, and music that moved us.

My sister and I had a big social circle, and we went out a lot. It didn't make us special, but some of our friends and boyfriends were in the streets getting up to stuff for which they went to prison or to their graves. And like in most dope-boy narratives, the lead-up to tragedy was wildly grimy, and it was more fun than it ever should have been. On group outings, instead of Whoppers, we scarfed seafood platters at Berkeley's bayside restaurants. Rib racks with multiple sides instead of link sandwiches with pickles and fries. We were hardly *Scarface,* but real bullets did fly, and loyalties—to a way of life, to a particular set of friends—were difficult to let go.

What came in handy was what I'd learned in childhood: hysteria gets you labeled weak and melodramatic. I was deeply familiar with anger, and I was comfortable calmly arguing with people. In Oakland, the local news counted murders. They were mostly "gang" or "drug" related, and it was depressing—especially since I knew the neighborhoods. And knew of some of the victims. So I started writing about how the evening news built the same story for every killing: dehumanize the victim, go in tight on the wet-faced, wailing mother, then talk again about ongoing violence—with zero context.

Oakland was wearing me down. I was falling out with people I thought were my friends. I started running away from home daily to the city. Doing my shifts, taking random classes at San Francisco State. After work I ate alone at Tad's Steak House. It was like a steak cafeteria, but I had on my Saks name tag and Perry Ellis pumps purchased on my discount, and I bought my fifteen-dollar steak with my own money. Felt like a baller.

Since I couldn't afford UC Berkeley, the school where I'd been accepted, music was keeping me sane—Karyn White's "Superwoman," Regina Belle's "Baby Come to Me," and New Edition's "Can You Stand the Rain." I noted that the sophisticated Caron Wheeler—who sang lead on Soul II Soul's two biggest singles—was not mentioned as often as producer-bandleader Jazzie B, but I was too distracted by the music scene in Oakland to really complain. Digital Underground was bubbling under, and there was MC Hammer, Too Short, En Vogue, Tony! Toni! Toné!, the Coup, Paris, K-Cloud and the Crew, Premo, MC Ant. And the Bay Area radio station KMEL was beyond hype at that time.

I felt like we were never not listening to KMEL. Headed up by Keith Naftaly and Hosh Gureli (who both eventually left to work for Clive Davis at Arista), the influential KMEL was problematic with regard to how it treated rap music, and I reported on it for *SF Weekly*. But the station brought hip hop out of the college and community radio station milieu and into the Bay Area's mainstream. KMEL premiering any record was a huge deal.

It was bright on the Bay Bridge the day Jackson's "Miss You Much" was set to drop for the first time. KMEL personality Theo Mizuhara had been teasing all morning that he was going to DROP THE NEW JANET SINGLE! When he finally played "Miss You Much," I screamed from the window, "This is a *perfect song*!" Janet was twenty-three. I was twenty-four. My opinion about the record has not changed.

"The creative team was simple," Jimmy Jam told *Billboard* in 2014. "Me, Janet, Terry and John McClain—and Rene Elizondo also. . . . If the ideas weren't flowing from that group of people, they weren't really being listened to." A backup dancer for her sister, La Toya Jackson (who has recorded regularly since 1980), René Elizondo met Janet in 1982, when she was sixteen. Five years later, with her marriage to James DeBarge in the rearview, Janet began referring to Elizondo as a "special person." In 1994, Jackson told me of Elizondo, "He keeps me sane."

"The 'rhythm nation' idea hadn't even been hatched at that point," said Jimmy Jam in 2014. "But 'Miss You' and 'Love Will Never Do,' those were the first two we had ready. . . . I just knew that it needed to be something danceable, up-tempo—and happy and mad. And that was kind of what it was."

The thing is, the now dominant mix of hip hop and R&B was just taking hold. "That particular sound [at the start of 'Miss You'] was a drum machine called an SP-1200, which is famous in hip-hop circles because of the way it sounds like an attack," said Jam. "It was the first time I'd actually used a drum machine on a record." Janet was no longer on *Dream Street*. She was, like Jody Watley, Neneh Cherry, Tone Lōc, and Bobby Brown, making a new, hip-hop-laced pop world.

"On 'Miss You Much,' yes, we [were] aware that there's a broad audience listening to her now, and we can't ignore them," said Jimmy Jam. "So, we're going to make a record that is . . . as universally appealing as possible. That's what we tried to do with Janet. It wasn't so much, make it *cross over,* but it was that you have an audience that loves you, obviously, in the black community. You have an audience that loves you in the pop community. Let's make a great record that should appeal to everybody. And 'Miss You Much' did. It was number one black and number one pop. . . . We were just trying to make the best record we could make."

Janet's father is more blunt. "She came out of a black situation," Joseph Jackson said in 1987. "Those are her roots. You can stay black and still sell millions of records."

"Miss You Much" is a torch that burns from a position of strength: *I'll tell your mama / I'll tell your friends / I'll tell anyone / Whose heart can comprehend / Send it in a letter / Baby, tell you on the phone / I'm not the kind of girl who likes to be alone.* Clear in Janet's indelible "Miss You" dance are the genes, the commitment to being the best in her family, the best in the world. "She felt guilty about admitting that she did feel competitive," said John McClain in 1987. "She'd been scared that she'd try, and fail. Well, Michael may not have wanted her to be *as* big, but it's no sin for *her* to want it."

From the first moments of the Herb Ritts–directed "Love Will Never Do (Without You)" video, you can see Janet simultaneously building and shrinking herself—becoming a pop star. It was around the time of the "Pleasure Principle" video that she decided to make changes. "I went on a crazy diet," Janet told me in 1994. "I shouldn't say *crazy,* because it worked, but I don't know if I could go through that again. I was going to this doctor, getting medications that would curb your appetite. I remember times when my heart would race." Janet said her hands would tremble. "I'd be shaking the entire day, and I started thinking, That's not good."

But hers wasn't solely an early version of #transformationtuesdays. Janet, like Tina Turner and Josephine Baker before her, understood the power of the Black female body in motion. Janet also knew she was us. Stephanie Mills got us through the breakups, but Mills was our big sister. Jody was our sophisticate, but we hadn't known Jody since she was a kid. Janet was Gen X Black girl youth energy; she was both a superstar and shy girl-next-door.

She'd been tucked into tailored black overcoats. She'd crowned sleek ponytails with a forward-facing ball cap. There had been the key dangling from a hoop earring. But in the video for her fifth number-one pop single, boyfriend jeans sit loosely on a new wasp waist. Spaghetti straps brush Janet's collarbones, and the dangling key is somewhere with the other artifacts of adolescence. She enters "Love Will Never Do" in a lower and more sensual register. Antonio Sabáto, Jr., and Djimon Hounsou appear, as matte and benign as the undie models they were. Music fans were smitten anew.

In 1994, Janet told me, "[Michael] has done so much. I feel like I haven't even gotten close to what he's done. When someone says, 'Oh my God, you've done this, you've done that,' I think, Yeah, that's nice, but Michael's done *this*."

It was breathtaking to see her doing her own thing. "Why the blond wig?" was the think-piece-y question of the time, but her look not only recalled Bardot and Ronnie Spector, it set off the powerful waist-grazing wigs and weaves of the future, from the multihued styles of Lil' Kim and Nicki Minaj, to the glorious tresses of Tyra, Beyoncé, and sisters going to work on the train every morning looking like movie stars.

It was a relief to see that Janet's more overt Michael mannerisms— see the smooth criminal leans in the choreography for "Miss You Much"—were to be preserved as allusions rather than building blocks. Michael had marched in front, kicking open the doors to integration-resistant organizations like MTV. Janet had the benefit of a clearer path, but hers was by no means a Saturday in the park.

———

Madonna Ciccone, with dark brown hair kicked up to platinum, stepped into 1983 with her debut, "Holiday," being promoted by Sire Records to Black radio stations. The sound of Madonna's debut album was so deeply R&B that many, including me, thought Madonna (sight unseen) was Black.

I loved "Holiday." It reminded me of songs like Aretha Franklin's "Day Dreaming," and Eddie Money's "Two Tickets to Paradise"—songs with a "hey, baby, let's get away" attitude. "Like a Virgin" was produced by Nile Rodgers. "Express Yourself" was produced by Stephen Pate Bray. Bray and Madonna co-produced "Into the Groove." All my faves.

While Jellybean Benitez is the name most associated with Madonna's emergence, Sire's first call was to Reggie Lucas when they wanted help creating music with Madonna. Lucas, who died in 2018, played with Miles Davis until he and James Mtume left to create the successful and influential band Mtume. He also co-wrote songs like Roberta Flack and Donny Hathaway's number-two pop hit, "The Closer I Get to You," and Stephanie Mills's biggest pop hit, 1980's "Never Knew Love Like This Before." Janet was set to go toe to toe, as had her brother, with a woman built in Blackness and POC imagery to be a queen of pop. Janet and Madonna were both selling millions of records, and their tours were historic. But Madonna's usage of Black, Indian, and Latin cultures was as relentless and superficial as it was successful. The "Love Will Never Do" hair also functions as a note from Janet regarding the full range of blonde ambition.

In 1994, I asked Janet if it was true that she couldn't stand Madonna. I alluded to the idea that because Janet is Black, she's perceived as capitalizing on what comes naturally—as opposed to Madonna, who gets cultural credit for intellectually creating herself.

" 'Can't stand'?" Janet asked me back, smiling. Then she rolled her eyes up to the ceiling. "How does my mom say it? If you don't have anything good to say, don't say anything at all."

Then Janet said, " 'Hate' is a strong word."

I'd never said "hate."

"But," Janet said, "if I did hate her, I'd have valid reasons."

Elizondo, for one, apparently wanted Janet to be even louder about herself. "Anybody who has been around Janet for any period of time will tell you the same thing," René said in 1990. "That she's humble to the point of fault. . . . She will not take credit for the things she is responsible for. . . . She will always say 'We did it' instead of 'I did it.' That's what we've been trying to point out to her. . . . It's the way she was brought up. I've told her, 'Part of the perception people have is your fault, because you won't tell them what you did.'"

A 1989 *New York Times* review of *Rhythm Nation* sees little but cynicism in the creation of the album—and comes off as little but cynical itself. Tellingly, Janet is mocked for being "calculated," and for her "transparent ambitions." The underlying ask is for the wildness and imprecision of a soul music with no drum machines, no keyboards, and with purely accidental appeal. *Rhythm*'s antiracism mood is written off as "convenient." We all get that pop is an evil marketing machine, but to approach a body of such elevated work with a complete disregard for its magic, and with outright disdain for its ambition—is heartbreakingly dismissive. And shortsighted.

Because our hero was on a yellow brick road to the future. "'Pleasure Principle' was basically the last song off of *Control*," according to Jimmy Jam, "and that led into what was 'Miss You Much.' I think 'Love Will Never Do,' being the last single on *Rhythm Nation,* led to *janet.* That was the transition."

Jackson began recording *janet.* two years after the Rhythm Nation World Tour, which made headlines for selling out arenas in an hour, or even minutes. And by this time Janet was so successful that A&M Records could no longer afford her. After a bidding war, it was Richard Branson who signed the check for an estimated $40 million. The deal with Virgin was announced on March 12, 1991, as the largest and the shrewdest deal in recording history.

That lasted for about one week. On March 21, it was announced that

Janet's brother Michael had renewed his contract with Sony for $65 million and an unprecedented share of profits. At the time, though, much of the industry talk was about how labels were "vesting too much importance in individual performers."

Not so much about how two siblings were the most successful pop acts in history. Not so much about how—just twenty-five years after something as basic as the Voting Rights Act was signed, and while hip hop was still being denied its true cultural standing—these children of Motown tapped the net-gain button for a combined $100 million. There was almost no place to be where Janet and Michael were not serenading. And the fascinating story of Black siblings going head to head for global domination in a recently segregated country via an industry that normalized that very segregation? It went, and still goes, virtually untold. "I've studied the best," Janet said in 1990. "Michael Jackson was just down the hall."

Michael settled with his 1993 accusers for more than $20 million. In May 1994, a Los Angeles County grand jury disbanded without handing up an indictment, and while Michael was not charged, he was not absolved. The previous December, Michael—in a normcore button-down and stagy makeup—appeared on television screens breathing like both hostage and kidnapper. "If I am guilty of *anything,*" he said, "it is of giving all that I have to give to help children all over the world. It is of loving children of all ages and races. It is of gaining sheer joy from seeing children with their innocent and smiling faces. It is of enjoying, through them, the childhood that I missed myself."

In June 1995, Michael's double album *HIStory: Past, Present and Future, Book I* was released by Sony. It featured "Scream," a duet with his sister. Her solidarity screamed that Michael was not a child abuser. He needed her desperately, and she showed up strong. It was hard to see then, but for Michael, it was the middle of the end.

Check in the mirror my friend / No lies will be told then / Pointin' the finger again

—JANET JACKSON, FROM 1998'S "YOU"

When I saw Janet Jackson in New York City the summer of 1997, she was exhausted by her relationship with Michael. We were in her suite at the Four Seasons Hotel, a hot spot for everyone from Martha Stewart to Antonio "L. A." Reid to John F. Kennedy, Jr. I was pleasantly surprised that Janet had requested me as interviewer, as she and I had not remained in touch between conversations.

Not only was this the era before people exchanged mobile numbers, this was the era before mobile. And even so, I used to think it was unprofessional to have a relationship with a subject. I'd tried it and had not experienced an upside. In my professional roles I was confident and could be ruthless. Personally, I was more of a pleaser, and I had no desire for my colleagues or interview subjects to see all that.

Were there champagne toasts with Mariah Carey on a private island off the coast of Antigua? Yes. Was I backstage with Beyoncé in Philly, in Paris, in Cleveland, in Brooklyn? All of it. Have I cruised the Upper West Side in a vintage Cadillac convertible with Queen Latifah? Yes, indeed. But, though I chalked it up to not wanting to get too close to creatives, I would have to cover as a writer or an editor—I actually did not feel worthy of such friendships. The underdog Oakland survival mentality brought me much success. It has also stunted me deeply. I was raised to believe that my happiness and accomplishments mattered little. Not only did I feel awkward, even aloof—I was distant from my own self.

Janet and I ease back into familiarity at the Four Seasons, amid the hand-knotted rugs and crisp views of Manhattan that, in the late nineties, still make me feel brand new. She tells me about having met a "cowboy in a desert" who is white, in his fifties, and full of wisdom. She considers him her "Obi-Wan Kenobi." I tell her, "We should all have one."

I ask Janet if she is feeling competitive with Michael. She says, "Yes."

I ask her if that is hard for her. She says, "No, because it's business." She says that she loves him, and that he knows that. She says, "I know he loves me. That was hard for me to come to. I didn't realize how much business it was with he and I until a few years ago."

I tell her what she already knows. That Michael is a legend in his own time. There will never be another Michael Jackson. I tell her that the Jackson right now, though, is Janet.

"The voice inside my head starts talking," says Janet, "and I ask myself, Why me? What did I do to deserve this?"

"The adulation?"

"Yes," Janet says. "I called my mom and asked her. She told me to be thankful. [Mom] says, 'Try not to question it.' I used to question it, because I felt guilty."

"Guilty for being a winner?"

Janet Jackson says she feels very guilty for being a winner. "When maybe someone else in my family wasn't doing as well as I was. There are a lot of times I would ask God, 'Why can't you make us all be on the same level? Why is one of us excelling more than the other?'"

But did she feel this way before *Control*? When Michael was Mr. MTV and Mr. *Thriller*? Did she wish everyone could be the same then?

Janet says, "No!" Like that. An exclamation.

I'm talking to the woman who, at the age of seven, opened for her brothers in a sequined gown and a boa before tens of thousands of people. I say, "You wanted to be a star." It matters to me, probably too much, to hear her intention. For her to confirm she is no accident or side project.

"Yes! I wanted to be a star!"

I, too, wanted to stand out and be lifted up for my accomplishments. A *Vibe* COO—a white woman who's name I cannot recall—said in passing to me, "Well, you're an ambitious girl, so I'm sure—" something or other, blah, blah, blah. Embarrassed, I said to her, and I was serious, "You consider me ambitious? I wouldn't say that."

The woman was about fifteen years older than me. She had a precise, shoulder-length bob that was just starting to gray. The woman wasn't a witch about it, but she laughed outright. I had not articulated real goals for myself.

I just wanted what was next. I wanted more decision-making power. I wanted Black music to win. I wanted hip hop to be forever. I wanted to depend on myself for living well. I still don't know if that adds up to proper "ambition." When Janet says, "But, I was . . . happy for Michael," I hear both respect and a desire to make him see that she is ruthless. I hear my desire for *Vibe* to win at the newsstands, to have the most and the most expensive ad pages, for our readers to be overserved with writing, photography, and design, and for *XXL, Rolling Stone, Spin,* and *The Source* to be irrelevant.

Janet tells me that when Michael was finishing up *Thriller,* he played her the album in his car, which had a "serious sound system." She says she'd never heard anything like it. She was a teenager, and she was "stoked" for him.

I ask if her brother gets excited about her work.

She says, "From what I hear, he does."

"From what you *hear*? Have you had any good talks recently?"

Janet does not respond. I ask, "Are you and Michael friends right now?"

She says, "Are we friends? Yes. Are we enemies? No. Have I spoken to him recently? It's kind of embarrassing—no, I haven't. I hate to say how long it's been since I've seen my brother. Two years. But he's on tour."

I think, *There are phones in the world.* I say, "Are you guys going to be all right?"

"Yes," she says, "It's nothing like that. . . . The last time I saw my brother, or even spoke to him, is when he was in the hospital."

In December of 1995, there was to be an HBO concert special called *Michael Jackson: One Night Only*. Even as *HIStory* struggled on the charts (after starting out at number one), HBO relentlessly publicized a global audience of 250 million. Taping was set for December 8 and 9, with the show to air December 10. At New York City's Beacon Theatre, on December 6, Michael collapsed during a rehearsal. When paramedics arrived he was given oxygen and an IV of saline and rushed to Beth Israel Medical Center.

Janet also happened to be in New York City.

"It was the night of the 1995 *Billboard* Awards," she says to me. "I was supposed to receive an award. I didn't even go to accept my award. I went straight to the hospital." Janet was to have received the prestigious Artist Achievement Award—recognition both for her overall artistic excellence and her historic *Billboard* chart accomplishments. Michael was to have received an award for his performance on the pop singles chart over the course of the year. Shaquille O'Neal accepted on Janet's behalf.

The next day, Janet's brother was diagnosed with low blood pressure. Hypotension can be caused by dehydration or low blood sugar, and it is a side effect of both OxyContin and Demerol. *One Night Only* was canceled. "I haven't seen him since then," says Janet. "I haven't spoken to him since then."

I ask if the distance between them has anything to do with their "Scream" duet. Janet, along with Michael, Jimmy Jam, and Terry Lewis share writing credit on what is essentially a rage against the press machine reporting on child abuse allegations. A descendant of Michael's "Just Leave Me Alone," the song is afire, and the siblings—cadaveric, chic, twin-like—give the camera the finger at the end of the video. It's Black and punk and united against the world. It's award-winning. It's a global pop hit.

But in the song, Janet's vocals are mixed way under Michael's. I wanted to understand how and why Michael is louder than Janet for the entire song. It bothers me still, this sonic shrinking of Janet Jackson by Michael and his team, just when Janet's stamp of loyalty was most needed. "I was wondering why I couldn't hear you," I tell Janet.

"I was wondering why you couldn't hear me," she says. "We went back after the session and put my vocal up and it sounded better. That's pretty much all I can say, because I don't know what happened. I wasn't there."

Jimmy Jam and Terry Lewis produced the record. "I mean, even when we first agreed to do the record," Jam told me in 2014, "I was like, 'Janet, are you cool with us doing this?' She said, 'No.' [Then] she said, 'It's fine.' She said, 'I want to help my brother out.' Because, at the time . . . remember, she was coming off of *janet*. She's much bigger than he is."

But it was also just the tune itself. "The song was wrong," according to Jam. "Everything was done for Michael. The song was written in his key. It was his melody. . . . We had to figure out, how are we going to make this work for Janet?"

When we spoke in 1997, Janet recalled recording her part after Michael, and not liking it.

In 2014, Jimmy Jam recalled it a bit differently. "Michael recorded his vocal at the Hit Factory in New York," he said. "Janet was supposed to record her vocal right after him. After he got done singing, she leaned over to me and she said, 'I'll do my vocal in Minneapolis.' I said Okay, no problem. Michael's like, 'Where are you guys going?'"

Jam told him they were headed west. "We do Janet's vocal in Minneapolis," Jam said. "Janet kills it. We send it to Michael. Michael goes, 'I want to come to Minneapolis and do my vocal.' *Why, Michael? Your vocal's done.* 'No, I think I can get it better.' Okay, so competitive."

Janet remembered, "He re-sang his, but his first pass had been better."

The shenanigans went on, right on through the mix. As Jam told it, "Michael said, 'We can use your engineer to mix the record.' I said, 'Michael, I don't care if my engineer mixes the record, but my engineer's got to do Janet's vocals.' We heard a version where her vocals were . . . stripped down and didn't sound right. I called Michael—'What's up with these vocals?' He said Bruce [Swedian] must have remixed it. I said, 'No, we already agreed, our engineer was going to do Janet's vocals. You don't touch Janet's vocals.' [Michael:] *That's right, I'm sorry—blah, blah, blah.*"

When the record was done and mastered, Jam, who happened to be at Neverland, got a call from Janet. She asked if he'd heard a new mix for "Scream" Michael had just sent her. He had not. Janet told Jimmy her vocal had been turned down—again. "I said, That's impossible. . . . I said, Michael's right here. Michael: 'I don't know how that could have happened.' We basically fought through . . . the whole thing, culminating with the actual video."

On set, Jam said, Janet was pissed but polite. "But in her mind, he's the older brother. He asked her to be—to do this. . . . Whenever something weird went down, she'd default to 'It's not really my record, anyway.'"

The song debuted at number five on *Billboard*'s pop chart and went even higher around the world. "I think it was the best record out," she told me. "But it didn't have anything to do with me, or anything like that."

Every pop star's run comes to an end, but in the wake of what was called Nipplegate, as opposed to Ripgate or Justingate, Jackson fell victim to a vast music-industry conspiracy.

One of Janet's accomplishments is a five-album streak of number-one pop albums: *Control, Rhythm Nation 1814, janet., The Velvet Rope,* and *All for You.* All of these albums feature multiple number-one pop songs. *Damita Jo* (2004) was released around the time of Super Bowl XXXVIII. During the game's halftime show, Justin Timberlake ripped a small shield from Janet's breast. Her nipple was exposed for literally one half of a second. The fines levied against CBS and the show's producer, MTV, were the highest in FCC history.

As *Rolling Stone* reported, "CBS and MTV's parent company Viacom, angered that an unannounced addition to the Super Bowl performance has now cost them all future halftime shows, hits back at Janet by essentially blacklisting her, keeping her music videos off their properties MTV, VH1, and radio stations under their umbrella. The blacklist spreads to include non-Viacom media entities as well. . . . Thanks to the radio and music television blacklist, *Damita Jo* underperforms compared to Janet's previous releases."

Damita went to number two on *Billboard*'s pop chart, but there were no big singles. In 2006, *20 Y.O.* was a number-two album, but there were no huge singles. *Discipline,* released in 2008, was Janet's first non-platinum album since before *Control.* In 2011, the 3rd U.S. Circuit Court of Appeals in Philadelphia ruled that the FCC was not only wrong to fine Jackson and CBS half a million dollars, but that the decision was "arbitrary and capricious."

Control is one of the most deeply imagined and well-executed concept albums in the history of recorded music. It is boldness in a bottle, the legend of a runaway child successfully living wild. The details are specific to Janet's life, but the journey is familiar to all women. And for Black women, the journey is not just toward success or enlightenment but also to freedom.

"My influence came from my family," Janet says to me over morning sushi at the Blue Ribbon. "I used to listen to Tower of Power, and *The Secret Life of Plants* . . . the classics. That's really what I had."

That can't be all. She grew up, after all, around Motown.

"I loved them all," she says of the Motown community. "I remember being a kid, and they'd come over, and you take so much for granted. . . . You're not thinking about the fact that it's Marvin Gaye over all the time, or Diana [Ross], or Smokey [Robinson]." Janet's descendants—Beyoncé, Rihanna, Ciara—they all had Janet Jackson videos to watch, over and over again. The videos helped these artists to create themselves.

Me, half thinking, and half speaking: "From where, Janet, did you pull *Control*? And *Rhythm Nation*? Who are you?"

"There were so many people that I loved," she says, "but was there a major influence, someone that I studied?" Janet Jackson answers her own question, and then literally sips tea. "No," she says. *No.*

MARIAH

The way that I am: I get pushed to a wall and then I attack.
It's a gradual process for me, because I am so cautious, and
so careful. But once you get me to that point, it's over, and I
can't turn back—that's been my defense mechanism my
whole life. I give people a chance. I would love to have
someone in my life that I trust fully. But I guess we all kind of
re-create what we saw was wrong when we were children.

—MARIAH CAREY TO DANYEL SMITH, NOVEMBER 1998

When I moved to New York in early 1993 to become R&B
editor at *Billboard*, R&B/hip hop charts director Terri
Rossi took me aside early on. Terri wore pantsuits in jewel tones. She
had an office with glass walls, and when she walked the maze of cubicles
with her smile and her random knowledge about most any staffer, I was
not alone in staring. This was when *Billboard* was at 1515 Broadway, on
Times Square. Terri was her own kind of famous, and this was my first
corporate job.

In Terri's office one morning, I told her I was going to try to get
home earlier, and to cook more, as I had in Oakland. "Lamont loves
smothered pork chops," I told Terri. "And biscuits." I waited on confirmation of this idea. Terri told me without looking up from her work
that there were not enough homemade biscuits in the world.

In 1993, I was about all musics, because I was at *Billboard*, but at
home my life was:

Salt-N-Pepa's *Very Necessary*
Whitney Houston's "I Will Always Love You"
Ice Cube and Das EFX's "Check Yo Self" remix
P.M. Dawn's "I'd Die Without You"

A Tribe Called Quest's "Award Tour"

MC Lyte's "I Cram to Understand U"

Xscape's "Just Kickin' It"

Shai's "If I Ever Fall in Love"

The cover art for Queen Latifah's *Black Reign*

Tupac's "Holler If Ya Hear Me"

Tupac's "I Get Around"

The video for Aerosmith's "Cryin'"

"Dazzey Duks" from Duice

Cypress Hill's *Black Sunday*

TLC's "What About Your Friends"

SWV's "Right Here (Human Nature Remix)"

Every single moment of *Guru's Jazzmatazz, Vol. 1*

Every single moment of Tony! Toni! Toné!'s *Sons of Soul*

Author and *Billboard* editor-in-chief Timothy White, who wrote 1983's *Catch a Fire: The Life of Bob Marley,* was presiding over the magazine and charts in the new SoundScan era, and the industry was still agog at the "new" strength of R&B, hip hop, and country. Black women truly ran the year. Minus a week here and a week there from Eric Clapton and Depeche Mode, Whitney Houston's *Bodyguard* soundtrack pretty much dominated the first half of 1993. Janet Jackson's *janet.* took over for eight weeks, and then there were brief stints at number one for U2, Cypress Hill, Garth Brooks, Pearl Jam, and Snoop Dogg. Mariah Carey's *Music Box* closed out the year with eight weeks in the number-one slot. So it was really about Mariah, Janet, and Whitney.

Tim White made it clear to me, via his pops by my cubicle, that gangsta rap was a menace, and that it made sense to cover it from that stance. Tupac's *Strictly 4 My N.I.G.G.A.Z* was offensive. As was Onyx's *Bacdafucup.* I resisted White's commentary. I'd been resisting, one way or another, since I'd written a cover story about Bay Area rap in 1989. I reported out a cover story while at *SF Weekly* about how local pop radio was broadcasting lots of rap, yet not reporting that fact to advertisers as being among the reasons the ratings were high. I'd reported out a story proving the de facto ban on hip-hop performances at Bay Area night clubs and arenas. My *SF Weekly* publisher told me, when I was music editor there, that I couldn't run a promo shot from Ice Cube's 1990 platinum *Kill at Will* EP on the opener of a back-of-the-book live music section.

"He's holding a pistol on us," *SF Weekly* publisher says.

Me: "Look at it. Truly look at it. He's *handing you the gun*. He's calmly holding it by the barrel, and handing it to you."

At *Billboard,* Terri Rossi, who was no fan of gangsta rap herself, said we should get out of the office—break bread. I met her at B. Smith's when it was on Forty-Seventh and Eighth Avenue in Manhattan. A lot of Black folks from the music industry lunched there, and when Ed Eckstine, then president of Mercury Records, stopped by the table to say hello, Terri introduced me like I was a cross between her favorite niece and Ida B. Wells. At the time, the only Black heads of major labels were Eckstine and Sylvia Rhone.

Terri told me I should go far. I tried not to be emotional about how she was lifting me. Terri told me also that in order to go far, I must avoid the classic pitfalls of women in the music industry. I recall her words as follows:

> It's easy in this business for us to fail. To get run out of town. You have to avoid the alcoholism—and it will be difficult. Because in your job . . . this one, the next one . . . you have to go out. You know this. You'll probably never have to buy yourself a drink again. You have to avoid the fat, the obesity. Everything is craft services, canapés. People will put their card down for you—breakfast, lunch, dinner—so you write about their artists. The fat will kill you. And you have to decide how you're going to conduct yourself. With regard to sleeping with men in this business. My advice is to avoid it completely. But you're going to do as you feel.

I reminded Terri I was happily married. I laughed. I'd been married for almost two years. Terri didn't miss a beat.

Life is long. And negros love to talk. Handle yourself well or . . . it'll be—not impossible, not impossible—but it'll be more difficult to get done the things you really want to get done.

One of my early *Billboard* columns was about Tag Team and their 1993 "Whoomp! (There It Is)." The author Havelock Nelson, then rap editor of *Billboard,* was shooting me side-eyes. Atlanta's Tag Team was not considered cool. But the song was my favorite, had more bass than the law allowed, and more importantly, was a number-two pop record. As I use Grammy nominee/win ratios to gauge older white music profession-als' connection with songs and artists, I use post-SoundScan-*Billboard* pop success as a strong indicator of the people's choice.

Four years later, as editor in chief of *Vibe,* my first official cover was the gospel artist Kirk Franklin. This was around the time of the 1996 "Stomp" remix featuring Cheryl James, aka Salt from Salt-N-Pepa. My CEO, Keith Clinkscales, was not alone in thinking it would be a soft cover in terms of newsstand sales. And that we were veering away from edgy, and into *Ebony* territory. He was not crazy for thinking any of these things.

My logic: the Notorious B.I.G. and Tupac Shakur are dead, and "Stomp" is the second line after the hearses. Also, previous editor-in-chief, Alan Light, who came to *Vibe* from *Rolling Stone,* had taught me that if you give your audience 70 percent of what they want, they will trust you with giving them 30 percent of what they need. I felt that Franklin was in both the 70 and the 30.

And our grouchy Time Inc. corporate director, Gil Rogin (who ran *Sports Illustrated* at its peak and launched *Vibe* with Quincy Jones), told me that when a cover story was not naturally emerging from the zeit-geist for *SI, People,* or *Time,* the trick was to choose a subject with a fa-natic fan base that feels underserved. Shit—*Vibe*'s whole fan base was underserved. But what Gil meant, and this was before nerdism broke wide, was to go with something like a glorious image of the cast of *Star Trek*.

To me, the gospel audience—evangelical, zealous—was more Trekkie-like than had been considered. The Kirk Franklin cover was a success. And it gave me the confidence in myself to do everything from hiring nontraditional creatives I thought best, to considering interns as important members of the teams, to dealing with colleagues who undermined me and/or didn't respect my taste or position or both.

I had a lot of work to do. I was told by Keith that I wasn't ready to write an editor's letter for months after I was named editor in chief. Then I was told I was too busy and had too much on my plate. Years later I was told that my *Vibe* bosses thought I was a bit too 'hood for my job—but there was really no one else as senior, or as familiar with the brand. I hadn't gone to NYU, or Columbia, or Brown. In fact, I had no college degree. I was unmoved by Basquiat. I did not view New York City as the center of the cultural universe. I could feel the energy, though, of fools feeling I was an inch too East Oakland, years before I was told.

I've written everything but the cover songs that I've done. Since the beginning.

—MARIAH CAREY, TO CHARLIE ROSE, 1999

In August 1997, I attend a Columbia Records gathering at the Royalton in Midtown, New York City. Basically the hotel's whole lobby, Bar 44 is a long, firelit lounge. People tongue-kiss over caipirinhas. Endure postwork thrashings. A disappointed hum rises from folks itching to rise fifteen floors to where life-changing things are happening.

But you can't step on the elevator without an invitation.

On the fifteenth floor, I wave at people, but mostly I stand in one place. I never was a relaxed networker. The late Andre Harrell, founder of Uptown Records, had noticed my awkwardness when he saw me buzzing around a small reception at New York's Bowery Ballroom one night.

The fuck you doing? Jesus. Find you a good spot and sit tight. You running that magazine? Or what? One of these negroes will bring what you need to know. And who you need to meet and shit. Why you running up on people? You Cali niggas funny. Get you a drink and watch the plays.

So, at the Royalton on the fifteenth floor, I'm watching the plays. Someone up front is saying something official. This is during the run-up to *Butterfly,* Mariah Carey's sixth album. Mariah is to be presented with platinum plaques for her previous album, *Daydream*. *Daydream* sold twenty million worldwide. In May 1995, Mariah announced her separation from Sony Music CEO Tommy Mottola. The buzz at the Royalton event is that Carey is coming back to Black.

This event is likely the one Sandra Bernhard referenced in a Mariah Carey joke from that era: "Now she's trying to backtrack on our asses," goes the bit. "Gettin' real niggerish up there at the Royalton Hotel suite with Puff Daddy and all the greasy, chain-wearing Black men. 'Oooh, yeah, Daddy . . . I got a little bit of Black in me, too. I didn't tell you that?' . . . Do *not* try to compete with the fierce ghetto divas. Because they will go down, in, around, and *off* on your ass!" Bernhard is also known for saying that Carey is "only Black when it helps her sell music." Which denies Carey her authenticity and humanity, and is also a super-rich comment, considering that the statement could be a motto for many white recording artists over the course of history.

At the Royalton, I see a guy. Guy sees me. Guy introduces himself— full name, no company or title. He looks familiar, but the room is shadowy, and he's standing too close for sharp focus. I introduce myself—full name, no company or title. The no-title thing does double duty. It's meant to convey that each of us should know who the other is. And meant to convey that not every interaction is or has to be completely about business. We're both smiling. Signaling: I see you. I'd been divorced over two years.

I am working and I am curious. Guy looks like he could be running a bar at any Nikki Beach. Looks like he could be holding down any Brooklyn corner. He also looks like he was a cog sci major at Williams College. So. We talk. But he keeps an eye on the front of the room, like he's waiting for a specific thing to happen.

Me: "Mariah fan?"

Guy, with big energy: "Big Mariah fan."

I don't say it, but I'm a big fan of Mariah's, especially her midtempo projects. The agility of her voice, the vocal arrangements, the bright emotion. I'm a Mariah fan for 1993's "Dreamlover" video, when Mariah goes up, up and away in her beautiful balloon. I'm a fan of the 1995 remix of "Fantasy" featuring Ol' Dirty Bastard (and the sample from Tom Tom Club's 1981 "Genius of Love"). For the remix, producer Puffy Combs loops from the low end. During my high-school-dance era, it was the part that sent us into a sweaty frenzy.

When Mariah was shut out of the 1996 Grammys, my fanship solidified. Carey was up for Best Female Pop Vocal Performance for "Fantasy." She was up for Album of the Year for *Daydream*. And, with Boyz II Men, she was nominated for Record of the Year and Best Pop Collaboration with Vocals for "One Sweet Day." "Always Be My Baby" was nominated for Best Female R&B Vocal Performance. Nominated for six awards, Carey did not win one.

As music editor of *Vibe* at the time, I was at Los Angeles's Shrine Auditorium that February afternoon. Mariah and the Boyz opened with "One Sweet Day." The guys walked onstage in white shawl-collar dinner jackets. Carey floated out in a full, black, floor-length skirt and a sparkly black corset tank. When she hit the high notes, she made all the gawky hand gestures that we used to mock her for. When Carey and Wanya Morris sing together—Morris had removed his sunglasses and had them in hand—the performance was better than the recorded song.

And it was a victory lap. It was not just that *Daydream* was on its way to selling over twenty million copies, and that Mariah was on her path to being second only to the Beatles in terms of number-one singles. It wasn't just that Carey and Boyz II Men, at the time of the Grammy performance, were sitting on the new milestone of most consecutive weeks at *Billboard* number one for "One Sweet Day." It was also that Boyz II Men's 1992 "End of the Road" broke a record set in 1956 by Elvis Presley's "Don't Be Cruel." This, along with the way hip hop was clawing its way onto pop radio playlists, was a cannonball landing on America's pop canon. Yes, it was a competitive year. But for Carey to lose six of six Grammys on such a huge album in such a huge year—it was a shaming.

In June 2008, when I arrive at Eagles Landing in Jumby Bay, Antigua, it's for a Mariah Carey *Vibe* cover story being written by Shanel Odum. Outside of seeing Paul McCartney jogging on the beach with a bodyguard, the first person I recognize is Nick Cannon. He's beautiful in a white tank and a light sweat. This is before they were out as a couple. Though they were playing platonic, speculation is rampant, and the energy between them was fire.

"Dan-*yel!*" Mariah yells out, flute of champagne in hand. It's both a call for me to relax like she knows I can relax, and an appreciated confirmation of my role in the room. It's my shoot, at her villa, and she loves it.

Me and Mariah met via the event at the Royalton. The guy with the big energy, who kept watching the front of the room—we lightweight stayed in touch. And I'd kept my ear to the ground about him. The Guy knew everyone who was anyone.

So, in August 1998, when Wyclef Jean pulled a gun on an editor I was working with—an incident Jean denies happened—I called Guy and asked him to speak to Wyclef on my behalf. To let him know, frankly, that he needed to stop. The call itself would let Wyclef know that I had friends.

Guy did me this solid. I remember he said, "My question is, why did you reach specifically to me for this favor?" It was because I knew that some people who deal in violent worlds have a specific stance, and Guy had that stance. It's not fearlessness, or even bravery. It involves charm. And awareness of backup. But mostly it's a predisposition to crisis management. This last one I see in myself.

In Oakland, the boys I liked road-managed rap groups, or rode fluorescent Ninjas at ninety miles an hour on long stretches of predawn highway. So maybe I was a little 'hood for my role. I do know I knew who to call. And I called Guy again when I needed to get to Mariah Carey. At the time, I'd never met Mariah. And my best Columbia Records contact was not feeling me. In June of 1998, I'd made a deal for Wyclef to cover *Vibe*'s August 1998 issue. As it was coming together, I kept staring at the cover image of him leaping, with a guitar, in a cowboy hat. I got the coldest of feet.

We were close to the end of production, and my gut told me the cover was going to tank. When they passed by the mock pages, the mood of the *Vibe* staff was iffy at best. And my boss, Keith, didn't like the Wyclef cover either.

So I told my publicist contact at Columbia that I needed to get a Lauryn Hill interview done right away—for another issue. I was not telling the truth. Our idea was to crash in a Lauryn cover as a split. "Wyclef Rocks" was one cover. "How Lauryn Rolls" was the other. Karen Good did the interview and wrote the story. We found an amazing image of Hill and got through editing, fact-checking, and copyediting in maybe forty-eight hours. The golden Lauryn cover carried us to victory. And is the cover everyone remembers.

It's possible that Wyclef, in addition to being mad at a bad Canibus album review in *Vibe*'s more youthful brother magazine, *Blaze,* had ill feelings toward *Vibe* when he pulled that gun. Wyclef co-executive-produced Canibus's much-anticipated debut.

So while Columbia had good reason to keep me on punishment, I knew Guy had access to Carey's business, because when he finally did step away for a moment at the fall 1997 Royalton event, he returned with four teenagers, who he quietly introduced to me as Beyoncé, Kelly, LeToya, and LaTavia. They'd signed to Columbia a few months before. They were teenagers. Though I'd just met Guy, he leaned over and whispered something to the effect of "Mariah specifically asked that this group not attend this event."

Me: "Okay, so why are they here then?"

Guy: "Tommy suggested I bring them here. Just to fuck with her."

I glanced at the girls. Beyoncé might have been sixteen. You could see it, though. The future.

We never had even met Mariah until I think it was . . . the [1999] Rainbow album. And that was because, for whatever reason, she said she'd always wanted to work with us. And for some reason, Tommy Mottola didn't. I think Mottola just wasn't a fan of ours . . . I was a little reluctant to work with [Mariah], because I enjoyed her, but I wasn't a fan. . . . I didn't feel like, I want her to sing my songs. . . . So when we actually met—she came with the . . . big entourage and the whole deal, private jet . . . I was like, Here we go. And then we actually got in the studio with her. . . . She was the most focused, savvy—particularly savvy. She knew her way around the hook like nothing else. Like . . . you would go to a chord, and she'd go, "No, that's not going to work for Top 40." Or you'd put a beat in and she'd go, "No, the hip-hop crowd won't like that." . . . She was so aware of who her audience was . . . what they wanted, what they expected, and what she wanted it to be. I turned into the biggest Mariah fan, me and Terry [Lewis] both, and I still am to this day. She . . . doesn't come across the way we know her in public . . . as very kind of lightweight, and . . . a diva. . . . She's not like that. In the studio, she's absolutely not like that at all.

—JIMMY JAM TO DANYEL SMITH, 2016

The Guy that brought young Destiny's Child to Mariah's platinum-plaque extravaganza at the Royalton—I called him and told him I needed to speak to Mariah. Like, right now I needed to speak to her.

Guy: "Why?"

"Why would I tell you why?"

"Because you're asking for a number."

"Do you have it?"

"You know I have it. How would I not have it. It's why you're calling me."

"It's a cover."

"Whoa."

"I know you're friends with her enemies."

[Laughs] "I have no friends. Mariah has no enemies."

He gives me Mariah's mobile number. I'm asked to not say how I got it. I call it. I have no speech prepared. I tell her who I am. That I am from *Vibe*. I make my pitch. She sounds bored.

Mariah: "Listen, I'm in a weird place. Like, geographically. You could never get here. But if you can get here I'll talk to you. But it's remote."

"Where?

She tells me she's in a super-unknown spot called Sonoma County, California.

What. Remote?

I'm from Oakland. I've been to Sonoma County many a time.

I tell my boss, Keith, I have Mariah. Keith puts me on a flight first class to SFO. No luggage. I leave the office. Get my interview.

And once I got it, Columbia *had* to work with me with regard to photos Mariah told me they owned, which would definitely work for the *Vibe* cover. As she told me that night, over too many glasses of merlot:

"I've always had this very . . . I don't want to call it ambitious, but an anxious state of being. Like, if I don't do *this,* then maybe something will go wrong. Like, maybe I better do this . . . if you know what I mean."

Oh yes, Mariah Carey. I know just what you mean.

OUTRO

I'll run away tomorrow
They don't mean me no good
I'm gonna run away
Hafta leave this neighborhood
—AS WRITTEN AND RECORDED BY GERTRUDE "MA RAINEY" PRIDGETT

his project. It was difficult to begin. It has been a long and uphill journey. And like a climb where you know every new plateau will be even more sunlit and blossom-rich than the last, it has been hard to stop. I want to keep going.

You have arrived here with me, at this "ending," with Mariah, so you know that music connects everything and is connected to everything in my life. At this moment: The late morning is cool in Los Angeles. I'm seated in a leafy patch of Venice that's near, but not on, the beach. When we were kids, my sister and I would ride through this 'hood on our bikes. It was different then:

The music booming from storefronts is L.T.D. and Rose Royce. Natalie Cole and Diana Ross. With ashy ankles and sun on my face, I hear the song to which I'll walk down the aisle. I hear songs that will be sampled by artists I'll write about for a living, and for the love. The Venice air is stank with ginkgo fruit and exhaust fumes. I am a sponge and a magnet, and everything—fallen palm fronds, not enough money for Fatburger—makes me feel a way. I am half on the run, and half free. I'm pedaling as fast as I can.

Now I ask you to blink once, and slowly. And see me in Venice, four decades later. The ginkgo remains redolent. My sister is now a popular

elementary school teacher with her own two genius teenagers who think their Aunt Dany makes boss grilled cheese sandwiches and plays music too loud and profane for her age. After decades in Oakland, New York, and Washington, D.C., I ride my bike through here again. Music still booms from souvenir stores, people's cars—and now, my earbuds. All of it feeds me. And the connections in music, like a map in murky times, comfort a girl who is finally telling her own stories with the kind of passion and rigor she has been telling the stories of others.

My fave playlist—which my husband named "K-DNY"—serves up Martha Wash singing *the music is my life* on "Gonna Make You Sweat (Everybody Dance Now)." And so my brain jumps to *My Life* being the name of Mary J. Blige's 1994 sophomore album. The second single from *My Life* is "I'm Goin' Down," which is a cover of Rose Royce's 1976 "I'm Going Down," which was on the soundtrack to the motion picture *Car Wash,* which was produced entirely by Norman Whitfield, who produced "Cloud Nine" and "Papa Was a Rollin' Stone," truly the most riveting songs from the Temptations, half of whom were originally called the Primes and inspired a girl group called the Primettes who changed their name to the Supremes, a culture-shifting trio of Black women from which Diana Ross emerged as the blueprint for Black women in pop. The Supremes' story is the inspiration for *Dreamgirls* (1981 Broadway production and 2006 film), and for both versions of *Sparkle* (1976 and 2012). The Supremes are the model for, among others, the Pointer Sisters, Sister Sledge, En Vogue, TLC, SWV, 702, Xscape, Total, and Destiny's Child. From Destiny's Child emerges Beyoncé. So you see how my mind works. And the beginnings of why Diana Ross is on the cover of this book.

I did not, at the Mariah Carey Royalton celebration I write about in the last chapter of *Shine Bright,* imagine the many revolutions of the genius Beyoncé Knowles Carter. I didn't foresee the strength of her light. Even after the giant sparkler that is her 2003 "Crazy in Love" debut—the hot pants, the silky tank top, that high-heeled walk down that alley and into history—I did not foresee the earthquake of "Formation" at Coachella in 2018.

"Formation" is the headline, and I get it. When Beyoncé sings *I grind 'til I own it!* I see a crystallization of Diana and Whitney and Tina and Janet. I even see Mahalia collecting driftwood from the Mississippi River. I hear the ferocity of a woman who hails from a space ("Texas Bama") that is literally erasing, right now, slavery from its history books. Beyoncé is the personification of difficult lessons well learned. She is a sponge and a magnet and a maker. "Formation" is a miracle merge of lyrics, vocals, dance, justice work, and placing women way on top. And as in the video for "Crazy in Love," Beyoncé's festival strut is discipline-crisped confidence. But even with all this being said about Beyoncé and her dancers' performance of "Formation" at Coachella, it's actually Beyoncé's Coachella entrance for me. To paraphrase her lyrics, Bey's cocky is indelibly fresh.

She is the first Black woman to headline the Coachella Valley Music and Arts Festival, which takes place in the Colorado Desert of California in a city called Indio, which is the Spanish word for "Indian," but I'll stop this toponymy thread because this really is the outro of *Shine Bright* and I must stop writing, at least for now. But suffice it to say, the ironies are many and mountainous. And only add to the glory of Beyoncé gliding to the sound of her own HBCU band playing the last and horny bars of Con Funk Shun's 1977 "Ffun." It's a number-one R&B hit from a Black band from Vallejo, California. A classic cookout jam sampled by West Coast artists like Ice Cube and DJ Quik and so, yes: there's some stomp in her glide. There is a reclamation of the desert. Beyoncé is talking to us on multiple levels, and the subtexts aren't even really that sub.

She's actually super literal when as a part of her entrance, Beyoncé breaks out with the first verse of "Lift Every Voice and Sing." To a Coachella audience that is typically less than 5 percent Black, Beyoncé sings our Black national anthem in slow motion. This is the woman whose husband, Shawn "Jay-Z" Carter, was told in 2008 that he should not headline Europe's largest and most beloved music festival. "Glastonbury has a tradition of guitar music," said Oasis's Noel Gallagher. "And . . . I'm not having hip hop at Glastonbury. It's wrong."

So Beyoncé's Coachella entrance occurred ten years after Jay-Z was treated with such disrespect. Beyoncé's Coachella set occurred three years after Sandra Bland was found hanging in a Texas jail cell after an unnecessary traffic stop. Beyoncé stomped into Coachella two years before the murder of George Floyd, as he begged for his life, by a police officer in Minneapolis. As a part of her Coachella entrance, Beyoncé reminded everybody—in perfect pitch and in vivid historically Black costume—to march on, until victory is won.

This is why I want to keep writing. The facts of Black women creating music is everything to me. I want to never stop thinking about when and where these women enter. Paula Giddings's 1984 *When and Where I Enter: The Impact of Black Women on Race and Sex in America* has inspired me throughout my entire career, and through the making of *Shine Bright.* I'm so grateful for Giddings's work, which, along with the rest of my amazing homemade curriculum, made me feel so educated through my twenties and thirties. I was without a college degree until the age of thirty-eight, yet Giddings's work gave me the courage to think about when and where I enter. That Black girl on the bicycle who grew up to be the first Black and first woman editor in chief of *Vibe.*

I already hear questions from fans of the women who are not, in big ways, in *Shine Bright. Sis, where are* my *faves? Where is your fairness? Why her? Where's ya taste?* As a writer, editor, producer, and now a podcast creator and host, my work has been about answering questions about my choices. It's hard, but I have practice doing it. What's more difficult is when the questions are about my own story. *Why her?* Exactly. Why me.

Why, for example, did I leave out that I played flute for eight years? Or that I used to usher at concerts before I could pay to get in, or enter with press tickets? Where's the story of the editor who pressed his fingers into my wrist after he manipulated a situation so I was the last to be dropped off after a work event? Where is the story of the male rapper who calmly inserted himself between me and a male boss of mine who was aggressively trying to Walk Me to My Hotel Room. Where are my stories about running around with Digital Underground, and going to Oakland diners with Tupac Shakur? What about the times I interviewed Queen Latifah in Manhattan, Foxy Brown in Miami, Simone

Biles in Qatar, Wesley Snipes that time here in Venice, California? Did I miss the part where my husband and I don't have children, and the many whys of that stark fact?

Where are my stories about covering the murder rate in Oakland in the late eighties? My memories of talking to a white bar owner in Emeryville about the politics and unwritten policies of segregated drinking spaces. What about 2012 when I was in Paris with my husband, backstage with Jay-Z and Beyoncé and Spike Lee and Gwyneth Paltrow for the *Watch the Throne* dates at what was then called Palais Omnisports de Paris-Bercy. On one of those Paris nights there was a celebration for *Throne* producer Hit-Boy's birthday. Ell and I walked into the after-/birthday party like we were Lorraine Bracco and Ray Liotta going in through Copacabana's kitchen in *Goodfellas.*

There are so many connections in this map of music and of my life in it. My husband, Elliott, was with Jay-Z that day in Glastonbury. There were credible threats to Jay's safety. Ell—who since 2016 is chief content officer at TIDAL, and before that was the longtime editor in chief of the hip-hop magazine *XXL*—was there as a journalist. But as my hub has said to me, "In that moment, we all felt like Jay's security."

So there were the real security guards, some friends, label people, and Elliott. They all walked with Jay to the stage in a loose huddle. The performance was epic. Jay placed an American flag on the mic. Elliott was on assignment for *Vibe,* where I was editor in chief. I still work with and/or am friends with so many of the creatives who worked on that historic fifteenth-anniversary edition of *Vibe.* One of our cover lines was "This is what it looks like."

"It" is American culture. And if it's American music culture? It's Black. As the team says about my podcast, *Black Girl Songbook:* it's the place where Black women in music receive the credit we are due—and sometimes I'm the Black girl in the songbook.

Gladys Knight is a hero of mine. I imagine her often, singing at her Mount Moriah church, which in turn takes my heart back to the days I spent with my friend Dianita, who was bussed to our John Burroughs

Junior High School from her Watts neighborhood. Dianita and I wore longish skirts for whole weekends because we almost never left her church, where women didn't wear trousers, and choirs were never not singing.

In the rec room downstairs at the church I ate piles of potato rolls. Cold cucumber in Wish-Bone Italian. Chicken legs baked in Wish-Bone Italian. I walked outside with Dianita, pear cake on a napkin, just to watch men smoke. Just to watch women in cars with the doors open, crocheting, listening to the service from crackly outdoor speakers. At Dianita's church I went to funerals of people I didn't even know. Leaned for hours on forward pews, clapping and caught up. White-gloved ushers passed us tangerines. White-gloved ushers held trays with paper cones of water. We needed it all. We were thrilled and exhausted by the music.

On May 19, 1979, there was an event at Dianita's church billed as "The Living Gospel Young People's Choir Presents a Musical Concert." A tenor named LaFayette was on lead as the choir sang "God Is Not Dead." The song was written by composer and educator Dr. Margaret Pleasant Douroux, who toured with Mahalia Jackson, and the choir sang that one song for what had to be an hour. The zealous dare of the *if-God-is-dead* lyric had me wound up and empty of argument. As I would with that autumn's "Rapper's Delight," I wrote down the gospel by hand, memorized it, and still know it. I still have the program from that May 1979 night. My ballpoint is faded but I wrote in: "LaFayette's song." He must have stood out. Or he must have been my friend.

I was in need of friends. Because if the duplex on Hi Point Street was a bomb, the wick was blazing, and as much as I loved being at Dianita's church, it functioned as an escape from my real life. My other ways of avoiding home included staying late at my junior high school, pretending to anyone who asked that I needed tutoring. I was always on the run from the aggression of my mother's lawyer-but-not-a-lawyer boyfriend, Alvin, and the toxic passivity of everyone else. Me and my sister were in pain as we crisscrossed Los Angeles's Miracle Mile, walking the long way home.

For my mother and Alvin, I fabricated band practice (the flute!) so I had "reasons" for being late back to that hellish Hi Point duplex after school. It was easy to lie about band rehearsal because I loved band. I'd been reading music since I was seven or eight, and it was clubby in that big airy room where we all knew this musical language. And Mr. Cooper—so decent from behind his conductor's podium—loved to lead us through Chuck Mangione's 1977 "Feels So Good." Mocked by critics as vapid, the composition optimism was a salve on my soul.

The seventies and even the early eighties were one of the many times in the United States when jazzy instrumentals held the country's imagination. In my girlhood these songs were featured as themes on television shows like my favorites *Sanford and Son* (Quincy Jones, 1972) and *Taxi* (Bob James, 1978). I felt a part of the world in Cooper's class. And woodwinds sat up front. I recall no faces or names from my row, but there was coziness among us.

Alvin came up to John Burroughs because he'd overheard kids on Hi Point Street, the Crispy Critters, talking about our "Ninth Grade Court," a strip of playground with benches and umbrellas for the "seniors." He'd repeatedly told me this "court" was "exclusionary." Alvin walked on the playground at the end of that day. It was right after band, my last class of the day. I had not been successful hiding my joy: Alvin knew I loved band.

I was standing there on the playground with my friends. We were fresh off making music together—playing Herb Alpert and Herbie Hancock. My sister, Quel, was standing next to me, but I've forgotten what we were doing, and I doubt I'll ever remember.

I caught the last of Alvin's heaving march toward the group of us. He hadn't brushed his teeth. Drunk Alvin berated a trembling horseshoe of kids for their snobbery. Alvin interrogated me about what? The rules and regulations of the Ninth Grade Court? My constant lies about my whereabouts? And then he slapped me down to the playground of my school in front of everyone.

Old black bubble gum flattened hard into gray ground. That's what I remember because my face was on it. I was vaguely aware of the kids around me. A few students were frozen with shock. A few defied Alvin with stares. Somebody finally ran for a yard teacher.

Alvin demanded my bus pass. Told me I could *Walk! Get home however you get home.* I had my flute case in hand. Alvin snatched Quel by the arm and stomped off with her. At the age of twelve she looked ten. He was talking to himself and to her as they walked away. I was failing my sister. But I knew then I had to go.

That night plays out in my memory like a silent film. Manic and jerky and Scott Joplin backing. Intertitles in all caps—IF I DIE RIGHT NOW NO ONE WOULD CARE—in my own hand. I never played the flute part of Joplin's "The Entertainer" with assurance, and it's why I love the song so much. I can hear what makes it difficult, and I heard its high short notes in my head all night. I hear it often even now, in my dreams. I still want to hit hard those short high bursts of sound. I want truly to rest in the rests. But I don't recall the last time I played a song on the flute. Some things, you just put down.

I stayed out until morning, mostly on the campus of UCLA, trying to blend with students on Westwood's clean streets. I was acting weird in a Baskin-Robbins, and a girl, or it could have been a boy, offered me ice cream. When the retail shops closed, I rode the bus. Pamela, one of the defiant kids—I think I knew her from student government—had given me a dollar or maybe it was five dollars when I stood up from the ground. So I didn't need my confiscated bus pass. My friend Taylor had been on the playground that day, too, near Pamela, and he offered to hold my flute. Taylor and I have remained off-and-on long-distance friends for forty years, and at the age of twenty we talked about marriage. But Taylor and I have never, that I recall, spoken about that day on the playground. He must know how ashamed I was. Taylor's family was so kind to me back in those times.

I understand from my sister that my mother and grandmother were worried when I was gone that night. Undone, even. It didn't seem so, to me. I would speak only to my grandmother, and she and I negotiated my return home. My grandmother: detached but trustworthy. Me, in a preview of the rest of my life: disoriented by depression, coolly desperate, goal-driven, and methodical. My mother's first words to me, in the front seat of her Monte Carlo: "What's up, Runaway?"

Within that arch tone is relief. Is the tic she has of chuckling in the face of despair. Is irritation at the fact that I'd made myself more important than our routines of hate and belittling and explosion and explanation. Is a desire to put things back as they had been before the playground slap-down, before she couldn't go to art school because my sister and I were born, before whatever traumatized her, scarred her, before my grandmother became a widow with two daughters under the age of seven, before the coming decades looked as if they might have more room for me than makes her comfortable—and that I might have nerve enough to make demands of this new world.

I recall no music from the morning of my return from the streets of Westwood and the exhausted vigilance of staying mostly awake on a public bus overnight. I was fourteen and suddenly a whole adult with the realization that no one would be swooping in, as the Supremes sing, to see about me.

And so I say thank you for the food, water, and shelter, for the beautiful life I lived until I was ten and began to have boobs and friends and ideas of my own. That careful part of my upbringing—with the blackberries and the kumquats and the Big Wheel—gives me solace every day of my life. Me and my sister remember it to each other like a movie only the two of us have ever seen.

Keyshia Cole's 2005 debut single, "I Changed My Mind," is the tale of a young Oakland woman deciding she is *done* done, and is going to leave a man she loves. But the song rings off because Keyshia sings it like she has changed her mind about everything. There's hesitation in some of the lyrics—in that, *I don't know!* But the big energy of the record is that if you are not going to encourage my creativity, if I am not going to feel reciprocity, if you are not going to help me on my journey to becoming well-known for my talent and hard work, well then, I will make my own way.

And that is all of us Black women, from Phillis Wheatley to Ma Rainey to Jody Watley to Donna Summer to Keyshia Cole to Nicki Minaj to Rihanna to Cardi B. It's this relentless drive to keep going and doing and building and naming and singing and designing and arranging and playing and conducting and managing and leading and drinking water and mothering and aunting and helping and contributing and running for office and for health and doing squats and giving flowers and receiving flowers and rehearsing and writing and working. There is this deep fear of stopping. Of resting in the rests. I didn't and still don't want to stop writing this book.

Because if we stop, we will be forgotten. That is the fear. And it's not an irrational fear, because so many Black women and so much of Black women's work is undervalued and strategically un-remembered. We cannot sit quietly while everyone dresses like us and sings like us and writes like us and just kind of steals us from ourselves. That's the part that makes us tired. But what's even more heartbreaking than that is the thought that people may not truly know us, or the details of our lives. What if no one ever gets us right? What if our spirits and stories are never truly known? It could so easily be that we—except for our songs, our art, our children—were never here at all.

But we can't keep living like that—or, at least, I can't. Always vigilant, waiting on the other shoe. Waiting on that person to slap me or snatch me out of my own story. Waiting on somebody to apologize, or say, "Here, girl, is your honorable mention." Nope. Not anymore. Here's a truth: waiting on that other shoe does not stop it from dropping. We gotta shine bright. We gotta also rest our minds and souls and voices and pens. Our lives and work dazzle and beam for eternity. We gonna keep being we.

I have written about this moment on the playground and this era so many times. From my childhood and adult journals through my first novel, *More Like Wrestling,* to countless creative writing class exercises, to now, in *Shine Bright.* I have allowed that afternoon to rule large parts of my life—this idea that whenever I want something, or love something, or whenever I am good at something, it will be taken from me, with gleeful violence, and it will not be spoken of ever.

Well, I am done with it now. I have to be. One, I'm way in my fifties. And also: I must make space in my brain to write about things I have left out of *Shine Bright.* I must make space, period, for things I have not allowed to be big in my own life. It has taken me this long, though, to make any of this so. I am tired of living the story of that playground, and everything for which it is a metaphor. I have therapy. I have my bus pass (of a sort). And my flute (it's a pen, but still!). I have friends who will defy fools on my behalf. I have my sister and my husband and an awesome family. I have music.

And it feels, actually, so good.

GRATITUDE

My editor, Christopher Jackson, is a genius. He constantly reminds me of my strengths, and without his guidance and attention this book would not have included my own stories. Without my agent, Ayesha Pande, who sees beyond what I see, this book might not exist at all. Far more than an attorney, the brilliant Jacqueline Sabac is an inspirer of imaginations. The writer and researcher Sabrina Ford not only functioned as fact checker for *Shine Bright,* her enthusiasm sustained me. Donovan Ramsey was with me as a research assistant when this book was a whole other book—and even as he became an author himself, Donovan never stopped pushing me to go deep, and to finish strong. So many people have helped me. So many people talked to me and encouraged me. Many spoke on the record about their lives and work. Many spoke off the record. While some interviews are not included in this volume, your conversations helped me see our creativity more clearly, and I thank you.

I am grateful to my family. My parents, Janelle and Reginald Jones. My other parents, Berta and Elliott Wilson, Sr. My sister, Raquel Smith, brother-in-law Christopher Beene, niece Parker Williams, and nephew Hunter Williams. Nicole Jones. My aunt Victoria Jones, and Calvin Synigal. Brandon Jones and his family. Damaris and family. Gail

Brooms. Marjorie Brooms. Khalief Brooms and her family. Amorette Brooms and her family. My great-aunt Betty Reid-Soskin and her family. My brother-in-law Steven Wilson. My brother-in-law Kenneth Wilson and his family. My godparents, Cherry Carter and Robert D. Carter. My goddaughter Lenox Cecelia Wiggins, and her parents, Danielle and Jonathan Wiggins. Educators (ret.) Rose Lutjen-Larson and Linda Walsh of St. Mary's Academy. I'm grateful for the memory of my grandmother Lottie Charbonnet Fields, and the memory of my great-grandparents Lottie and Dorson Charbonnet, and Dorothy Balugo. Grateful for the memory of my great-aunt Vivian Allen and my play aunts, Louise Latimore and Mary Fletcher. Grateful for the memory of my cousins, Thurman Brooms and Pedro Balugo.

There is also:

Sylvia Rhone and her family
Shawn "Jay-Z" Carter and Beyoncé Knowles Carter
Candi Castleberry
Karen Good Marable and Maurice Marable
Ileana Lagares and Benjamin Meadows-Ingram
Kevin Merida
Kelley L. Carter
Justin Tinsley
Aaron Dodson
David Dennis, Jr.
Joe Caramanica
Sean Fennessey

I am grateful for my memories of Patches, and Rose, and Alto.

NOTES

INTRO

xx **"The men and the women answering each other"** Marcus Rediker, *The Slave Ship: A Human History* (New York: Penguin, 2007), p. 287.

xx **"We have no Property"** "Africans in America," Public Broadcasting Service.

xxv **"because of her progressive ideas, commitment to social change"** Kani Saburi Ayubu, "The Phillis Wheatley Monument," *Black Art Depot Today,* Feb. 1, 2013.

THE DIXIE CUPS

6 **"only such facility available to African American children"** "Rosenwald Center to Be Demolished," statement from the office of New Orleans Mayor Mitch Landrieu, Jan. 7, 2013.

20 **A jury awarded the Dixie Cups** Matt Reynolds, "EMI Sued for Dixie Cups' 'Iko Iko' Royalties," Courthouse News Service, July 25, 2017, www.courthousenews.com.

LEONTYNE + DIONNE + CISSY

32 **"unofficial anthem of those trying to stamp out AIDS"** Ron Givens, "Artists Raise Money for AIDS," *Entertainment Weekly,* updated Apr. 13, 1990.

34 **"It was a musical family"** *Mojo* magazine, Oct. 2012.

42 **"There was a cousin who was a drinker"** Cissy Houston, The National Visionary Leadership Project, oral history, 2008.

43 **"I never let people know I listened"** Mahalia Jackson with Evan McLeod, Wylie, *Movin' On Up* (New York: Hawthorn Books, 1966), p. 36.

48 **"We used to sit and say"** Steve Hochman, "Mom Can Carry a Pretty Mean Tune," *Los Angeles Times,* Feb. 28, 1995.

49 **Estelle Brown says** "Elvis Presley Estelle Brown Sweet Inspirations Backup Singer Interview," Spa Guy, YouTube, Feb. 10, 2020.

50 **Cissy mimics her Inspirations** Cissy Houston, The National Visionary Leadership Project.

50 **Estelle Brown was clear** *This Time,* 2012.

52 **"When we finished rehearsing"** Cissy Houston, The National Visionary Leadership Project.

53 **"[She] taught me how to sing"** Danyel Smith, "When Whitney Hit the High Note," *ESPN The Magazine,* Feb. 1, 2016.

MISS ROSS

57 **"We were poor"** Diana Ross interview, *Parkinson,* BBC, 1981.

58 **"I guess [it's] being a second child"** *The Barbara Walters Special,* ABC, Nov. 29, 1978.

58 **"breaking windows, burning crosses"** Thomas J. Sugrue, "A Dream Still Deferred," Op-Ed, *New York Times,* Mar. 26, 2011.

58 **In 1978, when describing** *The Barbara Walters.*

58 **"I was very influenced by windows"** Jill Hamilton, "Q&A: Diana Ross," *Rolling Stone,* Nov. 13, 1997.

63 **"Diana Ross really went"** "Behind the Scenes," Bonus Materials, *Lady Sings the Blues* [DVD], produced by Paramount, Feb. 23, 2021.

64 **"The drug problem"** Diana Ross interview, *Parkinson.*

65 **"Disco music was black music"** Hadley Meares, edited by Sam Dresser, "The Night When Straight White Males Tried to Kill Disco," *Aeon,* Feb. 28, 2017.

65 **"We were not raised by nannies"** Barbara Hoffman, "How Diana Ross' Daughter Learned Her Dad Was Berry Gordy," *New York Post,* May 2, 2015.

GLADYS

78 **"Miss Fitzgerald is the epitome"** Randy Cordova, "Diva Salutes Diva," *The Arizona Republic,* Oct. 19, 2006.

81 **Gladys recalls her mother** *Tavis Smiley,* PBS, Sept. 16, 2006.

82 **"for African Americans"** "Top Hat Club/Club Beautiful/Royal Peacock," sweetauburn.us/peacock.htm, accessed July 1, 2021.

86 **"We got intricate with our dream"** *Tavis Smiley,* PBS, Sept. 16, 2006.

90 **"She went to Motown"** "Bubba Knight of Gladys Knight & The Pips Talks with Tom about His Family's Musical History," interview with Tom Meros, YouTube, July 1, 2014.

91 **"Motown wanted everything"** Trevor Anderson, "Rewinding the Charts: In 1973, Gladys Knight & The Pips Took the 'Midnight Train' to No. 1," *Billboard,* Oct. 27, 2017.

91 **"I filed away the song"** Marc Myers, "Anatomy of a Song: 'Midnight Train to Georgia,'" *Wall Street Journal,* Aug. 8, 2013.

DONNA

102 **"I grew up with a very good outlook"** Elliot Mintz, "The Penthouse Interview: Donna Summer," *Penthouse,* July 1979, transcript available at http://www.donnasummer.it/interview.html.

102 **"I went to school with"** Mikal Gilmore, "Donna Summer: Is There Life After Disco?" *Rolling Stone,* Mar. 23, 1978, available online dated May 17, 2012.

103 **"He was a real dominating father"** Mintz, "The Penthouse Interview."

103 **"Basically, Donna Summer was"** Richard Buskin, "Moroder: What a Feeling," *Studio Sound,* Oct. 1997, available at https://worldradiohistory .com/Archive-All-Audio/Archive-Studio-Sound/90s/Studio-Sound-1997 -10.pdf.

107 **"I'd suggested doing a sexy song"** Angus MacKinnon, "Der Munich Mensch Machine—Giorgio Moroder," *New Musical Express,* Dec. 9, 1978.

111 **"There's more to me"** Gilmore, "Donna Summer: Is There Life After Disco?"

112 **"I had three bodyguards"** Soledad O'Brien interview with Donna Summer, *American Morning,* CNN, Oct. 22, 2003, transcript available at http://edition.cnn.com/TRANSCRIPTS/0310/22/ltm.17.html.

113 **"People don't give her enough"** Degen Pener, "How Donna Summer and Barbra Streisand's Famous Duet 'Enough Is Enough' Came Together," *Hollywood Reporter,* May 18, 2012.

113 **"[This all] comes from"** Mintz, "The Penthouse Interview."

MARILYN + PEACHES

119 **"Some bands have pop voices"** *Delaware State News,* Apr. 2, 2016.

120 **"They had problems categorizing us"** Mark Mussari, "Marilyn McCoo

and Billy Davis, Jr.: The 5th Dimension Belong in the Rock and Roll Hall of Fame," *Pop Entertainment* (blog), Apr. 17, 2020.

STEPHANIE + THE WIZ

142 **"The area's high schools"** Keith Williams, "Bed-Stuy: A Very Brief History," *The Weekly Nabe* (blog), June 23, 2012.

142 **"I'd been singing in church"** Andrew Davis, "Stephanie Mills: R&B Legend Talks about New CD, Gay Families," *Windy City Times* extended online edition, Aug. 11, 2010.

JODY + DENIECE

166 **"We were the only area"** Heikki Suosalo, "Soul Express Interview/Article: Deniece Williams," *Soul Express,* 2007.

167 **"He is one of my dearest"** Heikki Suosalo, Deniece Williams interview, *Soul Express.*

170 **"I'm not . . . boasting"** Michael P. Coleman, "Stacy Lattisaw: 'There's Nothing Like the Peace You Experience When You're Doing What God Has Planned for You to Do,' " *Sac Cultural Hub,* Nov. 10, 2014.

WHITNEY + ARETHA

195 **"emotional dynamic"** David Ritz, *Respect: The Life of Aretha Franklin* (New York: Little, Brown and Company, 2014), p. 67.

199 **"allowed to burn"** "Chase Ends at the Stake," *Los Angeles Times,* Feb. 8, 1904.

203 **"bruised cheek and a cut lip"** Todd Peterson, "Bobby Brown Sentenced to Jail Time," *People,* Feb. 27, 2004.

212 **"part of a generation that changed"** Leslie Kaufman, "Lois Smith, Publicist Who Mothered Star Clients, Dies at 84," *New York Times,* Oct. 9, 2012.

JANET

233 **"When someone says"** Robert Hilburn, "Janet Jackson Finally Learns to Say 'I,' " *Los Angeles Times,* Apr. 15, 1990.

237 **"She came out of a black situation"** J. C. Stevenson, "Janet Jackson: Our 1987 Cover Story," *Spin,* July 13, 2019 [reprinting original story from January 1987].

237 **"She felt guilty about admitting"** Stevenson, "Janet Jackson: Our 1987 Cover Story."

241 **"vesting too much importance"** Alan Citron and Chuck Philips, "Michael Jackson Agrees to Huge Contract with Sony," *Los Angeles Times,* Mar. 21, 1991.

IMAGE CREDITS

INDEX

ABOUT THE AUTHOR

DANYEL SMITH is the author of *Shine Bright: A Very Personal History of Black Women in Pop*. She is also the creator and host of the forthcoming *Black Girl Songbook*, a music + talk show that centers Black women in music (exclusive to Spotify). Smith was a senior editor and producer at ESPN, and before that, a 2013–14 John S. Knight Journalism Fellow at Stanford University. She has served as editor of *Billboard*, editor at large at Time Inc., and editor in chief of *Vibe*, in its classic era. Danyel is cofounder of HRDCVR, a hardcover media project created by diverse teams for a diverse world. She has written two novels—*More Like Wrestling* (Crown, 2003) and *Bliss* (Crown, 2005). Among other outlets, her nonfiction has appeared in *The New York Times Magazine* and on NPR and CNN. A proud Oakland native and a New Yorker by choice, Danyel lives in Southern California.